THE RISE OF NORMATIVE CHRISTIANITY

THE
RISE
OF
NORMATIVE
CHRISTIANITY

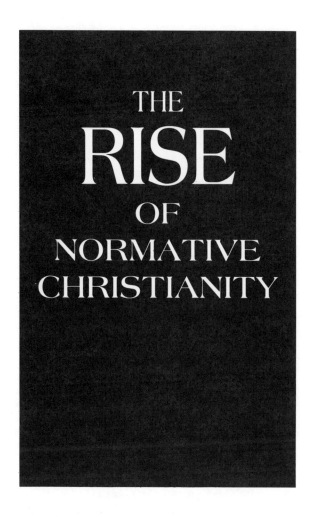

Arland J. Hultgren

Fortress Press/Minneapolis

THE RISE OF NORMATIVE CHRISTIANITY

Cover design: Allan Haag Design

Library of Congress Cataloging-in-Publication Data

Hultgren, Arland J.
    The rise of normative Christianity / Arland J. Hultgren.
       p.   cm.
    Includes bibliographical references and index.
    ISBN 0-8006-2645-1 (alk. paper) :
    1. Theology—Early church, ca. 30–600. 2. Bible. N.T.—
Criticism, interpretation, etc. 3. Christianity—Origin.
4. Bible. N.T.—Canon. 5. Church history—Primitive and early
church, ca. 30–600. I. Title. II. Title: Normative Christianity.
BT24.H85   1994
270.1—dc20   93-14307
                                                                      CIP

The paper used in this publication meets the minimum requirements of American National Standard for Information Sciences—Permanence of Paper for Printed Library Materials, ANSI Z329.48-1984.   (∞)™

Manufactured in the U.S.A.   AF 1-2645
98   97   96   95   94   1   2   3   4   5   6   7   8   9   10

Contents

Preface

PRECISELY AT A TIME WHEN SOME SCHOLARS ARE EXPRESSING doubts about the value of the historical-critical method in the interpretation of the New Testament, others are challenging the validity of the study of the New Testament itself as a discipline. What they call for is the histor cal-critical study of "early Christianity," not just the New Testament. That entails the investigation of a vast range of ancient literatures that give expression to many different forms of Christianity. The New Testament, it is said, gives only a partial view of early Christianity, even a biased one.

No scholar of our time, as far as I know, claims that the New Testament represents the total diversity that existed in the various first- and second-century movements and sects whose origins relate in some way to the ministry of Jesus of Nazareth. What the New Testament represents, rather, are expressions of Christian faith and life in documents that came to be considered "canonical" or "normative"—synonyms of Greek and Latin derivation, respectively.

The purpose of this book is to investigate the rise of "normative" Christianity within the complex and bewildering world of "early Christianity" in which it had its origins. A normative tradition did arise, a tradition that had tremendous breadth from the outset. But there were outer limits to diversity, beyond which religious systems and traditions became less recognizably Christian. One of the tasks of our day should be to discern those limits—fine lines in the sand, to be sure—in order to define Christianity as a religious system and tradition, both in antiquity and today.

Much of the research and writing of this book took place in two settings during a sabb atical in the 1990–91 academic year. The first was Uppsala, Sweden, where I was a visiting scholar at Uppsala University during the

fall and winter. The gracious hospitality of faculty members of the De-
partment of Theology there, plus that of the library staff, will long be
remembered. The second location was back at Luther Northwestern Theological Seminary where the unusually fine library personnel and resources
proved themselves superb once again. Thanks are extended to all these
persons and for these institutions. Thanks are also extended to Dr. Marshall
D. Johnson, Editorial Director at Fortress Press, for his encouragement in
this project and for the work that he and his colleagues did in the editorial
process.

It is hoped that the volume produced here will contribute to greater
understanding of early Christianity. The investigations undertaken go well
beyond the New Testament to include many noncanonical documents. By
ranging widely in the sources, the various factors contributing to the rise
of normative Christianity should be seen more clearly.

Abbreviations

Ancient Sources

Old Testament Pseudepigrapha

Pss. of Sol.	Psalms of Solomon
Sib. Or.	Sibylline Oracles
T. Judah	Testament of Judah
T. Levi	Testament of Levi

Philo

Deus Imm.	Quod Deus sit Immutabilis
Ebr.	De Ebrietate
Leg. All.	Legum Allegoriae
Quaest. Gen.	Quaestiones et Solutiones in Genesin

Josephus

Ant.	Jewish Antiquities
J. W.	The Jewish War

Dead Sea Scrolls

CD	Damascus Document
1QH	Thanksgiving Hymns
1QM	War Scroll
1QS	Manual of Discipline
1QSa	Rule of the Congregation

Early Christian Literature

Barn.	Epistle of Barnabas
1 Clem.	The First Epistle of Clement
Eusebius,	
Hist. eccl.	Ecclesiastical History
Hippolytus, Ref.	Refutationis Omnium Haeresium
Ignatius, Eph.	Epistle to the Ephesians
Magn.	Epistle to the Magnesians
Phld.	Epistle to the Philadelphians
Pol.	Epistle to Polycarp
Rom.	Epistle to the Romans
Smyrn.	Epistle to the Smyrnaeans
Trall.	Epistle to the Trallians
Irenaeus, Adv. Haer.	Adversus Haereses
Oxy. Pap.	Oxyrhynchus Papyri
Ps. Clem. H.	Pseudo-Clementine Homilies
Tertullian,	
Adv. Marc.	Adversus Marcionem
De Praesc. Haer.	De Praescriptione Haereticorum

Nag Hammadi Tractates

Ap. Jas.	The Apocryphon of James
Ap. John	The Apocryphon of John
Apoc. Peter	Apocalypse of Peter
Gos. Eg.	The Gospel of the Egyptians
Gos. Phil.	The Gospel of Philip
Gos. Thom.	The Gospel of Thomas
Gos. Truth	The Gospel of Truth
Interp. Know.	The Interpretation of Knowledge
Soph. Jes. Chr.	The Sophia of Jesus Christ
Testim. Truth	The Testimony of Truth
Treat. Res.	The Treatise on the Resurrection
Treat. Seth	The Second Treatise of the Great Seth
Tri. Trac.	The Tripartite Tractate
Val. Exp.	A Valentinian Exposition

Journals, Reference Works, and Serials

AB	Anchor Bible
ABD	The Anchor Bible Dictionary, ed. David N. Freedman, 6 vols. (New York: Doubleday, 1992)

ACNT	Augsburg Commentary on the New Testament
AJA	*American Journal of Archaeology*
BAGD	W. Bauer, W. F. Arndt, and F. W. Gingrich, *A Greek-English Lexicon of the New Testament and Other Early Christian Literature*, 2d ed., rev. F. W. Gingrich and F. W. Danker (Chicago: Univ. of Chicago Press, 1979)
BAR	*Biblical Archaeology Review*
BETL	Bibliotheca Ephemeridum Theologicarum Lovaniensium
BEvT	Beiträge zur evangelischen Theologie
BK	*Bibel und Kirche*
BJRL	*Bulletin of the John Rylands Library*
BZ	*Biblische Zeitscrift*
CBQ	*Catholic Biblical Quarterly*
CBQMS	Catholic Biblical Quarterly Monograph Series
ConBNT	Coniectanea Biblica, New Testament
CR	*Classical Review*
CS	Coptic Studies
CPSSV	Cambridge Philological Society Supplementary Volume
EKKNT	Evangelisch-katholischer Kommentar zum Neuen Testament
EncRel	*The Encyclopedia of Religion*, ed. Mircea Eliade, 16 vols. (New York: Macmillan, 1987)
ETL	*Ephemerides Theologicae Lovanienses*
ExpTim	*Expository Times*
FBBS	Facet Books, Biblical Series
FBHS	Facet Books, Historical Series
FFF	*Foundations and Facets Forum*
FRLANT	Forschungen zur Religion und Literatur des Alten und Neuen Testaments
GTA	Göttinger theologische Arbeiten
HDR	Harvard Dissertations in Religion
HNTC	Harper's New Testament Commentary
HorBT	*Horizons in Biblical Theology*
HTR	*Harvard Theological Review*
HUCA	*Hebrew Union College Annual*
ICC	International Critical Commentary
IDBSup	*The Interpreter's Dictionary of the Bible: Supplementary Volume*, ed. Keith Crim (Nashville: Abingdon Press, 1976)
IESS	*International Encyclopedia of the Social Sciences*, ed. David L. Sills, 17 vols. (New York: Macmillan, 1968)
Int	*Interpretation*
IRT	Issues in Religion and Theology

JAC	*Jahrbuch für Antike und Christentum*
JBL	*Journal of Biblical Literature*
JR	*Journal of Religion*
JSNT	*Journal for the Study of the New Testament*
JTS	*Journal of Theological Studies*
LCL	Loeb Classical Library
LXX	The Septuagint
NCB	New Century Bible
NGS	New Gospel Studies
NHLE	*The Nag Hammadi Library in English*, ed. James M. Robinson, 3d ed. (San Francisco: Harper & Row, 1988)
NHS	Nag Hammadi Studies
NICNT	New International Commentary on the New Testament
NIGTC	New International Greek Testament Commentary
NovT	*Novum Testamentum*
NovTSup	Novum Testamentum, Supplements
NTAbh	Neutestamentliche Abhandlungen
NTS	*New Testament Studies*
NTTS	New Testament Tools and Studies
PC	Proclamation Commentaries
PSB	*Princeton Seminary Bulletin*
PTS	Patristische Texte und Studien
PTMS	Pittsburgh Theological Monograph Series
PWSup	*Supplement to Paulys Realencyclopädia der classischen Altertumswissenschaft*, ed. G. Wissowa (Stuttgart: A. Druckenmüller, 1903—)
QD	Quaestiones Disputatae
RadRel	*Radical Religion*
RevQ	*Revue de Qumran*
RSR	*Religious Studies Review*
SANT	Studien zum Alten und Neuen Testament
SBEC	Studies in the Bible and Early Christianity
SBLDS	Society of Biblical Literature Dissertation Series
SBLMS	Society of Biblical Literature Monograph Series
SBLSBS	Society of Biblical Literature Sources for Biblical Study
SBT	Studies in Biblical Theology
SC	*The Second Century*
SEÅ	*Svensk Exegetisk Årsbok*
SHA	Sitzungsberichte der Heidelberger Akademie der Wissenschaften: Philosophisch-historische Klasse
SHR	Studies in the History of Religion
SJLA	Studies in Judaism in Late Antiquity

SJT	*Scottish Journal of Theology*
SNTSMS	Society for New Testament Studies Monograph Series
SNTU	*Studien zum Neuen Testament und seiner Umwelt*
SPS	Sacra Pagina Series
Str-B	H. Strack and P. Billerbeck, *Kommentar zum Neuen Testament aus Talmud und Midrasch*, 6 vols. (Munich: C. H. Beck'sche, 1922–61)
TDNT	*Theological Dictionary of the New Testament*, ed. G. Kittel and G. Friedrich, 10 vols. (Grand Rapids, Mich.: Wm. B. Eerdmans, 1964–76)
TJT	*Toronto Journal of Theology*
TSK	*Theologische Studien und Kritiken*
TZ	*Theologische Zeitschrift*
TU	Texte und Untersuchungen
USQR	*Union Seminary Quarterly Review*
VC	*Vigiliae Christianae*
WBC	Word Biblical Commentary
WMANT	Wissenschaftliche Monographien zum Alten und Neuen Testament
WUNT	Wissenschaftliche Untersuchungen zum Neuen Testament
WW	*Word & World*
YJS	Yale Judaica Series
ZNW	*Zeitschrift für die neutestamentliche Wissenschaft*

1

Normative Christianity
as a Problem and Issue

EARLY IN THE FOURTH CENTURY OF THE CHRISTIAN ERA THERE
was a form of Christianity that could be labeled "orthodox."[1] Moreover,
that form was not only recognizable far and wide but was considered by
its adherents and proponents as traditional as well, representing the legacy
of Jesus' apostles and guarded by their faithful heirs. According to modern
historical research, of course, the matter was not so simple, since orthodoxy
was not in fact a summary statement of apostolic teaching. Yet it is fitting
to raise the question whether there was a "normative" Christianity that was
set on its course in apostolic times, providing basic norms for the flowering
of orthodoxy later. The contention of this book is that there was, and that
it can be described.

The contention just stated sounds rather innocent, but it is not. To speak
of *normative Christianity* demands an explanation. And once the explanation
is given, a major issue has to be faced.

The Problem with Normative Christianity

At one time there was no hesitation to use the word *normative* in the discussion
of religious traditions. Early in the twentieth century, for example, George
Foot Moore used the term *normative Judaism* in his classic three-volume study
of ancient Judaism.[2] His interest was to describe what he considered a
standard, mainline, dominant Judaism in the first centuries of the Christian
era, which was the Judaism of the Pharisees and their successors in "rabbinic"
Judaism. But in recent years the term *normative Judaism* has been judged as
misleading.[3] The point made in criticism of the term is that there never
was a standard, mainline, dominant form of Judaism in antiquity. Instead,

one must recognize that Judaism had many forms of expression. The discovery of the Dead Sea Scrolls (1947) was a major factor in that shift of perspective.

Can one speak then of a *normative Christianity*, as the title of this book suggests? There are arguments pro and con. Against use of the term, the old dictum of Ernst Troeltsch applies wherein he declared that "the Christian religion is in every moment of its history a purely historical phenomenon, subject to all the limitations to which any individual historical phenomenon is exposed."[4] One must recognize that there never has been—even in the New Testament era, and some would say *especially* in that era—a standard, mainline, dominant form of Christianity. The diversity of early Christianity has been amply documented.[5] It has been difficult for scholars to find a common core in the message of the New Testament writings,[6] and it has been argued that there never was unity among the churches of the New Testament era.[7]

Moreover, the books of the New Testament are studied today, as never before, within a broader context, including the writings of the Apostolic Fathers, the New Testament apocrypha, and other sources. In this larger setting the diversity of early Christianity becomes even more evident. And if the discovery of the Dead Sea Scrolls in 1947 called for a new perspective on ancient Judaism that allows for seeing and acknowledging more diversity within it than previously, the discovery of the Nag Hammadi documents in 1945 has required more than ever before a perspective that is sensitive to all the diversity that existed among ancient Christian communities around the Mediterranean Sea and deep into the far reaches of Egypt, Syria, Asia Minor, and the European continent.[8] Perhaps, then, one should speak of *formative* Christianity, recognizing that there was an era (roughly the first three centuries A.D.) when Christianity assumed its classic form, plus other forms, and leave the question of norms aside.

Nevertheless, in spite of the variety of expressions of faith that existed, a *normative* form of Christianity arose during the first three centuries after the historical, earthly ministry of Jesus of Nazareth. Certain documents written and preserved for use primarily in worship and teaching were canonized—that is, they were considered normative far and wide in Christian communities.[9] The history of the canonization process is lengthy, and it shows that what was finally considered normative literature for the church was by no means self-evident from the start.[10] Yet there is a "family resemblance" among the documents that make up the New Testament. In point of origin they are among the oldest texts we have, or even know of, from the ancient church. In spite of their differing theological emphases, they share in affirming that the man Jesus of Nazareth, crucified and raised from the dead, is the incomparable revealer of God and redeemer of humanity.

Of course not all the canonical books are the oldest literature we have; certain noncanonical documents were written earlier than some of the New Testament books. For example, *1 Clement*, not in our New Testament, may have been composed about A.D. 96,[11] and it could very well be older than the Pastoral Epistles (1 and 2 Timothy and Titus), which are often dated around A.D. 100 or even later,[12] and it is likely to be older than 2 Peter.[13] And in terms of doctrine, there are extracanonical books—again, one can point to *1 Clement*—which affirm that Jesus is the revealer and redeemer; they resonate with the canonical books. The point being made is not that the most qualified books got into the canon (which may be true), but rather that a *normative* type of Christianity arose that is exemplified in the twenty-seven books of the New Testament and in other early Christian literature. This type of Christianity was the precursor of, and then the dominant voice at, the ecumenical councils, beginning with the Council of Nicaea in A.D. 325.

What to call the type of Christianity that developed and became dominant in the first three centuries, and was given further and decisive form by the ecumenical councils, is a problem. One is tempted to use the word *orthodoxy*, but that is not satisfactory.[14] Orthodoxy is, in usual parlance, a doctrinal consensus that developed in and among major centers of Christianity after the New Testament and the Apostolic Fathers,[15] and that is opposed to "heresy."[16] It is not clear at what point in time or place the term is appropriate. It is found in the writings of Eusebius (early fourth century),[17] but orthodoxy was still in the process of development in his time and was given further shape in the ecumenical councils. And if we mean by orthodoxy what the councils hammered out, such as the doctrine of the Trinity or the two natures of Christ, then even the New Testament writings do not measure up to the doctrinal standard of orthodoxy. The term *proto-orthodoxy* could perhaps be used, but that should probably be reserved for the theological systems of major Christian writers located on the eve of orthodoxy.[18]

Other terms have been proposed. Some scholars have used the term *early catholicism*, referring to developments within early Christianity that became evident in later catholicism (the fading of the expectation of an imminent parousia; the rise of authoritative teaching and ecclesiastical offices; and the linking of the Spirit to the institutional church), and they have maintained that these developments can be found already within certain New Testament writings, especially Luke-Acts and the Pastoral Epistles.[19] But that term is unsatisfactory for our purposes, since it is applied only to the later books of the New Testament, and pejoratively.

What is needed is a term that is capable of embracing elements of Christianity found in earlier books of the New Testament that are not normally included under the designation *early catholicism*.[20] Another term sometimes used is simply "the Great Church,"[21] referring to the church that came into being after the New Testament and that canonized the latter. But that term will not suffice either, since our interest includes the churches of the New Testament era itself, and its focus is on theological emphases as well as on institutional life.

The term *normative Christianity*, for all its risks,[22] is the most satisfactory.[23] In spite of the diversity of early Christianity, an expression of Christian faith arose in the first three centuries that claimed continuity with the faith of the apostles and is exhibited in the classic texts that came to make up the New Testament. Alternative expressions of faith, such as Marcionism, Montanism, Ebionitism, and Gnosticism, arose and made—to one degree or another—the same or similar claims. But there were factors within them—confessional and communal—that made those claims difficult to sustain. The purpose of this book is to investigate what factors contributed to the rise of normative Christianity and its distinction from current alternatives.

The Rise of Normative Christianity as an Issue

No doubt many factors were at work in the rise of normative Christianity. Nevertheless, an important trend has developed in some sectors, in both scholarly and popular works, to focus primarily on one factor as decisive. That is to claim that the rise of normative and then orthodox Christianity was the achievement of certain powerful leaders who could not tolerate diversity, and whose works have given us a one-sided view of how things came to be. These early Christian leaders, it is said, had "imperialist" and "exclusivist" attitudes, and they imposed their wills on others, coercing some into conformity, and condemning those who refused.[24] These leaders appealed to tradition and claimed to represent the apostolic legacy, but their claims had political implications.[25] Their teachings "legitimized a hierarchy of persons through whose authority all others must approach God."[26] Alternative forms, such as gnostic Christianity, were "forced outside" the mainstream "to the impoverishment of the Christian tradition."[27] But today, it is said, scholars in the field of Christian origins know that the views about Jesus espoused in the orthodox tradition are simply those that "triumphed over the views of 'losers' in ecclesiastical struggles," and that the books of the New Testament canon are those "approved by the 'winners.' "[28] The origins of Christianity must be reassessed in light of all the extracanonical materials of early Christianity now available, since "canonization" was in fact a "process of selective 'memory,' "[29] not giving the true picture. The problem and its resolution have been stated pointedly:

> The [New Testament] canon was the result of a deliberate attempt to exclude certain voices from the early period of Christianity: heretics, Marcionites, Gnosticism, Jewish Christians, perhaps also women. It is the responsibility of the New Testament scholar to help these voices to be heard again.[30]

Such views are of course not without foundation. A reading of the New Testament and other early Christian literature provides plenty of evidence of struggle, claims, and counterclaims in the rise of normative Christianity and orthodoxy. The development of the New Testament canon is a complicated story that does not reach its conclusion until well into the fourth century, and even then it was not at its end in certain sectors of eastern Christianity. Moreover, it is evident that incumbents in ecclesiastical offices sought to have their positions "legitimized," and early Christian writers were not slow in providing it. Early in the second century, for example, Ignatius exhorted his readers: "Be zealous to do all things in harmony with God, with the bishop presiding in the place of God and the presbyters in the place of the Council of the Apostles, and the deacons . . . entrusted with the service of Jesus Christ."[31] Other examples can be cited also.[32]

Having said that, however, it is fair to ask whether there may have been discernible factors having to do with belief and conduct that favored the survival and development of certain forms of Christianity along the path of the normative consensus, broadly conceived, and the dissent and eventual isolation, or even demise, of others. Each form of early Christianity prescribed ways of believing and behaving. Therein lies the basis for diversity and, in some cases, the parting of ways. What those prescriptions for believing and behaving were deserve our attention as factors that were decisive in the multiple developments of early Christianity.

2

Before Orthodoxy: Four Approaches

THE QUESTION OF LINES OF CONTINUITY FROM THE PROC-
lamation of Jesus to developments in early Christianity, and then on to
orthodoxy, is an old one. It has been dealt with in various ways—some
more interesting and important than others. There are four avenues of
approach that are perhaps the best known and that have captured the
historical imagination down through the ages. The first, which could simply
be designated the "traditional view," has been dominant through the centuries, holding its ground well into the twentieth century. The other three
arose in the twentieth century and challenged the traditional view in one
way or another. Reviewing these four approaches is instructive, since it can
bring major issues to the surface, and helps to set the stage for the chapters
that follow.

Truth Preceded Error

The traditional approach to the question of continuities between Jesus and
developments in early Christianity is stated well by Clement of Rome.
Writing near the close of the first century (ca. A.D. 96), he says:

> The Apostles received the Gospel for us from the Lord Jesus Christ, Jesus
> the Christ was sent from God. The Christ therefore is from God and the
> Apostles from the Christ. . . . Having therefore received their commands,
> and being fully assured by the resurrection of our Lord Jesus Christ, and
> with faith confirmed by the word of God, they went forth in the assurance
> of the Holy Spirit preaching the good news that the kingdom of God is
> coming. They preached from district to district, and from city to city, and
> they appointed their first converts, testing them by the Spirit, to be bishops
> and deacons of the future believers.[1]

7

Clement was not the first to paint a picture of continuity of teaching from Jesus to the apostles and then to their successors. Already the apostle Paul wrote in the middle of the first century about traditions that he had received traceable back directly to the earthly Jesus (1 Cor. 7:10-11; 9:14; 11:23-26) or at least to those who were apostles before him (1 Cor. 15:3-7). Moreover, the evangelist Luke claims at the outset of his Gospel that he is writing an "orderly account" concerning Jesus' ministry, death, and resurrection based on information delivered by "eyewitnesses and ministers of the word" (Luke 1:1-4).

The traditional view concerning the rise of false teachings is that, after the death of the apostles, evil and crafty persons perverted the teachings of the Lord and his apostles. Hegesippus (ca. A.D. 100–180), in a work preserved by Eusebius, writes as follows:

> When the sacred band of the apostles had in various ways reached the end of their life, and the generation of those privileged to listen with their own ears to the divine wisdom had passed on, then godless error began to take shape, through the deceit of false teachers, who now that none of the apostles was left threw off the mask and attempted to counter the preaching of the truth by preaching the knowledge falsely so called.[2]

The basis for such a view regarding the origins of false teaching is older than the second century. It can be found in the Acts of the Apostles where, according to Luke, the apostle Paul predicted on his departure from Ephesus that "fierce wolves" would enter the flock to destroy it, and that members from within would also speak perverse things in order to draw disciples away from the truth (20:29-30). Indeed, according to the Gospel of Matthew, Jesus himself had warned against false prophets who would come in sheep's clothing, but inwardly would be ravenous wolves (7:15).

The traditional view—that "the truth must of necessity precede the false [teaching]" (Tertullian)[3]—is not altered a great deal by data from the New Testament that shows greater complexity. The letters of Paul contain passages where he refers to opponents who, in his view, teach or practice error (2 Cor. 11:4-5, 13-15; 12:11; Gal. 1:7; 5:12; Phil. 3:2). These passages can be taken as examples of the rise of heterodox opposition to an apostle during his lifetime. Yet the traditional picture can accommodate the complexities, for the apostle Paul comes off as the inspired defender of the truth, maintaining it to the end. As long as there were apostles, the truth could be maintained. But after the death of the apostles, even false teachers could appeal to Jesus, the apostolic tradition, or the Spirit without rebuttal from an apostle.

Heresy Preceded Orthodoxy

The traditional view concerning continuity between Jesus' proclamation and developments in early Christianity was discarded vigorously by Walter Bauer in his book *Orthodoxy and Heresy in Earliest Christianity*,[4] which was published in its first German edition in 1934. Bauer's work is provocative, controversial, and influential. Its influence continues to exert itself in ways both explicit and implicit in New Testament scholarship and studies in early church history. Some of the main points of the book will be summarized here.

Bauer does not look for possible connections between Jesus and early Christianity, but deals with issues this side of the cross in early Christianity itself. The thesis of his book can be stated quite succinctly. Over against the traditional view that "orthodoxy" was early and widespread, and that "heresy" came later, Bauer argues that in many geographical areas of antiquity that which would be called "heresy" at later times was actually the original manifestation of Christianity.[5] The implication is that in many geographical areas, so-called heresy was prior to orthodoxy. "Orthodoxy," he says, "represented the form of Christianity supported by the majority in Rome"[6] that became ascendant in the second century and victorious in other areas to the east around A.D. 200.[7] It should be added that Bauer does not provide theological definitions of "orthodoxy" and "heresy" but says only that in his book these two terms "refer to what one customarily and usually understands them to mean."[8] Moreover, he declares that he prefers to make use of sources after the New Testament since "the New Testament seems to be both too unproductive and too much disputed to be able to serve as a point of departure."[9]

Bauer's method is to survey the history of Christianity in major geographical areas: Edessa (located in eastern Syria east of the Euphrates River), Egypt, Asia Minor, Macedonia, Crete, and Rome. His work demonstrates major differences among the manifestations of Christianity in these various locations. And while his work is obviously important for our understanding of Christianity in the second and third centuries, it also has far-reaching implications for our understanding of early Christianity from its very beginnings. The so-called heretical groups of the second century were, in Bauer's picture, simply the theological descendants of first-century varieties of Christianity. They were not deviations from a unified Christian faith common to churches of the first century.[10] The writings of the New Testament reflect only a part of the total picture.

Bauer begins his survey at a place that, in the view of modern scholarship, has no apparent connection with any of the books of the New Testament. The place is Edessa. After sifting through the legends about the founding of Christianity there, Bauer concludes that the earliest form of Christianity there was Marcionism, and that it arrived there in the last part of the second century.[11] The first orthodox leader (Pâlut) appeared there about the year A.D. 200,[12] although it was not until about A.D. 300 that orthodoxy was definitely secure.[13] Thus, in the case of Edessa, heresy preceded orthodoxy.[14]

Subsequent chapters echo the refrain of the first. In Egypt, says Bauer, Christianity existed already in both Jewish and gentile forms in the first two centuries, but both were gnostic.[15] Orthodoxy was not evident until the third century with Bishop Demetrius of Alexandria.[16] When he turns to Asia Minor, Macedonia, and Crete, Bauer enters territories referred to in the New Testament and Apostolic Fathers. The letters of Ignatius portray the rise of monarchical bishops in Asia Minor, who are customarily assumed to be orthodox, at the beginning of the second century. But according to Bauer, Ignatius himself did not have a secure position as bishop of Antioch,[17] and his letters bear witness to his *desire* for order and orthodoxy in Asia Minor, "but not to the existing reality."[18] Several of the churches there, he says, had heretical leaders.[19] Moreover, the churches founded by Paul in Macedonia were dominated by heresy at the turn of the century.[20] In the final analysis, and drawing primarily on *1 Clement*, Bauer claims that the only church free of gnostic influences was the church at Rome.[21] It was an opponent of Gnosticism from its very beginning[22] and, claiming the authority of both Peter and Paul, exerted its influence in the east during the second century:

> Supported by the conviction that Rome constituted the church founded in the world capital by the greatest apostles, Rome confidently extends itself eastward, tries to break down resistance and stretches a helping hand to those who are like-minded, drawing everything within reach into the well-knit structure of ecclesiastical organization. Heresy, with its different brands and peculiar configurations that scarcely even permitted it to be united in a loose association reflecting common purpose, had nothing corresponding to this by way of a similar offensive and defensive force with which to counter.[23]

The work of Bauer is impressive in its detailed information, argument, and thesis. Nevertheless, it has received considerable criticism,[24] and its flaws have become even more apparent with the passing of time. Too often Bauer argues from silence and, in other cases, pushes aside evidence that works against his thesis. Concerning his account of the rise of Christianity in Edessa, his claim that the earliest form to appear was Marcionism does little to support his overall thesis that far and wide, except for Rome, "heresy" preceded "orthodoxy." If he is correct about Edessa, that only means that Marcion's "heresy," which was a departure from "orthodoxy" according to early sources,[25] was taken to an area that had not otherwise been evangelized previously. The traditional view, that orthodoxy preceded heresy, does not require that orthodoxy existed in every conceivable place prior to heresy.[26]

Bauer's picture about the origins of Christianity in Edessa has been challenged on other grounds. It has been argued that the earliest form of Christianity there was an ascetic and Encratite expression of Jewish Christianity indigenous to Syria, and that that version of Christianity arose within and then out of the Jewish community of Edessa, which had been evangelized by missionaries from Palestine.[27] It has been suggested further that the *Gospel of Thomas* and the *Acts of Thomas* were produced in that community.[28] That the latter was produced at or near Edessa early in the third century is widely accepted.[29] That the former was produced in Syria has also gained widespread, if not unqualified,[30] support as well.[31] But how early that Gospel was composed is debated. Although some seek to place its origins in the first century,[32] the view that it was actually composed near the middle of the second century (ca. A.D. 140) is more commonly held.[33] If the *Gospel of Thomas* can be taken as representative of the form, or *a* form, of Christianity that existed at Edessa already by the middle of the second century, it provides witness to a Christian community whose expression of Christian faith would not be considered "orthodox" by contemporary and later standards elsewhere. But that expression could have been indigenous to that part of Syria.[34] Even if those who evangelized the area brought traditions of Jesus' sayings that formed the basis for the eventual production of the *Gospel of Thomas*, one cannot on those grounds pass judgment on the relative orthodoxy or heterodoxy of the missionaries themselves, for the sayings may not have been the sum total of their proclamation. If the missionaries were indeed heterodox, one must then ask whether they came from a milieu that was isolated from, and secondary to, the primary apostolic communities.[35] The Edessa milieu must also be taken into account. Edessa was the home of a strongly Hellenized sycretistic Judaism prior to the rise of Christianity there, and the documents produced by Edessa Christians were strongly influenced by it.[36] Rather than drawing immediate, direct links between Palestine and Edessa, it is more plausible that Palestinian traditions in the *Gospel of Thomas* were transmitted through other Syrian Hellenistic Christian communities (for example, at Antioch) prior to their arrival at Edessa in eastern Syria. The result is that the Bauer thesis is too simplistic, and there are several considerations based on evidence, however slight, that speak strongly against it.

In the case of Egypt, the picture has changed drastically since the work of Bauer. First, some ten biblical manuscripts, or fragments thereof (including seven from Old Testament books, three from New Testament books) have been discovered in Egypt that are dated as second-century texts. The texts are demonstrably from a Christian community, and the presence of Old

Testament texts speaks loudly in favor of the nongnostic character of that community.[37] No gnostic texts have been discovered from so early a time as these.

Second, it has been argued persuasively that the gnostic Christians of Egypt in the second century made use of books obtained from nongnostic Christians that were destined to become part of the canonical Scriptures of the church, particularly the Gospels and the letters of Paul.[38]

Third, the document known as the *Epistula Apostolorum*, discovered in 1895, may be evidence of a remarkably "orthodox" community in Egypt either prior to or contemporaneous with gnostic Christianity. This document is widely thought to have been written in Egypt.[39] It is from the second century, either at the middle or earlier.[40] It opens with references to Simon and Cerinthus (both Gnostics) as "false apostles" and affirms the teachings of "catholic" Christianity (using the term *catholic* in the Ethiopic version, chapter 1). Whatever the merits of the *Epistula Apostolorum* in the issue, at least the other evidence provided here speaks in favor of the existence of "orthodoxy" (nongnostic Christianity) prior to, or at least along side of, gnostic Christianity in Egypt.[41] Moreover, it has been argued that numerically this community was greater than the gnostic Christian community in the second century, for the Gnostics themselves considered their community (the "pneumatics") to be the few among the mass of ordinary Christians.[42]

Bauer's treatment of territories for which there is evidence in the New Testament and Apostolic Fathers is particularly one-sided. He creates a picture of conditions based on a reading between the lines of the texts we have—and ignoring the lines that we do have. To claim, as he does, that Ignatius lacked a secure standing as bishop of Antioch as evidence that heresy preceded orthodoxy there is untenable. The alleged weakness of Ignatius would indicate only an embattled orthodoxy and a mixed (orthodox/heterodox) situation at most, not a chronological priority of heresy.[43] Further, along the same lines, one should not think of the so-called monarchical bishop (the Ignatian ideal) as a diocesan bishop, but rather as the overseer of a local congregation, or a small cluster of congregations at most, who may well have had rivals in other congregations. The presence of major gnostic teachers in Antioch, such as Menander and Saturninus, is well enough attested in second-century sources to provide grounds for thinking that orthodoxy would have been challenged.[44]

But Bauer is just plain wrong when he says that there was no "credible list of bishops" and "ecclesiastical tradition" at Antioch,[45] for Eusebius provides the names of the early bishops there, and there is no apparent reason to doubt his credibility.[46] Moreover, there is the New Testament evidence for an "ecclesiastical tradition" at Antioch. Early stages of the history of the church at Antioch are attested in Acts 11:19—13:3; 14:26—15:35; 18:22 and Galatians 2:11-21, in which the apostles Peter and Paul have important roles. The legacy of each continued at Antioch into the second century. The legacy of Pauline Christianity continued to have an impact, as reflected in the so-called Paulinism of the letters of Ignatius.[47] And the legacy of Peter was continued in the Gospel of Matthew, which is widely held to have been composed in or around Antioch during the last quarter of the first century (partly because Ignatius alludes either to the Gospel of Matthew itself or at least to traditions peculiar to it[48]),[49] and in which Peter is portrayed as preeminent among the apostles (cf. 16:13-20).[50] These attestations of Pauline and Petrine Christianity at Antioch prior to the episcopacy of Ignatius speak against the Bauer thesis.

Evidence concerning the churches of the Pauline field in Asia Minor and Rome refutes the Bauer thesis as well. The letters of Paul were most likely collected in Asia Minor (probably at Ephesus) in the last decade or two of the first century within a "Pauline school."[51] Further, the Pastoral Epistles were most likely composed in or around Ephesus about A.D. 100,[52] and if the term *orthodoxy* can be applied so soon, the Pastorals rank among the most orthodox writings of the New Testament. And as for Rome, the situation is more complicated than Bauer lets on. From Paul's Epistle to the Romans in the middle of the first century to *1 Clement* at the end, what may be called *orthodoxy* is attested. But Rome was the destination of various "heretics," including the gnostic teacher Simon in the first century (arriving as early as the time of Claudius, A.D. 41–54),[53] and Marcion and Valentinus in the middle of the second.

It should be apparent, on the basis of the foregoing, that a simple developmental approach does not finally serve well in tracing continuities between the mission of Jesus and his disciples and developments in early Christianity. Bauer says at the outset of his book that the traditional view, which he calls "the ecclesiastical position,"[54] is inadequate, namely, that Jesus revealed "pure doctrine" to his disciples, the latter preserved it, and then heresy arose. But his own thesis—which posits the existence of "heresy" virtually everywhere except in Rome at the beginning of the second century, followed by the rise of orthodoxy—does not hold up either. And in fact it does not actually destroy the traditional view, for it takes the early second century for its starting point, and the heretical forms he claims to find there would have necessarily been preceded by the apostolic era.

His description of "the ecclesiastical position" is also a caricature. Scarcely anyone would say that Jesus revealed "pure doctrine" (Bauer's term) to his disciples. Doctrine developed on the basis of Jesus' ministry, death, and resurrection as early Christians reflected on the meaning of the Christ event within the overall purpose and work of God.

Fixed and Flexible Elements

A different kind of approach to the matter of orthodoxy and heresy in early Christianity was taken by H. E. W. Turner in his book *The Pattern of Christian Truth*, published in 1954.[55] Turner devotes a chapter to an analysis and refutation of Bauer's work,[56] and yet he does not try to revive the traditional view. He speaks of orthodoxy as "a confluence of many tributaries into a single stream."[57] Already in the New Testament, he says, "there exists a considerable variety of theological traditions." Indeed, "different interpretations of the ministry of Jesus are contained in the Gospels."[58] Further, he says:

> This fluidity extends into sub-apostolic times. . . . We note the practical authoritarianism of I Clement, the Paulinism of St. Polycarp, the apocalyptic of Hermas and the *Didache*, the gnostic tinge of Barnabas and 2 Clement, and the Johannine features of the letters of St. Ignatius.[59]

Turner goes on to propose a way of conceptualizing the rise of orthodoxy. He suggests that "the development of Christian theology . . . may perhaps . . . be interpreted as the interaction of fixed and flexible elements."[60] The "fixed elements" are "the religious facts themselves, without which Christianity would have no ground for its existence."[61] These include (1) belief in God as Creator, Christ as historical Redeemer, and his divinity; (2) the centrality of biblical (Old Testament) revelation; and (3) creedal traditions.[62] The "flexible elements" are differences in idiom (such as differences in eschatological and metaphysical interpretations) and differences in the individual characteristics of various early theologians, leading to different emphases.[63] Turner sees the development of orthodoxy as a confluence of traditions kept alive through the corporate devotional life of the church (its *lex orandi*).[64] None of the "tradition-lines" was adequate by itself to express the church's experience as a whole, but each made its contribution to the formulation of doctrine. "The sole theological criterion by which they were to be judged was their adequacy to express in all its fullness the religious tradition to which the Church was heir."[65] Heresy arose "when the defined forms of the Church [were] transgressed" or "when the specific religious content of the Christian faith [was] substantially impaired."[66]

Turner's approach has much to commend it. Like Bauer, he covers an enormous amount of material. But, again like Bauer, his attention is given almost totally to the post–New Testament era, ignoring earlier developments. He does not discuss the various "tradition lines" at all that, he says, flowed from earlier stages into the making of orthodoxy. He seems to assume that they were simply fitted together, like pieces in a jigsaw puzzle, in the formation of orthodoxy. And although he speaks of orthodoxy as evolving,[67] he also speaks of it in one place as having an "essential autonomy,"[68] which seems to betray his true view—that is, that orthodoxy was not so much an achievement as a given, a deposit of faith that heresy assaulted. But the main weakness of his work is that, even though he asserts that fixed and flexible elements were at work in the development of orthodoxy, he does not show how either actually played a role. Instead, he switches to the roles of Scripture, tradition, and reason as "the three principal sources of orthodoxy."[69] One misses in his work a sustained presentation and unfolding of the approach promised at the outset. Turner's critique of Bauer is perhaps the main value of his work. But in the end he does not provide a satisfying alternative.

Diverse Trajectories from the Beginning

A much more dynamic picture is presented in the essays published in their jointly authored book *Trajectories through Early Christianity*, by James M. Robinson and Helmut Koester, which appeared in 1971.[70] Both authors give credit to Walter Bauer for providing foundations for their own thinking and research leading to the essays contained in this volume.[71] The trajectory-critical approach followed in the work of Robinson and Koester is not given a precise definition by its proponents, but it is a way of investigating developments in early Christianity that takes seriously the dynamics of historical and cultural forces upon traditions from and about Jesus.[72] Rather than thinking in terms of static "backgrounds" of early Christianity (for example, apocalyptic Judaism, rabbinic Judaism, Hellenism, Gnosticism, and the like), the researcher recognizes that there is movement across the board.[73]

Thus, for example, Judaism, Christianity, and Gnosticism developed writings of the same genre almost simultaneously. Similarities among these various developing traditions must be attributed to influences of the cultural conditions in which they were being produced.[74] In short, the method calls for a radical contextualization of investigations, which recognizes that context is dynamic, not static. This will mean that a particular document (for example, the hypothetical Q document, a collection of miracle stories, a collection of revelatory sayings, and so forth) may function differently at one point in time and place than at another—and thus have a different meaning in each context.[75] The Q material, for example, would have one function and meaning in the so-called Q community, but it has another function and meaning once it has been incorporated into the Gospel of Matthew and still another in Luke's Gospel. Or the apostle Paul, facing one set of opponents, may use conceptualizations that another set of opponents

elsewhere would consider their own, but Paul would oppose those conceptualizations when writing to the latter opponents.[76]

But there is another aspect of the trajectory-critical approach that is
more pertinent to our concerns here. It has long been recognized in New
Testament studies that both written sources and collections of traditions
stand behind our present canonical Gospels, including collections of sayings
and of miracle stories. These sources and collections can be classified
according to genre, which is one of the major achievements of form criticism.[77] But what is striking is that documents exist among the New Testament apocryphal books and other early Christian literature, which represent these and other genres in their entirety. The *Gospel of Thomas*, like
Q, is a collection of sayings of Jesus. The *Infancy Gospel of Thomas* is a
collection of infancy narratives. *The Dialogue of the Savior* is a revelatory
discourse. These and other examples demonstrate that the presentations of
Jesus familiar in the four canonical Gospels, regardless of their differences,
were by no means the only way to proceed.

Nor, as the earlier collections and sources behind our Gospels show,
were those presentations necessarily the earliest. Koester, in one of his
essays, asks the question, "Do apocryphal and 'heretical' gospels have their
origin in very early layers of the gospel tradition, perhaps even in certain
aspects of the words and works of the historical Jesus himself?"[78] Robinson
proceeds in the same direction of thought in one of his essays. He suggests
that trajectories can be traced in which "words of the wise" are preserved
and handed on in Jewish, Christian, and gnostic communities.[79] According
to his analysis, the total pool of sayings of Jesus would have contained
wisdom sayings, and these were brought together into collections. Such
collections were transmitted orally in different localities. The Q material
is one of the earliest known instances of their transmission in literary form,
and the *Gospel of Thomas* is a later one. The sayings collection is thus a genre
(or *Gattung*) that, "though apparently not gnostic in origin, was open to a
development in that direction, once a general drift toward Gnosticism set
in."[80] One might conclude from this that one stream within early Christianity
consisted primarily of a sayings tradition, that that stream was a version of
Christianity existing from the beginnings of Christianity as a whole, and
that it was "suppressed" by the "orthodox" point of view that got the upper
hand. In fact, such an account of things has been given.[81]

The trajectory-critical approach calls for the rejection of lines of demarcation between canonical and noncanonical, orthodox and heretical,[82]
even though both Robinson and Koester use these terms frequently in their
essays. That which the church has come to judge as canonical and orthodox
is only one portion of the legacy of Jesus and his followers. If the earliest
sources were collections of traditions from and about Jesus, it is possible

that both "heretical" and "orthodox" forms of Christianity are simply, in the words of Elaine Pagels, "variant interpretations of the teaching and significance of Christ."[83]

On the descriptive level, that is correct. The impact of Jesus upon later generations exceeds those circles that produced the documents that came to be canonized by the church of the ecumenical councils. Koester has given an account of how, in his view, different traditions and affirmations about Jesus produced various patterns of church life and literature, including those of the orthodox church and the canonical writers. Not surprisingly, it was the creed of Jesus' having been raised from the dead that was the "central criterion of faith for the 'canonical' writers" and the orthodox church.[84]

The insights of the trajectory-critical approach are well grounded in the methods and results of historical-critical study. Like the History of Religions School of previous generations,[85] it serves notice that the writings of the New Testament emerged from a context where boundaries between religious traditions and movements were not as fixed as some modern scholarship has assumed or suggested. But the approach has assumptions and suggestions of its own that need to be tested. Its fixing of a particular text within a particular trajectory is determined by later developments of a genre as much as by earlier ones. For example, Koester attributes to a "very primitive" version of Q certain "gnosticizing tendencies" that were developed into a gnostic theology. He argues his case on the grounds that, according to him, the hypothetical "primitive" version was used in the composition of the *Gospel of Thomas.*[86] Robinson likewise takes the *Gospel of Thomas* as evidence that the genre of Q (a "sayings of the sages" collection) moved along a trajectory that led to Gnosticism.[87]

In these judgments Koester and Robinson do not entertain the possibility that, while the contents of an early version of Q (Koester) may indeed have been amenable to a gnostic interpretation at a later stage, and while Q and the *Gospel of Thomas* shared the same genre (Robinson), a gnostic outcome of neither the content nor the genre was inevitable any more than gnostic interpretations of the letters of Paul or the Gospel of John were, even though they were given such in gnostic communities.[88] In the proposals of Koester and Robinson concerning Q and its genre, the trajectory-critical approach has a retrojectory character. It is fair to say that the approach as a whole is under the spell of Bauer's view of orthodoxy and heresy, retrojecting his picture of early Christianity after the New Testament into the New Testament era, indeed to traditions behind the New Testament documents themselves. Needless to say, that is a questionable method. As Robert McL. Wilson has remarked, "It is dangerous to . . . use second-century material for the elucidation of first-century documents."[89] Nevertheless, the assumptions and proposals of the trajectory-critical method rank among the most stimulating of our time for research into Christian origins. But they should be tested by further historical and theological analysis by means of still other approaches.

3

Confession and Community in Christian Tradition

WHATEVER ELSE CAN BE SAID, THE RELIGIONS OF THE WORLD have two primary expressions—belief and practice. That statement, which appears self-evident in a moment's reflection, applies to tribal religions, religions intertwined with the history and saga of nation states, ancient or modern, and religions whose origins can be traced to specific founders. Belief, when articulated, is given expression in primary language—such as prayer (private or corporate), creedal formulas, and testimony—and in secondary language of a more theoretical, reflective kind, such as in doctrine. Practice includes cultic acts, the social expression of belief, behavior in accord with beliefs, and the formation of community life.[1]

Religion is both a personal matter and a social phenomenon. In regard to the latter, there are two primary types of religious tradition.[2] First, there are "natural" religious traditions in which religion and social organization—such as class, ethnic group, or nation—are closely allied; a person is simply born into the social and religious alliance. Examples include the Israelite religion during the monarchy or, to some extent, Shinto tradition in modern Japan. Second, there are "specific" religious traditions in which membership is by choice—even if the choice is attributed to divine call—and such membership is based on commitment to beliefs and a community that shares those same beliefs. Examples include the mystery religions of the Greco-Roman world and Christianity both in antiquity and in modern pluralistic societies. In the latter type of religious tradition, the formation of community is a common, almost universal, feature. The obvious exception is the rejection of community by the hermit.

The Fusion of Confession
and Community Ethos

Since the work of Ferdinand Tönnies (1855–1936), it has been customary and helpful to make a distinction between the larger society and the communities in which persons live. At a minimum, the former can be conceived as "public life," the "mere coexistence of people independent of each other," while the latter is characterized by intimacy, solidarity, and shared beliefs among its members.[3] Indeed, a community can be spoken of as a "living organism."[4] There is a symbiotic relationship between beliefs, values, or worldviews and the character of the community that is formed in any given instance. A religious community embodies a worldview and a way of life.

The relationship between worldview and life in community has been addressed by cultural anthropologists, sociologists, and historians of religion. Gerardus van der Leeuw has written about the close connection between "outward action"—the social manifestations of religion—and "inward action"—that is, matters of belief and experience.[5] In his analysis of religions, he maintains that each religion assumes specific historical forms and manifests particular characteristics that are related to the "specific experience of Power" at its foundation.[6] He describes a dozen varieties, integrating the claims and manifestations of each. That a linkage exists between convictions and community forms has also been asserted by the sociologist of religion Joachim Wach. He has written concerning the reciprocal relationship between the "spirit and attitudes of a religious community" as a whole and the "individual attitudes and concepts" of its members.[7] The cultural anthropologists A. R. Radcliff-Brown and E. E. Evans-Pritchard have also written about the correspondence between religious beliefs and the way a society (or community) is constituted.[8]

More specifically, Clifford Geertz has used the word *congruence* in his discussion of the relationship between the specific metaphysic of a religious community and its particular style of life.[9] He maintains that a major role of religion is the "fusing of ethos and world view."[10] "Ethos," in his view, has to do with "the tone, character, and quality of [a people's] life, its moral and aesthetic style and mood," while "worldview" is "their picture of the way things in sheer reality are."[11] "Whatever else religion does," he says, "it relates a view of the ultimate nature of reality to a set of ideas of how man is well advised, even obligated, to live. . . . Thus do received beliefs, essentially metaphysical, and established norms, essentially moral, confirm and support each other."[12] Geertz goes on to propose that the scientific analysis of religion should give attention to the clarification of this mutual confirmation.[13]

Illustrations of the fusion of worldview and ethos can be drawn from the history of religions. They can be seen, for example, in cults of ancestor worship, wherein the ethos of care for and solidarity with members of the clan are related directly to the conviction that one's behavior can either please or offend one's departed ancestors.[14] The ethos of certain Hellenistic cult associations, which became the primary groups for many uprooted people in the Greco-Roman world, was in many ways comparable to that of a household. Not surprisingly, there were moral codes concerning the relationship between members and the subordination of the individual to the group.[15] And within Judaism, particularly in the case of ancient sects (such as the Qumran community and Pharisaism), the correspondence between worldview and a prescribed way of life (an ethos) can be detected. In one of his methodological essays on the study of Judaism, Jacob Neusner has suggested that the description of Judaism in any of its forms requires attention to the correspondence between worldview and ethos on the part of the investigator.[16] Indeed any religious system is made up of the worldview and way of life characteristic of a particular social group.[17]

Confession and Community in the Analysis of Christian Traditions

If linkages between beliefs and ethos are evident in religious traditions in general, and are capable of description, they should also be evident in early Christianity in all its forms. Yet, while much attention has been given to early Christian beliefs (theologies) in all their diversity,[18] relatively little has been given to the ethos of the various communities that held those beliefs,[19] and virtually none to the fusion of the two. The result is that our picture of early Christianity is one of many competing, disembodied voices represented in the New Testament and other early Christian literature. And, as indicated in the previous chapters, there is a widely held view that the triumph of orthodoxy was a rather late and even highhanded achievement of ecclesiastical leaders representing one strand, however diverse that strand was, who appealed to apostolic tradition to give legitimacy to their own position.

The question is worth raising whether the picture might be altered somewhat if it is granted on methodological grounds that a more appropriate analysis of early Christianity requires attention to both the confession of faith and the ethos of each of the various Christian communities. That is the method of analysis adopted in this study. Such an analysis recognizes that diversity within early Christianity was not simply a matter of differing convictions, and that controversy was not simply a matter of competing ideologies of legitimation. Another, and very significant, ingredient was the question how people sought to live together—the kind of ethos that theological convictions both generated and reflected. What is confessed has a direct bearing on how persons conduct their lives. That is why what is confessed is so important. But in the final analysis it is behavior that builds up or destroys community.

Succeeding chapters of this book consist of probes into several Christian communities of the first and second centuries. It will be shown that there was considerable diversity of confession of faith and community ethos among them. But there was a stream of Christianity—which was indeed a *broad* stream—that claimed that there were limits to diversity, and that persisted from the beginning on into the second century, providing the foundations for orthodoxy. That stream did not consist simply of a collection of ideas guarded and perpetuated by a core of ecclesiastical leaders. Instead one can observe a succession of faith and life over time, a faith lived in working communities, capable of sustaining itself, while other expressions of Christian faith and life could not sustain themselves, since they were prone to disintegrating factors. What emerged as orthodoxy was but the ecclesiastical validation of a broad stream of convictions and ways of living that had staying power. A question that motivates much of the enterprise in the following chapters is, What were the factors that contributed to the rise and resilience of normative Christianity?

Before turning to the analytical work, however, it is fitting to draw some boundaries. In current study it is no longer self-evident where the label "early Christianity" applies and where it does not. The boundaries between Judaism and Jewish Christianity, for example, are not as fixed as one might expect, and the term *Christianity* itself may be anachronistic when applied to so-called *Christian* communities prior to A.D. 70. Nor can the boundaries between Christianity and Gnosticism be clearly drawn, for some forms of Gnosticism were Christian, while others were not. And some manifestations of Christianity may have had gnostic elements, or at least were affected by incipient gnostic influences early on. And what is the line of demarcation between the so-called Jesus movement and early Christianity?[20]

I shall propose here a rather loose, even exceedingly broad, definition. That is that the term *early Christianity* applies specifically to movements, traditions, and communities of the first two centuries A.D. in which Jesus—known to have been killed, but now considered living an exalted life—is confessed as the incomparable revealer of God and redeemer of humanity. One is tempted to add other points that can be considered implied claims: that the God referred to is the God of Israel, who is one, who created the world, elected Israel, and sent the Son; and that honorific statements and titles (such as Christ, Son of God, and the like) must be attached to Jesus.[21]

Yet, for our purposes here, that would be too restrictive. It would mean that certain figures, such as Marcion, would have to be excluded from consideration. Although Marcion was considered heterodox by major Christian writers in his time, he and his followers claimed to be Christians.[22] He considered Jesus as revealer of the Father and redeemer of humanity, even though he denied that the Father revealed by Jesus was the God of Israel. In order to include Marcion and other figures within our analysis, the definition of Christianity has to remain rather broad. Soon enough we shall have to describe *normative Christianity*, and there the definition will have to be narrower. But that can wait for now.

4

The Beginnings of a Normative Tradition

PRIOR TO THE JEWISH WAR IN PALESTINE (A.D. 66–70) A NUMBER of Christian communities came into existence. There is documentary evidence for the existence of such communities in Palestine, Syria, and regions north and west from Asia Minor on to Rome. In this chapter we shall focus attention on the confession and community ethos of those communities, as they can be observed from the sources, which came into existence from ca. A.D. 30 into the 60s. We begin with the earliest known communities, which were in Palestine, where the ministry of Jesus had taken place.

Before launching into the investigations, it may be necessary to comment on the use of the word *Christian*. It is debatable whether any of the communities investigated in this chapter would have used that term as a self-designation. The word appears only three times in the New Testament (Acts 11:26; 26:28; 1 Peter 4:16), and these documents are conventionally dated post-70 of the first century. It is possible that, as some have suggested, Acts 11:26 ("in Antioch the disciples were for the first time called Christians") is an anachronism.[1] But even if it is not,[2] it stands as a nickname conferred on the mixed (Jewish-gentile) community of those "belonging to the way" (9:2) by the gentile populace, who regarded its members as distinct from Jews and as followers of a man who had *Christos* as a personal name.[3] It is not, in any case, a self-designation at this point in Acts. The same applies to the other two uses of the term in the New Testament. In Acts 26:28 the term is used by Herod Agrippa in a derisive way, and at 1 Peter 4:16 it is mentioned as the indictment under which one might suffer. The first clear instances of the use of the term as a self-designation are in the letters of Ignatius of Antioch.[4] It is plausible that a nickname given by the public in Antioch eventually became a self-designation late in the first century and thereafter in the same city.[5] Nevertheless, even though it may not have been a self-designation, the term is used sparingly in this chapter as a descriptive shorthand for communities of faith that regarded Jesus as the one sent from God for purposes of revelation and redemption.

The Churches of Palestine

The main sources for Christianity in Palestine prior to the Jewish war are references in Paul's letters, which were written before the war (none later than the 50s),[6] and the Acts of the Apostles, which was probably written after the war in the 80s or 90s.[7] Other sources are either contested or later. One such contested source is the so-called Q document—that is, material common to the Gospels of Matthew and Luke that has not been derived from the Gospel of Mark. Proponents of Q as a document generally hold that it was produced by a Q community in either Palestine or Syria in the middle of the first century (see below). Because that document is hypothetical, and also because the proponents of Q often link it with Syria, rather than Palestine, I shall deal with that material and the Q community separately.

Another contested source for Palestinian Christianity is the synoptic tradition as a whole. In his study of the sociology of Palestinian Christianity, Gerd Theissen makes use of materials from the Synoptic Gospels as sources concerning the Palestinian "Jesus movement" of A.D. 30–70.[8] Since these Gospels were all written outside Palestine after A.D. 70, however, their use as sources on Palestinian Christianity pre-70 is highly problematic. I shall return to this issue later.

Finally, there are other sources on Palestinian Christianity from much later, which can be used in limited ways. The main sources here are brief accounts or references to leading apostles and the churches of Palestine within the *Ecclesiastical History* of Eusebius (fourth century) based on earlier sources, including writers of the second century such as Hegesippus and Clement of Alexandria.[9]

The sources provide evidence for the existence of Christian communities at several locales within Palestine prior to the death of Herod Agrippa in A.D. 44, which is recorded in Acts 12:23 and by Josephus.[10] Confining ourselves to this early period, the locales within Palestine recorded by Luke in his Acts include Jerusalem (Acts 1–8), Judea (1:8; 8:1; 9:31), Samaria (1:8; 8:14, 25; 9:31), Galilee (9:31), Caesarea (8:40; 10:44-48), Lydda (9:32-35), and Joppa (9:36-43). Paul refers to the church at Jerusalem (Rom. 15:25; Gal. 1:18; 2:1) and speaks—in the plural—of "the churches of Christ in Judea" (Gal. 1:22).[11]

Much of the material illustrative of early Christianity in Acts 1–12 consists of scenes in which major figures, especially Peter, preach and debate in public places (3:1-26; 4:8-12; 5:19-42). Yet there are traditions also of the fusion of confession and community. The earliest community in Jerusalem, according to Luke, consisted of eleven of the original Twelve, who are named (Acts 1:13), Mary the mother of Jesus, a group of women who are not named but must be those referred to in the passion and resurrection narratives (Luke 23:49, 55-56; 24:10), Jesus' brothers (Acts 1:14), and still others, totaling altogether a community of 120 persons (1:15). Peter is the leading figure in this early community.[12] We are to understand that the core of this community's confession proclaims Jesus' ministry, cross, and resurrection, for being an eyewitness to the ministry of Jesus from his baptism by John to his resurrection and ascension (the cross is presupposed in this sequence) is the prime prerequisite for the election of Matthias to be enrolled with the eleven remaining apostles (1:22), and Peter's preaching in Jerusalem regularly sets forth the kerygma of cross and resurrection (2:23-24, 32-36; 3:13-15, 18; 4:2, 10-11, 33; 5:30). In addition, in the case of Peter's Pentecost sermon, there is a call for repentance, which is to be followed by baptism for the forgiveness of sins (2:38; cf. later at 3:19 too).

Of course the question must be raised concerning the degree to which the speeches of Peter in Acts reflect the actual preaching of the historical apostle Peter. The speeches by Peter and Paul in Acts have been the subject of intense investigation. There is widespread consensus that, although they may well be based in part on traditions available to him, Luke has so edited them that in their present form they are virtually Lukan compositions.[13] It has been maintained by some interpreters that the speeches of Peter addressed to Jews in the early part of Acts appear to have been based on a pre-Lukan pattern concerning the rejection/crucifixion of Jesus, his vindication by God through resurrection, and a call for repentance.[14] But of course that pattern may also be as much Lukan as pre-Lukan, so the argument cannot be decisive. Nevertheless, that the preaching of Peter included the kerygma of the cross and resurrection of Jesus is confirmed by Paul's recitation of the tradition he had received as the core proclamation of the gospel (1 Cor. 15:3-7), which he most likely received from the primitive Jerusalem community while Peter was still the leading figure there (Gal. 1:18-19).[15]

As a consequence of Peter's preaching on Pentecost, Luke says that three thousand persons were added to the original nucleus (2:41). This community is portrayed as meeting in homes, as well as attending the temple, on a daily basis (2:46), devoted to the teaching of the apostles, fellowship, and prayer (2:42), and holding property in common (2:44-45). The community was thus brought together by the proclamation of Peter, which consisted primarily of a recital of the passion and resurrection. It understood itself as living in the era of redemption under the power of the Spirit. The ethos of the community is shown to be both shaped by and expressed through the thanksgiving and praise due unto God (2:46-47), the baptism of every member (2:41), and the celebration of the Eucharist (which the "breaking of bread" probably signifies in 2:42, 46[16]). Both baptism and Eucharist are reminders of being given over to death—one's own death in baptism, and Christ's death in the Eucharist. They are also the means of entering into and sustaining life within the community of faith. The ethos of the community, based on its confession, is thus one of sharing and caring for the needs of each member (2:45). Confession and community are fused in ideal fashion in Luke's portrayal of the earliest community in Jerusalem.

The ideal does not last. There are instances of dishonesty, as in the story of Ananias and Sapphira (5:1-11), and dissension, as in the complaint of the Hellenists against the Hebrews (6:1-6).[17] Nevertheless, the foundation story of the earliest community at Jerusalem sets the standard for other communities, as well as for later stages of the Jerusalem community itself. The apostles and others preach the word in Jerusalem (4:4, 31; 6:7), goods are shared, and the needy are taken care of (4:32-35). The community grows in numbers (3:47; 4:4; 5:14; 6:7; 9:31), and its members gather in homes (house churches, 2:46; 5:42; 12:12), even though the whole community is known collectively as one "church" (5:11; 8:1, 3; 15:4, 22). In fact, Luke refers to "the church" throughout Judea, Galilee, and Samaria in the singular (9:31), as though there was one Palestinian church.[18]

Luke provides relatively little information about the communities in the outlying areas of Palestine. He seems more interested in the drama of the apostolic mission, recounting the "mighty works of God" (2:11), than in the texture of the communities of Palestine. But there are traces. Communities of faith come into being through the proclamation of the word by the apostles, as in the case of the preaching of Philip at Samaria (8:5, 12) and that of Peter at Joppa and Caesarea (9:42; 10:34-43).[19] Believers are baptized, as in Samaria (8:12) and Caesarea (10:44-48). These believers continue together in fellowship in communities, as at Joppa (9:38; 10:23) and Caesarea (10:48; cf. 21:16).

In later phases of Palestinian Christianity the church at Jerusalem continues to have prominence, as both Acts and the letters of Paul show. The leadership role of Peter is superseded by that of James, the brother of Jesus. By the time of the Jerusalem conference of A.D. 48 (or 49),[20] James is the leading figure, even spokesperson, for the Jerusalem church (Gal. 2:9; Acts 15:13), a position he continues to hold when Paul arrives in the city near the end of his career (Acts 21:18). Later traditions bestow on him the title of bishop of Jerusalem (and he is considered the first bishop there in the same traditions),[21] and they relate his martyrdom (ca. A.D. 62).[22]

By combining materials from Acts and Paul's letters, the following can be said with fair certainty about James: he was considered one of those to whom the risen Lord had appeared (1 Cor. 15:7) and a member of the earliest Jerusalem community (Acts 1:14); he recognized the validity of Paul's mission to Gentiles (Gal. 2:9; Acts 15:19, 28), including the rejection of the view of certain Judean Christians (Acts 15:1; Gal. 2:4) that Gentiles must first become Jews (be circumcised) in order to be Christians (15:24).[23] But he did not approve of table fellowship between Jewish and gentile Christians in mixed (Jewish-gentile) congregations (Gal. 2:12-13).[24]

The picture sketched so far of early Palestinian Christianity does not correspond to that which has been proposed in the highly influential works of Gerd Theissen.[25] Theissen says that Jesus did not primarily found local communities, but called into being "a movement of wandering charismatics"[26]—that is, the so-called Jesus movement, which, he says, existed in Syria and Palestine between A.D. 30 and 70.[27] He contends that the disciples of Jesus, after his death, did not return to a settled life.[28] "The decisive figures in early Christianity," he says, "were travelling apostles, prophets and disciples who moved from place to place and could rely on small groups of sympathizers in these places."[29] These "homeless wandering charismatics" were the ones who "handed on what was later to take independent form as Christianity."[30]

The picture painted of the so-called Jesus movement is attractive. Its basis of support is primarily the synoptic tradition, which Theissen considers to be a mix of both genuine traditions coming from Jesus himself and traditions that originated in the post-Easter Jesus movement. "In either case," he says, "the result is the same: there is a correspondence between the social groups which handed down the tradition and the tradition itself,"[31] for "those who pass on a tradition must in some way identify with it."[32] Moreover, we may assume that those who handed down the traditions about Jesus "shaped their lives in accordance with the tradition."[33] The fact that these traditions speak of Jesus' disciples as leaving home, severing family ties, abandoning possessions, and traveling without protection is taken as evidence that the earliest Christians, the members of the "Jesus movement," were wandering charismatics.[34] Theissen also points to the existence of "wandering prophets and teachers" in the second century, to whom the *Didache* refers (11.3-6; 13.1-7; 15.2).[35]

Theissen's portrayal of early Palestinian Christianity should not, however, dominate our understanding. Wandering charismatics there may indeed have been; but if so, they do not show up in Acts or the letters of Paul.[36] Peter and Paul both travel, but they do not fit the description of the wandering charismatics. Paul, for example, resided in Corinth for a year and a half (Acts 18:11) and in Ephesus for more than three years (Acts

20:31), and he worked for a living. When Peter and other apostles traveled, they were accompanied by wives (1 Cor. 9:5). Even the synoptic tradition has emphases in the direction of settled communities, as in the case of giving children a place in the community (Mark 10:13-16 par.), preserving marital bonds (Mark 10:2-9 par.), resolving disputes and granting forgiveness to one another within the community (Matt. 18:15-22), and celebrating the Lord's Supper within the context of a common meal (Mark 14:22-25 par.). The wandering charismatics that Theissen speaks of must therefore have been a small minority at most.

More important historically are the communities of Jerusalem and elsewhere in Palestine that are mentioned in Acts. In his thoroughgoing critique of Theissen, Richard Horsley has written: "The most striking thing sociologically about the Jesus movement was that it seems to have taken the form of local communities."[37] Theissen, he says, portrays the wandering charismatics as "a few dozen itinerants" whose proclamation, consisting of the "hard sayings of Jesus," had no relevance for "ordinary social relations."[38] Horsley grants that there were itinerant missionaries in the earliest stages of Palestinian Christianity, but maintains that their mission was "the revitalization of local community life," and that their leaving home, possessions, and family would not have been a "way of life" but a temporary expedient, "an unavoidable but more incidental matter necessitated by their mission."[39] Their activities do not account for the formation of the communities themselves, nor was their way of life to be emulated by the members of those communities as a life-style.[40]

There are two other issues related to the Palestinian church that have a bearing on our discussion of confession and community. The first is the significance of the Hellenists, and the second is the question of lines of development between early Palestinian Christianity and later expressions of Christianity. The Hellenists, who are mentioned in Acts 6:1,[41] appear to have been Greek-speaking Jewish Christians.[42] The most we have concerning their beliefs is given in Stephen's speech to the Sanhedrin as rendered by Luke (Acts 7:2-53). The speech is a recital of the history of Israel from the time of Abraham to that of David and Solomon. The main point made is that the Jerusalem temple with its cultus was not instituted by God,[43] for God "does not dwell in houses made with hands" (7:48). Jesus is called the prophet like Moses and the righteous one (7:37, 52), whom the officers of the Sanhedrin have executed (7:52). It is likely that the view concerning the temple is based on the conviction that, since the death and resurrection of Jesus and the creation of the Christian community, the temple is obsolete. In any case, the Hellenists were dispersed from Jerusalem during the first few years (perhaps months) of the Christian movement (8:1), and they evangelized and founded Christian communities outside

Jerusalem, including that of Antioch of Syria (11:19).[44] It is possible that the Hellenists also reached Alexandria and founded a Christian community there.[45] Whatever the extent of the mission of the Hellenists, the type of Christianity represented by them, according to Stephen's speech and what can be known of the church at Antioch, provided for the propagation of the gospel in the Greek language and the inclusion of Gentiles at an early date.

Concerning later developments, from the outbreak of the war in Palestine (A.D. 66–70) and later, many Palestinian Christians emigrated. Some, according to independent accounts by Eusebius and Epiphanius, settled in the city of Pella and surrounding sites in the Decapolis and Perea.[46] It has been speculated that others may have settled in Asia Minor, including those who were to constitute the beginning of the Johannine community at Ephesus.[47] It appears that a remnant of a church continued to exist in Palestine at least to the end of the first century and on into the time of Trajan (A.D. 98–117) under the leadership of the grandsons of Jude, Jesus' brother.[48] In later times the Ebionites considered themselves to be the heirs of Palestinian Jewish Christianity, appealing to James as a major source of their teachings.[49] But whether the Ebionites actually originated in a circle of Jewish Christians associated with James is an open question.[50] Then too the canonical Epistle of James claims to stand in the tradition of James as well.[51] The various tributaries of Palestinian Christianity cannot be traced here. In a very literal sense, of course, every stream of Christian tradition goes back ultimately to Palestinian Jewish Christianity, directly or indirectly.

The Q Community

Material common to the Gospels of Matthew and Luke, which was not derived from the Gospel of Mark, has conventionally been designated Q (an abbreviation from the German word *Quelle*, meaning *source*).[52] Although a few scholars have rejected the view that Q existed as a written source for the two major synoptic evangelists,[53] they are clearly in the minority. While the Q hypothesis cannot be designated an "assured result" of modern scholarship, it is widely held as the most likely explanation for the high degree of similarities of content, wording, and sequence in over two hundred verses common to Matthew and Luke that are not derived from Mark. Dieter Lührmann has conveniently gathered up five points commonly accepted concerning Q research,[54] which I shall summarize: (1) Q consists of material common to Matthew and Luke, which is not from Mark; if additional material in either Gospel came from Q, that would not alter the picture significantly. (2) The language of Q must have been Greek; verbal agreements in the two Gospels speak against a common source in Aramaic (although the traditions go back to an Aramaic stratum). (3) Q has certain theological features, such as opposition to "this generation," a connection with wisdom traditions, and a Christology that is not modeled on the "kerygma type." (4) Q is indebted to traditions, but it is not agreed whether these were gathered in phases in ever-growing layers (a series of compositional steps), or whether they are simply from different, earlier traditions. (5) The final redaction of Q was around A.D. 60, since nothing in it shows acquaintance with the Jewish war (A.D. 66–70) or events leading up to it. Various scholars have provided reconstructions of the Q source, based on the material common to Matthew and Luke.[55]

Although it is possible to accept the hypothesis that Q existed as a document without going on to assume the existence of a discreet Q community, there is a widespread tendency today among scholars to speak of a Q community without reservations. In doing so, of course, scholars are stacking one hypothesis upon another. Yet no one will deny the importance of their scholarship in the study of Christian origins. Even those who have reservations about the existence of a discreet Q community must analyze and assess the various portraits of the Q community that are being offered. In the discussion that follows an attempt will be made at such as though the existence of a Q community can be taken for granted.

The tendency has been to locate the Q community geographically in either Palestine[56] or Syria.[57] Either of these is possible, and there seems to be no way of selecting one over the other.[58] What can be said is that the community consisted of Greek-speaking Christians, probably of Jewish background primarily,[59] but open to the inclusion of Gentiles,[60] who treasured traditions of Jesus' sayings, and who expected the imminent arrival of God's kingdom and the parousia of the Son of Man.

It is possible, as contended by various scholars, that Q in its final form is the result of a series of redactional stages that reflect theological developments within the Q community over time.[61] For example, John Kloppenborg has suggested three stages of development. According to him, the first written stage of Q consisted of a collection of "wisdom speeches" that were "hortatory in nature and sapiential in their mode of argumentation." At a second stage, this collection was expanded by additional sayings, which were prophetic and apocalyptic, and which "adopted a critical and polemical stance with respect to Israel." Finally, at the last stage, the story of Jesus' temptation in the wilderness (Luke 4:1-13//Matt. 4:1-11) was added, which introduced a "biographical dimension" into the collection.[62]

Positing stages of development of Q, and therefore of the Q community as well, increases the complexities of theological and social analysis. Whatever one says about Q or the Q community has to be coordinated with a particular stage. Beyond that, there is no clear agreement among scholars concerning the stages of composition;[63] the proposal of Kloppenborg is but one.

For our purposes it is sufficient to confine ourselves to an analysis of the theological themes of Q in the form it had when Matthew and Luke used it for the composition of their Gospels, allowing that both evangelists made redactional modifications of the material when they incorporated it into their respective Gospels. At least at that level the confession of the Q community was colored by strong twin eschatological expectations:[64] (1) God's kingdom is imminent (Luke 10:9-11//Matt. 10:7-14; Luke 11:20// Matt. 12:28; Luke 12:54-56//Matt. 16:2-3), and (2) the Son of Man will come soon (Luke 12:39-40//Matt. 24:43-44) and carry out the final judgment (Luke 12:8-9//Matt. 10:32-33). Those who belong to Jesus on earth will be confirmed for salvation by the Son of Man at his coming.

The question has been raised many times about the lack in Q of passion and resurrection accounts. Does that absence mean that, for this community, the proclamation of the death and resurrection of Jesus was foreign to its own? Did the Q community proclaim a version of Christianity that either knew nothing of, or chose to reject, the kind that one finds, for example, in the Pauline tradition? There are several issues to sort out here. We should ask, first, whether there are any indications that the Q community had some acquaintance with the accounts of Jesus' death and resurrection. Then we should ask what the results might mean.

Although it has been asserted that the Q community knew nothing about the proclamation of cross and resurrection,[65] the saying that one must "take" or "bear" one's own "cross" and "follow after" or "come after" Jesus in order to be a disciple (Luke 14:27//Matt. 10:38)[66] presupposes the cross of Jesus and recalls the carrying of Jesus' cross—either by Jesus himself (as in John 19:17) or by Simon of Cyrene (as in Mark 15:21//Matt. 27:32//Luke 23:26)— in the passion accounts. The metaphor of taking up one's cross in connection with following Jesus makes sense only within a context where the cross is a symbol of giving oneself over sacrificially, and therefore it most certainly echoes the passion.[67] Even the writer of the *Gospel of Thomas* recognized this by the insertion of a reference to Jesus' carrying his own cross: "whoever does not bear the cross *as I do* will not be worthy of me" (*Gos. Thom.* 55).[68] Luke's intensification "his *own* cross" (*ton stauron heautou*, 14:27) appears also to be an antiphonal accent in counterpoint to the cross of Jesus.

A second passage that echoes a refrain from the passion accounts is related, by Q itself, to Jerusalem, and that is the lament of Jesus over Jerusalem (Luke 13:34-35//Matt. 23:37-39). The quotation of Psalm 118:26 (LXX, Ps. 117:26), "Blessed be he who comes in the name of the Lord" (Luke 13:35//Matt. 23:39), may well refer in the Q context to the parousia of the Son of Man,[69] but elsewhere it is associated with the passion narrative

(Jesus' entry into Jerusalem) in both the synoptic and Johannine traditions (Mark 11:9//Matt. 21:9; Luke 19:38; John 12:13). There is no evidence that Psalm 118:26 was understood in a messianic sense in first-century Judaism.[70] The first such usage must have been in connection with the account of Jesus' entry into Jerusalem, where it is unmistakably messianic (which Luke and John underscore by the insertion of the term *king*). The fact that the usage has attestation in both the synoptic and Johannine traditions speaks in favor of its place in the Jerusalem entry tradition from very early times. The Q saying echoes the acclamation of the crowds at the coming of the Messiah to Jerusalem. It is preceded by Jesus' lament over Jerusalem for killing the prophets and stoning those whom God has sent; surely the rejection and killing of Jesus will follow.[71] The inhabitants of Jerusalem are told that they will not see him until their full acceptance of him, and that will be expressed in the acclamation that is fitting for the Messiah's coming to Jerusalem—namely, Psalm 118:26. The messianic interpretation given to that verse in the Q passage therefore presupposes knowledge of a passion tradition that appears in the Gospel narratives, and it provides further evidence that the Q community knew at least elements of the passion tradition.

Still other Q passages show evidence of acquaintance with the passion, death, and resurrection of Jesus. Although the tradition history of the parable of the pounds/talents (Luke 19:12-27//Matt. 25:14-30) is exceedingly complex,[72] it has long been recognized that it contains allegorical overtones. A wealthy man, addressed as *kyrios* ("lord"), departs to a far country (Luke) or on a long journey (Matthew), leaving his servants in charge of his property, and on his return settles accounts with them. Whatever its meaning at the moment of telling by Jesus, if it is authentic, the telling of it in the Q community would have had allegorical reference to Jesus' departure via death and exaltation, his parousia, and the final judgment.[73]

Further, the Q passages on Jerusalem's habitual killing of prophets and other emissaries from God (Luke 13:34//Matt. 23:37) and the homelessness of the Son of Man (Luke 9:58//Matt. 8:20) carry, within any Christian community knowing even the slightest details of the fate of Jesus, the meaning of the rejection and execution of Jesus. In the Q passage concerning the final judgment upon Israel by his disciples (Luke 22:28-30//Matt. 19:28), the Son of Man has been given a kingdom by his Father (Luke), or a glorious throne on which to preside (Matthew), indicating that he is the vindicated and exalted one. And of course Jesus can be the expected Son of Man, as portrayed in Q passages elsewhere (Luke 12:40//Matt. 24:44; Luke 17:26-30//Matt. 24:37-39), only on the basis of his resurrection, by which he received his transcendent status.[74]

On the basis of this review of Q passages, it can be concluded that the Q community was acquainted with traditions about Jesus' death and resurrection. But the question remains concerning the meanings the community would have attached to it. Here there is a wide range of scholarly opinion. There are two leading positions, however, with variations in nuance by those who hold them.

According to several interpreters, while it is granted that the Q community would indeed have known traditions about Jesus' death and resurrection, its christological and soteriological focus lay elsewhere. It gave no particular soteriological significance to those events in the manner of the kerygma proclaimed by Paul and others.[75] Kloppenborg, for example, has written that "Q seems curiously indifferent to both Jesus' death and a divine rescue of Jesus from death,"[76] and that "the notion of resurrection is absent from Q . . . because this metaphor is fundamentally inappropriate to the genre and theology of Q."[77] He has argued that every literary genre "carries within itself a hermeneutical framework" and is, so to speak, "genre-bound."[78] Since Q is primarily a collection of sayings, its meaning should be investigated within that hermeneutical framework alone without the importation of concepts from outside. He concludes that "Q was not influenced by either the passion kerygma or the passion stories."[79]

A similar point of view has been expressed by Helmut Koester. In light of Q's emphasis on the task of the disciples of Jesus to carry on his proclamation, he says:

> Any emphasis upon Jesus' suffering, death, and resurrection would be meaningless in this context. Thus Q can not be seen as a teaching supplement for a community whose theology is represented by the Pauline kerygma. Q's theology and soteriology are fundamentally different.[80]

What then is the theological and soteriological center of Q? On the basis of the material in Q itself, it is clear that the community that composed it sought to continue Jesus' proclamation of God's kingdom, both present and coming (Luke 10:9//Matt. 10:7; Luke 13:28-30//Matt. 8:11-12; Luke 16:16//Matt. 11:12-13; cf. Luke 7:28//Matt. 11:11; Luke 12:2-3//Matt. 10:26-27),[81] and it proclaimed that the Son of Man would come and carry out the final judgment (Luke 12:8-9//Matt. 10:32-33; cf. Luke 12:39-40, 41-46//Matt. 24:43-44, 45-51; Luke 17:22-25, 26-30//Matt. 24:26-27, 37-39). Those who belong to Jesus on earth will be confirmed for salvation by the Son of Man at his coming (Luke 12:8-9//Matt. 10:32-33; cf. Luke 10:16//Matt. 10:40; Luke 10:21-22//Matt. 11:25-27).[82] All this means that Jesus is then "the redeemer of the future."[83] The death of Jesus was understood as a feature of the last days (the forces of evil working against him).[84] According

to Kloppenborg, Jesus' death is understood in particular in light of deuteronomistic theology: "persecution and death are the 'occupational hazards'
of the envoys of God or Sophia."[85] Jesus' resurrection or exaltation was
understood, in the view of some interpreters, as the means of authorization
and inspiration of the risen Lord's prophets within the Q community.[86]
Kloppenborg, however, has contended that "the notion of resurrection is
absent from Q":[87]

> Q understands the authorization of Jesus' soteriologically intensified words
> by implying a functional identification of Jesus and Sophia. . . . No special
> moment of vindication is required. If one wishes to speak of Easter at all,
> one must say that what the Markan and post-Markan Easter traditions localize
> and particularize by narration, Q assumes to have always been a characteristic
> of Jesus' words as the words of Sophia.[88]

Other interpreters, however, have come to different conclusions regarding the theology and proclamation of the Q community. Essentially
they agree that Q, as we can construct it from our Gospels of Matthew
and Luke, may not reflect all of the christological convictions of the Q
community.[89] Heinz E. Tödt, who is often credited for being the pioneer
of recent Q research,[90] has contended that "the passion and resurrection
were not what had to be preached but what had enabled them to preach,"
for the "events of the passion and resurrection" were the foundation for its
existence in the first place.[91]

Various interpreters have held that Q would have had a specific function
alongside the ongoing proclamation of the cross and resurrection. According
to Tödt, the Q community took up and taught the teachings of Jesus,
convinced that the risen Lord was present in their fellowship, and that the
fellowship was itself the gift of salvation that would be valid before God
in eternity.[92] In the view of Ernst Käsemann, the function of Q was to
provide guidance in the mission of the community.[93] Werner Kümmel has
declared that "Q was organized for the need of the community itself, for
whose existence the primitive Christian kerygma was a presupposition."[94]
And Marinus de Jonge has written:

> It is extremely unlikely . . . that the communities in which the sayings of
> the Q collection were handed down knew no other traditions about Jesus'
> life, death, and resurrection/exaltation. Q's implicit Christology cannot have
> represented the whole understanding of Jesus in any Christian congregation.
> For one thing, one could not speak of Jesus' rejection by Israel's leaders
> without telling what happened afterward. One had to explain why the king-
> dom of God was a present dynamic reality and not an illusion of people
> who did not want to admit that their master had deluded both them and

himself. Those who handed down the Q material believed in a God who had vindicated Jesus, his work and his message, and they believed that he would come again to share with them the full bliss of the kingdom of God.[95]

The issues are complex, and viewpoints are maintained with considerable strength. But some decisions must finally be made. One can start, it seems, by maintaining that the issue is not whether the Q community knew, in however rudimentary form, that Jesus had been crucified and that it also shared the belief with other Christians that he had been raised from the dead. The issue is, instead, whether the Q community attached any soteriological significance to the death and resurrection *in the way* that others, particularly Paul, did.

Perhaps the first issue to face is the question of genre. How "genre-bound" (Kloppenborg) must one be in interpreting the theology of a given community? Although Q is a sayings collection that presents Jesus as representative of Wisdom, can one say that that exhausts the significance of Jesus for the Q community? It is one thing to describe the theology of Q as a document; it is another to declare that the community's theology as a whole is fairly represented by it; and it is still another to say that its theology is fully contained within it. The problem with using a "genre-bound" hermeneutic to interpret the theology of the Q community can be illustrated by reference to more recent works. For example, the most authoritative collection of the writings of Martin Luther King, Jr., runs some 676 pages in length.[96] But because of the issues addressed, and because of the genre of most of the writings contained in the volume, one looks in vain for references to the cross and resurrection of Jesus and their soteriological significance. Yet no one would claim that the King corpus available to us reflects the totality of the theology of King, his Atlanta congregation, or his followers in the civil rights movement he led.

The question must be asked concerning the origins of Q and then the function of Q within the Q community itself. Concerning its origins, its core could go back to the pre-Easter circle of disciples, and that would explain why its contents are limited to sayings.[97] Its later function within the Q community may have been a very limited one.[98] We simply do not know what other texts and traditions were available to the community in its inner life. If we look elsewhere at early Christian communities, such as those in which the Gospels of Matthew, Luke, and John were composed, we see that they were able to accommodate very different sources and traditions.[99] What makes them different from the Q community is that they finally produced documentary evidence of integrating their sources and traditions, giving them a final redactional stamp.

What seems particularly strange in some of the current discussions of Q is that, precisely at the moment when scholars far and wide are calling for the dismantling of long-standing conceptual walls between religious and cultural traditions of antiquity (for example, between Palestinian Judaism and Hellenistic Judaism or between orthodoxy and heresy), some are portraying the Q community as walled off from the rest of early Christianity, even though such persons will claim that itinerant missionaries went out from (and presumably returned to) the Q community, traveling about Palestine and Syria! Surely the theology and life of the Q community had dimensions that are not reflected in the Q document itself. Since it narrates no fellowship meals, must we assume that the community had none? Since it prescribes neither baptism nor the Lord's Supper, and since it contains no accounts of such, must we conclude that the community practiced neither? In short, it is one thing to say that there is no clear literary evidence for a soteriological interpretation of the cross and resurrection in the Q community; it is another to say that, therefore, the Q community (and each of its members) obviously attached no soteriological significance to them. This methodological point is actually granted in the following remark: "Obviously," Kloppenborg has written, the Q document "does not offer a complete catalogue of the group's beliefs."[100]

Nevertheless, to claim that the Q community had other sources, traditions, and theological emphases is to argue from silence no less than it is to say that Q contains all that the community thought significant about Jesus. It seems more fruitful to take another tack. The issue itself must be restated. Although it is agreed by interpreters generally that the Q community knew about Jesus' death and resurrection, the point that has been made is that for that community the passion, death, and resurrection were not understood as having soteriological significance. Here lurks the habit of measuring all forms of proclamation in light of the Pauline kerygma. It has long been recognized, however, that the portrayal of the passion, death, and resurrection of Jesus as having soteriological significance differs widely in the New Testament. Neither the author of Luke-Acts nor the author of the Gospel of John, for example, represents Jesus' death as an atonement for sin in the way that Paul does. In each case the passion and death of Jesus is primarily a prelude to his exaltation/resurrection. Yet they attach soteriological significance to the whole complex in one way or another.[101] In the case of Luke-Acts, the passion and death of Jesus are the means by which he might "enter into his glory" (Luke 24:26; see Acts 17:3; 26:23). It is the risen Lord who grants salvation through the forgiveness of sins of those who repent and believe in him in consequence of the proclamation of his witnesses (Luke 24:46-47).[102] And in the Fourth Gospel the lifting up of the Son of Man on the cross is the beginning of his glorification

(John 12:32-33; cf. 3:14; 8:28); "passion, resurrection, exaltation, ascension, and glorification are all seen together as one event."[103] The exalted Son has received power from the Father over all flesh and gives eternal life to those whom the Father has given him (17:2)—that is, those who believe (3:16; 5:24; 6:47).

As we have seen, there are allusions in Q to Jesus' rejection, death, resurrection, and coming again—the main points of the common Christian kerygma! These allusions presuppose that the community not only knew about the major christological "moments" of the common Christian tradition but also reflected on them. That point is agreed to by those who claim that Jesus' rejection and death were interpreted in light of deuteronomistic theology.[104] Further, the Q community most certainly considered itself to be living already in a new era, endowed by the presence and power of the Holy Spirit (Luke 3:16//Matt. 3:11; Luke 12:10//Matt. 12:32; and Luke 12:12//Matt. 10:19).[105] The new age was not considered to be entirely future; it had already begun.[106] According to traditional Jewish eschatology, the endowment of the Spirit is a sign of the advent of the messianic era and of one's inclusion among the redeemed.[107] Although the Q community awaited the parousia of the Son of Man as the final stage of its redemption, its very existence as a community of the Spirit, and therefore of the messianic age, was based on events that had taken place—the ministry, death, and resurrection of Jesus, followed by the Spirit's coming and vitality among its members—even if that community had not reflected on the meaning of the death and resurrection of Jesus along Pauline lines. Salvation may well have been understood as fellowship bestowed and renewed by the risen Lord, to be certified by his coming as Son of Man.[108] But it was possible then only as a consequence of Jesus' earthly ministry, death, and resurrection. And it is doubtful then whether one should look upon Q as evidence for the existence of a community whose Christology stood in actual contrast, or as an alternative, to those held in communities founded upon the kerygma of the death and resurrection of Jesus.[109]

How one describes the theological convictions of the Q community has a direct bearing on how the ethos of the community will be understood. In general the Q community has been described as having an ethic of radical discipleship, which was rooted in its conviction that the kingdom is dawning and that the Son of Man shall come quickly to execute the final judgment, and which had been delineated by the teachings of Jesus.[110] It has been suggested that the Q community may have consisted of two identifiable groups: wandering charismatic prophets who carried on a mission in Palestine or Syria, confronting their hearers with the words of Jesus, and a circle of fellow believers living in a settled community life, who composed the Q document.[111] Be that as it may, as soon as one speaks of the Q *community*, it is the settled, and presumably major, group responsible for the production of Q that one has in mind. That community, in spite of its expectation of the coming of the Son of Man in the future, knew Jesus in the present as the post-Easter exalted Jesus,[112] and also remembered him as the earthly Jesus of the past who had been a lonely figure, rejected and killed. The community considered discipleship a matter of following him. That is apparent above all in the saying that the disciple must bear his or her own cross and come after Jesus (Luke 14:27//Matt. 10:38) but elsewhere also.[113]

What that life looks like is not spelled out in detail. But it includes repentance,[114] faith,[115] a readiness to confess Jesus as the Son of Man,[116] and a life of dependence upon God for all things needful and its correlate, freedom from anxiety.[117] In relationship to God, persons pray for what is needed, both material goods[118] and the forgiveness of sins.[119] In relationship to others, the life of following Jesus entails withholding judgment,[120] love and generosity toward them,[121] a willingness to forgive,[122] and in particular a special regard and care for the poor.[123] Life becomes life when the disciple gives no thought about the enhancement of his or her own existence or standing before God and others, but when his or her life is given over to following Jesus in love and care for others (Luke 17:33//Matt. 10:39).

The Q material provides evidence therefore of congruence between confession and community. The community remembers the earthly Jesus and his teachings about discipleship. It affirms his crucifixion and his resurrection to transcendent status. And it expects his coming as the Son of Man who will exercise the final judgment. Implications for community life follow. The community recalls the teachings of Jesus to guide its common life, a life that is given shape also by the memory of Jesus' cross and his coming as Son of Man to judge. Discipleship does not consist of finding one's life by appropriating wisdom, as a purely Wisdom Christology might suggest, but consists primarily in following Jesus, which means conflict with the larger society, even rejection and persecution, and turning to both friend and enemy alike with love, generosity, and forgiveness.

The legacy of the Q community that is best known is the Q document, which was taken over by the evangelists Matthew and Luke and incorporated into their Gospels. But what can be said about the Q community itself? If it existed in Palestine in the middle of the first century, what became of it during or after the outbreak of the Jewish war (A.D. 66–70)? Did its members migrate from Palestine? Did they perish? If they migrated, did they continue intact as a community, only to pass out of existence later, or did they join other Christian communities? If the Q community existed in Syria, did it simply pass out of existence some time after the composition of the Q document? Or did its members share the fate of Q itself and become assimilated into Matthew's community, which was most likely located in or near Antioch of Syria?

The suggestion has been made by James M. Robinson that the genre of Q—that is, a sayings collection—moved along a trajectory that led to Gnosticism, and the *Gospel of Thomas* is taken as evidence for its development.[124] If that is so for the genre of Q, could the community of Q have moved along the same kind of trajectory, ending up in Gnosticism? There is no way that one can answer the question with certainty.

Nevertheless, the suggestion by Robinson itself has been called into question or modified, not least of all by Robinson himself. For one thing, apart from the *Gospel of Thomas*, a "gnosticizing tendency" is not evident in any other example of the sayings genre (*Pirke Aboth* and *1 Enoch*).[125]

Further, Helmut Koester and John Kloppenborg have introduced considerations that must be taken seriously. While Koester has suggested that the *Gospel of Thomas* may be dependent in part on an early version of Q, or upon clusters of sayings employed in its composition,[126] he has said that any gnosticizing tendencies that might have existed in Q were held in check by the introduction of the apocalyptic expectation of the Son of Man.[127] Kloppenborg has argued that, by incorporating the temptation story (Luke 4:1-13//Matt. 4:1-11) into the document, the final redactor of Q tilted it in a biographical-narrative direction, and that that process was furthered by Matthew and Luke when they incorporated Q within the narratives of their respective Gospels.[128]

It seems fair to say that the *Gospel of Thomas*—insofar as it can be considered gnostic at all (a view that needs to be substantiated)—can be taken as evidence that a portion of sayings it has in common with Q (some 78 verses of Q, or about a third of them[129]) *could* be used in a gnostic interpretation of the sayings tradition. But it cannot be maintained that Q, or even a portion of it, moved along a gnosticizing trajectory as though that was a natural development.[130] The evidence adduced by Koester and Kloppenborg, in fact, speaks against it, and it also speaks against the view that the Q community would have moved naturally toward or into Gnosticism. Finally, since Q actually alludes to the main points of the common Christian kerygma (Jesus' rejection, death, resurrection, and coming again), it would seem that the Q community could easily have made common cause with other communities of the "kerygmatic" type, either existing alongside them or being assimilated into one or more of them over time.

Given all these considerations, it is not likely that the Q community ended up in Gnosticism. The view of Walter Bauer that second-century heresies (in this case Gnosticism) were theological descendants of first-century varieties of Christianity (in this case, the Q expression of it) does not find a basis for support in this particular instance.

The Churches of Paul

The two main sources concerning the apostle Paul, his activities, his churches, and his theology are his letters and the Acts of the Apostles. Of these two sources, the letters have primary importance; Acts is to be considered a secondary source.[131] And of the various letters attributed to Paul, those that are of undisputed authorship are most important. Those that are considered deutero-Pauline must, like Acts, be dealt with as secondary sources.[132]

According to his undisputed letters, along with corroboration and further information from Acts, Paul can be considered the founder of churches in Galatia, Ephesus, Corinth, Thessalonica, and Philippi. He may have founded churches elsewhere,[133] but it is these congregations that can be investigated on the basis of Paul's letters. One can derive from these letters aspects of Paul's theology, the gospel he shared with the communities he founded, viewpoints that he opposed, and information concerning the ethos of the communities to which he wrote.

There are methodological issues to be addressed at the outset. In investigating the confession of faith of the Pauline churches, we must be aware (1) that the letters of Paul give Paul's views, not necessarily those of people in his communities, and (2) that the letters of Paul to his churches are occasional correspondence prompted by issues among his addressees. The point has been made in Pauline studies that, although there is a "coherence" to his thought, Paul's letters are "contingent"—that is, they are written for specific historical circumstances.[134] Therefore one cannot expect to find in them, singly or together, a systematic presentation of Paul's theology.

Regarding the first point, Paul's letters provide not only aspects of the apostle's thought but also his expectations that his churches will be of like mind with him (cf. 1 Cor. 4:14-16; Gal. 5:10; Phil. 4:9), above all in their confession of faith. In spite of inevitable differences between Paul and his communities, it is he who set the standard, the norm, by which the faith of the communities could be judged.

Regarding the second point, of course the letters of Paul are contingent, occasional pieces, for Paul works in ever-changing contexts requiring different responses. Yet every theologian and every proclaimer of the gospel works in historical and social contexts, and that does not preclude a descriptive grasp of his or her theology or message in other times or places.[135] In the case of Paul, it is clear that he considered himself an apostle (Rom. 1:1; 1 Cor. 1:1; Gal. 1:1), not a theologian in the sense of later figures (Origen, Aquinas, and others). Yet, elusive as it may be, his thought can be described—at least in its major affirmations.[136] We should be able to expect a good measure of coherence and consistency in his letters except where the texts prove otherwise.[137]

The confession of faith of Paul and his communities—made up mostly of persons of gentile background[138]—consists of elements from the legacy of Israel (such as monotheism, God's creation of the world, and the Scriptures of Israel as authoritative revelation) and elements from the common stock of pre-Pauline Christianity. Above all, there are the creedal formulas common to Paul and his predecessors that the apostle has included in his letters.[139] They consist of two types. One type—the *hyper* formula—has a three-part structure consisting of (1) Christ (or another christological title) as subject of the clause, (2) an aorist verb (such as "died" or "was put to death"), and (3) the preposition *hyper* ("for," "on behalf of," or "for the sake of"[140]) followed by a genitive noun (such as "sins" or "the ungodly") or pronoun (such as "us"). Although this type of creedal formula had pre-Pauline origins, as 1 Corinthians 15:3 demonstrates, it became a part of the apostle's own proclamation. The passages of this type—which all contain *hyper*—are as follows:[141]

Christ died for the ungodly (Rom. 5:6).
Christ died for us (Rom. 5:8).
Christ died for our sins (1 Cor. 15:3).
[Christ] has died for all (2 Cor. 5:14).
[Our Lord Jesus Christ] gave himself for our sins (Gal. 1:4).
[The Son of God] gave himself for me (Gal. 2:20).
[Christ became] a curse for us (Gal. 3:13).
[Our Lord Jesus Christ] died for us (1 Thess. 5:10).

The second type of creedal formula—the "sending" formula—has a four-part structure consisting of (1) God as the subject of the clause, (2) an aorist verb ("sent" or "gave up"), (3) the "Son" as the direct object, and (4) a statement of purpose for the sending or giving up, which is always a redemptive one. There are three such passages in Paul's letters:[142]

For God has done what the law could not do: . . .
    sending his own Son in the likeness of sinful flesh and for sin, he
    condemned sin in the flesh (Rom. 8:3).
He who did not spare his own Son but gave him up for us all (Rom.
    8:32).
God sent forth his Son . . . to redeem those who were under the law,
    so that we might receive adoption as children (Gal. 4:4-5).

These two types of formula have both structural and material differences. But the differences should not be pressed too far, since Paul can combine them, as he does in Romans 8:32, where a sending formula contains the preposition *hyper*. For Paul, it is clear that Jesus has given himself over to death for the sake of others, as the first type indicates. At the same time it is evident that the redemptive act carried out at the cross was an act of God for the sake of humanity, as the second type has it. Christ is the agent of redemption on the basis of God's initiative. Therefore Paul's redemptive Christology is primarily theopractic,[143] emphasizing God's action, for in Christ God was reconciling the world to himself (2 Cor. 5:19). God's judgment upon humanity has been carried out at the cross. The crucified Christ became a "curse for us" (Gal. 3:13), thereby liberating humanity from the judgment and sentence due. The alienation and hostility between sinful humanity and God has been overcome.[144]

Jesus' death and resurrection are at the center of Paul's consciousness and confession. To the Corinthians Paul wrote: "I decided to know nothing among you except Christ and him crucified" (1 Cor. 2:2). To the Romans he declared: "If you confess with your lips that Jesus is Lord and believe in your heart that God raised him from the dead, you will be saved" (Rom. 10:9). References to Jesus' sacrificial death appear not only in the passages quoted above as creedal formulas but in longer passages as well, such as in Romans 3:21-26; 5:6-21; 1 Corinthians 1:18—2:5; 11:23-32; 15:3-28; 2 Corinthians 5:14-21; and Galatians 6:11-16.

So important is the cross as the means of Jesus' death that Paul refers to it, or to Jesus' crucifixion, a dozen times in his letters.[145] It is quite likely that he added the words "even death on a cross" to the reference to Jesus' death within the Philippian hymn (Phil. 2:6-11) at 2:8.[146] Likewise, Paul's many affirmations of Jesus' resurrection focus on "the singularity of Jesus' fate."[147] Although on one occasion he speaks of Jesus as actor (that is, he says that "Jesus rose" from the dead, 1 Thess. 4:14), that is within a confessional statement that can be considered pre-Pauline in origin.[148] Normally and overwhelmingly Paul speaks of God as the actor; so God raised Jesus from the dead, or Jesus "was raised" (by God) from the dead.[149] Some of the passages appear to be pre-Pauline formulas (for example, Rom. 1:4; 4:25; 10:9; 1 Cor. 15:4), but affirming the resurrection of Jesus belongs to the fabric of Paul's message. Its implications are that God has established Jesus as Lord and Christ; that he is the vindicated redeemer; and that the new age has been inaugurated.[150]

Paul shared his confessional language with his churches, and he expected it to become their own.[151] He also expected that the ethos of the communities he founded would reflect their commonly held confession of faith. This can be observed in a variety of ways. Four of them will be illustrated here.

First, those who make up Paul's churches were baptized upon entrance into membership (1 Cor. 12:13; Rom. 6:4; Gal. 3:27). This initiatory rite recalled the death and resurrection of Jesus, and it had clear implications for the life of the believer. The person who was baptized was to consider himself or herself dead to sin, and to have left a former life; and to consider himself or herself to have become alive again by the power of the Spirit, and to have entered into a new life (Rom. 6:1-11; 1 Cor. 6:11). But the emphasis is primarily on crucifixion and being united with Christ in his death; Christ's own voluntary submission to death is a model for the other-regarding attitudes and actions of the Christian (Rom. 15:1-7; 2 Cor. 8:9; Gal. 6:2).[152] Although Paul speaks of Christ as having been raised from the dead in the principal passages (Rom. 6:4, 5, 8-9), he is careful not to say that Christians are already participants with Christ in his resurrection. That is still future, as the use of future tense verbs shows (Rom. 6:5, 8).[153] So baptism is not a means of entering into a new existence free of earthly troubles, a union with Christ above. On the contrary, it is entry into "newness of life" (Rom. 6:4) within the present world under the lordship of Christ, to whom the baptized person belongs (Rom. 14:8; 1 Cor. 1:12; 3:23; 2 Cor. 10:7; Gal. 3:29), and whose conduct thereafter is Spirit-led (Rom. 7:6; 8:4, 11, 14; Gal. 5:16-18, 25).

Second, the churches of Paul shared a self-definition with Paul that gave shape to their ethos.[154] Paul applies to his communities such labels as "the church of God" (1 Cor. 10:32; 11:22; cf. 2 Cor. 11:24-29), "the churches of Christ" (Rom. 16:16), or simply "the churches" or "the church" (1 Cor. 1:2; 2 Cor. 8:1; Gal. 1:13; Phil. 3:6). Whatever the precise origins of the term "church,"[155] it existed among Greek-speaking Jewish Christians prior to Paul,[156] and its background is the biblical phrase "assembly of God" (*qahal elohim*; Greek: *ekklēsia tou theou*) or "assembly of the Lord" (*qahal Yahweh*; Greek: *ekklēsia tou kyriou*).[157] Such terminology appears also in the writings of Philo and the Qumran community.[158] Within the letters of Paul, the term *ekklēsia* signifies an eschatological reality. That becomes clear through his use of modifiers. The churches are the assemblies of the saints (1 Cor. 14:33), persons sanctified in Christ (1 Cor. 1:2), who are called to belong to Christ (Rom. 1:6-7) at the beginning of the new age signaled by the resurrection of Jesus from the dead.

Members of the church are called "saints" in all Paul's letters, except Galatians, for a total of twenty-five times.[159] They are called "believers" ten times in four letters.[160] But above all, Paul uses the terminology of siblings, "brother" and "sister," which is used in singular and plural forms on 116 occasions in his letters.[161] The use of such language can be found in the

Old Testament and other literature of Jewish origin, in traditions of Jesus concerning his hearers or disciples, and in literary sources of gentile origin in the ancient world.[162] But the rarity of the terminology in these sources causes the frequency of its use in Paul's letters to jump out in even bolder form than a noncomparative reading might otherwise suggest.[163] Here Paul makes use of the language of primary groups, and such groups are typically characterized by intimate face-to-face association and cooperation, strong feelings of group loyalty and identification, and providing a place where members can be themselves without fear, rejection, or ridicule.[164] The evaluations imposed upon the members of such groups by outsiders can be dispensed with.[165]

Typically, according to Max Weber's analysis, a religious community that considers itself a brother-and-sisterhood has an ethic of relativization and reciprocity: there is a relativization of natural ties of family so that the spiritual brother-and-sisterhood is stronger than relationships between spouses, parent and child, and siblings; and there is reciprocity in the sense of mutual aid and support, based on the principle that the need of the other person today could be one's own tomorrow (*was heute dir mangelt, kann morgen mir mangeln*).[166] Although social and economic stratifications surely existed among the members of Paul's churches,[167] and probably reflected a cross section of most of Roman society,[168] these stratifications were relativized to insignificance in the Pauline churches—at least ideally, even if never quite successfully.[169] But even having such relativization as a goal made the churches of Paul different from various other cults and associations of the day, since the latter tended to be as homogeneous as possible in terms of the social and economic status of their membership.[170]

Third, the ethos of the Pauline churches—made up of persons baptized into Christ, and bound together as brother-and-sisterhoods—was shaped by corporate worship. Celebrations of the Lord's Supper were done "in remembrance" of Jesus (1 Cor. 11:23-26), specifically his crucifixion, in the breaking of the bread and the sharing of the cup. These acts were also considered moments of "communion" (*koinōnia*) in the body and blood of Christ (1 Cor. 10:16). The church itself is the "body of Christ"—a concept that must have come to the fore in part because of the "communion" of the congregation in the "body" of Christ.[171] In any case, Paul usually speaks of the church as the body of Christ in connection with worship, for it is in the worship service that the church assumes its form.[172]

Finally, the ethos of the Pauline churches was shaped by the exhortations of Paul, and also of other persons within, to be faithful to Christ and mutually supportive of one another. As indicated earlier, Jesus' death and resurrection were at the center of Paul's consciousness and confession. They were also prominent in his proclamation, as his letters attest. But for Paul the preaching of the death and resurrection had direct implications for the conduct of believers. As his correspondence with the church at Corinth shows in particular, Christian spirituality—no matter how elevated by wisdom from on high or by gifts of the Spirit—should never become detached from the message of the cross.[173] Paul confronts his readers' claims of wisdom (1 Cor. 1:20; 3:18) and their arrogance and boasting (4:7, 18-19; 5:2, 6; 13:5) with the reminder that Christ is the crucified one (1 Cor. 1:23; cf. Gal. 3:1). Those who make up the body of Christ, though having a variety of gifts, are to use their gifts for the upbuilding of the body, mutual service, and the common good (Rom. 12:4-8; 14:19; 15:2; 1 Cor. 12:7; 14:12, 26).

Paul's emphasis on mutual care within the congregation, and even among Christians of the church in its totality, is particularly important to underscore. When he speaks of the church as the "body of Christ," he gives a double message,[174] depending on his audience. On the one hand, when he writes to the church at Rome, he says that each member is expected to employ his or her gifts for the sake of the body, so that it will function (Rom. 12:4-8). At this point Paul's analogy of the body and its members is similar to what appears in Stoic literature.[175] But Paul gives a different twist in his second use of the metaphor when he writes to the church at Corinth. Rather than exhorting the individual to care for the body, he exhorts the body to care for the individual. The body as a whole is not to despise any of its members, but to care for each, so that if one member suffers, all suffer, and if one rejoices, so does the body (1 Cor. 12:14-26).[176] Very prominent in Paul's exhortations to readers everywhere is his call upon them to love one another,[177] to seek the good of each other,[178] and to live at peace.[179] The attitude and action of love toward other persons is, for Paul, the "most excellent way" of living as a believer (1 Cor. 12:31); twice he quotes the love commandment (Rom. 13:8-10; Gal. 5:14); and he says that all that one does should be done in love (1 Cor. 16:14).

Up to this point nothing has been said concerning opponents of Paul and developments that opposed Pauline teaching within his own communities. Paul's letters show signs of opposition and are the earliest sources available concerning the rise of heterodox Christianity. These and other sources were used by Walter Bauer to contend that "heresy" rose early in the Pauline field, that it was strong from the outset, and that it soon predominated in the post-Pauline situation. According to Bauer, "heresy" had taken over by the beginning of the second century in Macedonia, Corinth, and Ephesus.[180]

An examination of the sources shows that Bauer's claims are too sweeping and simplistic. According to Acts 16:12-40 and 17:1-9, Paul was present in Macedonia (Philippi and Thessalonica) shortly after the Jerusalem conference, and presumably he founded the churches there on those occasions, which can be dated ca. A.D. 50. In the case of the church at Philippi, Paul's relationship continued to be remarkably cordial. When he wrote his Letter to the Philippians, while imprisoned a few years later,[181] he speaks very positively about its fidelity to the gospel that he had proclaimed (1:3-11; 2:12-13; and 4:1). There are two indications of troubles there: a disagreement between two women (4:2-3), and a warning against false teachers, who are evidently from outside, whom he calls "evil-workers" and "enemies of the cross" who apparently teach the necessity of circumcision (3:2, 18). Yet Paul does not seem to consider the community to be unduly threatened.[182] This church continued in existence into the second century. Early in that century, Polycarp, bishop of Smyrna, wrote his Letter to the Philippians, providing evidence of its existence. In that letter Polycarp opposes a docetic Christology that is taught by "false brethren" (6.3—7.1), but there is no basis for concluding that docetism was the view of the majority in Philippi at the time (contra Bauer[183]). The polemic is, even in its wording, much like antidocetic passages in the Johannine letters and the writings of Ignatius,[184] thus sharing a common ecclesiastical tradition of the time.[185] In any case, opposing "heresy" was not the occasion of the letter.[186] The primary reason for it was that it served as a cover letter accompanying a collection of the letters of Ignatius, which the Philippian community itself had requested that he send (13.2). Members of the community had assisted Ignatius and his companions on their way to his martyrdom in Rome (1.1; 9.1). Polycarp also extols the apostle Paul from whom they had received "the word of truth" (3.2; cf. 9.1); he speaks often of Christian virtues; and he refers to persons who hold ecclesiastical offices at Philippi (presbyters and deacons, 5.3; 6.1). Insofar as the community could understand the antidocetism of Polycarp, it was not insulated from "heresy," but there is no basis for concluding that "heresy" dominated there in the early second century, much less in the time of Paul or in the immediate post-Pauline situation.

Regarding the situation at Thessalonica, the two canonical letters to the Thessalonians are primary sources from the first century. In 1 Thessalonians, probably written from Corinth ca. A.D. 50,[187] Paul takes up concerns of the congregation that had been reported to him in consequence of Timothy's return from there (3:6). He responds to inquiries regarding the fate of those who had died prior to the parousia of Christ (4:13-18) and the timing of the coming of the Lord (5:1-11). There are indications that certain critics of Paul troubled the community by calling Paul's apostleship into question (2:3-8), and it appears that these critics were members of the congregation, since Paul has to admonish the community to respect its leaders (5:12-13).[188] Nevertheless, Paul commended the congregation as a whole for its faith and love, as reported by Timothy (3:6). According to the letter itself, the congregation was strong in its loyalty to the apostle (1:3-8; 2:10; 3:6), and the tone of the letter is generally one of friendly parenesis.[189] The letter known as 2 Thessalonians—whether written by Paul shortly after 1 Thessalonians, or perhaps deutero-Pauline[190]—provides evidence that an "overrealized eschatology"[191] developed in the community, which the author opposes by means of an apocalyptic section (2:1-12). Here the author argues against the view that the "day of the Lord" has come (2:2), which had led to idleness and assembling to meet the Lord (2:1; 2:6-12). Although it has been contended that those who held such a view were Gnostics,[192] that is not likely.[193] They were persons who had taken the Pauline eschatology further than the apostle had intended, but insofar as the community awaits the coming of the Lord (2:1), it has not abandoned the temporal framework that Gnosticism could not accommodate. The letter provides no evidence of features present in the community that are typical of Gnosticism (docetic Christology, rejection of the body, and so forth).

Bauer claimed that Thessalonica was soon dominated by "heresy," since the letters of Ignatius and Polycarp at the beginning of the second century are silent concerning it.[194] It would be more appropriate for a historian to say that, since the sources are silent, nothing is known about the eventual fate of the community at Thessalonica—whether it passed out of existence, was taken over by heresy, or continued along normative lines. But there actually is evidence of the community's continued existence in the second century, however small. Bishop Melito of Sardis (ca. A.D. 115–85) mentions that the Emperor Antonius Pius (who reigned A.D. 138–61) prohibited the persecution of Christians there.[195]

In regard to the churches of Paul in Galatia, they had been infiltrated already by opponents of the apostle when he wrote his letter to them (Gal. 1:6-7; 4:21; 6:12). From the tone of the letter it appears that the opponents had received a hearing. This anti-Paulinism originated there not from within but from outsiders who taught a "different gospel" (1:6-7), and who had arrived after Paul had established a church or churches in Galatia. They seem to have been Jewish Christian missionaries who demanded circumcision and observance of the law.[196] Paul sought to reclaim these churches, calling them back to the freedom in Christ that they had through his proclamation of the gospel. If 1 Peter 1:1 can be taken as evidence, the inclusion of Galatia within the orbit of those to whom that letter was addressed implies that a Christian community continued to exist in Galatia later in the first century, and that a "Pauline" type of Christianity could still receive a hearing there.[197]

The sources yield more information on opposition to Paul when we turn to Corinth and Ephesus. As in the case of the churches of Galatia, but for different reasons, the church at Corinth was a troubled one, as Paul's letters to it indicate. After founding the congregation and having spent a year and a half there (Acts 18:11), ca. A.D. 49–51,[198] Paul moved on to Ephesus, from where he wrote a letter now apparently lost (see 1 Cor. 5:9) and then the canonical 1 Corinthians (16:8). The occasion for the letter was a report received from "Chloe's people" (1:11), a letter from the Corinthians themselves (7:1), and probably a report brought by three persons from Corinth (Stephanus, Fortunatus, and Achaicus, 16:17).[199]

According to information in Paul's correspondence, there is division within the congregation (1:12; 3:4, 22) and, above all, a spiritual "enthusiasm" that places a high premium on ecstatic phenomena (1:7; 12:1-13; 14:1, 12, 37), "knowledge" (*gnōsis*, 1:5; 8:1, 7, 10-11; 12:8; 13:2, 8), and being "strong" (4:10). Although it may be going too far to speak of Corinthian "opponents" of Paul at the time of writing this letter, there is a volatile situation that has risen not from the instigation of outside forces but from within the congregation itself.[200] According to some interpreters, a form of Christian Gnosticism was being manifested in the community.[201] The label "Gnosticism," however, should not be applied without qualification, since major features of Christian Gnosticism as commonly known from the second century are lacking, particularly in regard to Christology. Yet the importance attached to "knowledge" (*gnōsis*), wisdom (1:18—2:13; 3:18-19), present fulfillment of one's spiritual life (4:8), and the denial by some of future resurrection (15:12-19) point in the direction of an incipient Gnosticism, or at least proto-gnostic tendencies.[202]

Tracing further developments at Corinth becomes complicated because of literary and historical questions surrounding 2 Corinthians. According to a widely held view, 2 Corinthians is a composite of several smaller letters (perhaps as many as five) that were written by Paul after conditions changed at Corinth subsequent to the writing of 1 Corinthians.[203] Briefly stated, the course of events after the writing of 1 Corinthians may have been as follows:

1. An opposition arose in Corinth against Paul that was caused by Jewish Christian missionaries (2 Cor. 11:22) from outside (11:4), who claimed to be apostles (11:5, 12-13; 12:11), and who found fault with Paul for his lack of eloquence and miraculous powers (10:10; 12:12).

2. Paul wrote a letter to the church at Corinth that is contained in 2 Corinthians 2:14—6:13; 7:2-4, in which he defends his apostleship, a letter to which Paul refers at 7:12 and 10:10.

3. Having concluded that the letter made no impact, Paul made a hasty visit to Corinth, which turned out to be a "painful visit" (2:1; 12:14; 13:1).

4. In despair Paul wrote another letter, which is contained in chapters 10–13, a severe letter, which he sent to Corinth by Titus, hoping

that Titus could improve the situation. This letter is referred to at 2:4.

5. Before Titus returned to Ephesus, Paul left and met him in Macedonia and received good news of success in his mission (2:13; 7:5-7, 13).

6. Paul wrote still another letter, contained in 1:1—2:13; 7:5-16, which is a letter of reconciliation between Paul and the church at Corinth.

7. Chapters 8 and 9 consist of an additional letter or letters concerning the collection, which had been disrupted by the crisis.

Whether this hypothesis can be accepted in every detail or not, 2 Corinthians provides evidence of an opposition to Paul at Corinth which rose after 1 Corinthians had been written. As indicated, Paul has actual opponents, Jewish Christians from outside the community,[204] who had initial success at Corinth. But by means of his letters and the help of Titus, Paul was able to win back the loyalty of the Corinthians. From Macedonia, Paul went on to Corinth. There he wrote Romans (Rom. 15:25-27), and there is no indication in that letter that the crisis at Corinth still existed.

In the post-Pauline era the earliest information available concerning the church at Corinth is *1 Clement*, written ca. A.D. 96 by Clement of Rome, on behalf of the Roman church, to the church at Corinth. Although he says that there is no hint of Gnosticism at Corinth in this lengthy letter, Bauer contends that its reference to the removal of presbyter-bishops from office (44.3-6) must have been due to a "take-over of the church offices" by younger persons of gnosticizing viewpoint.[205] But that is a reading between the lines that exceeds what is permitted. Generally interpreters have denied that false teaching was involved.[206] Hegesippus (ca. A.D. 100–180), who says that he had visited Corinth on a voyage to Rome, states that "the Corinthian church continued in the true doctrine until Primus [fl. ca. A.D. 150] became bishop." He goes on to say that he had "spent some days with the Corinthians during which we were refreshed by the true word."[207] Moreover, one of the best-known second-century bishops of Corinth was Dionysius (fl. ca. A.D. 170), who was regarded by Eusebius as sturdy in his orthodoxy,[208] and who claimed that *1 Clement* was still being "read from time to time [at Corinth] for our admonition."[209]

Although the churches of Galatia and Corinth experienced troubles of many kinds, and opponents against Paul and his mission appeared in them, the church at Ephesus seems to have enjoyed relative calm by comparison. According to Acts 20:31, Paul carried on a ministry of proclamation at Ephesus for three years (perhaps ca. A.D. 52–55[210]). It was at Ephesus that Paul wrote 1 Corinthians, at least portions (if not all) of 2 Corinthians, and probably Galatians.[211] Ephesus may also have been the place that Paul wrote Philippians and Philemon, although that is less certain.[212] During his time in Ephesus, Paul was surrounded by co-workers, including Timothy (1 Cor. 4:17; 16:10; 2 Cor. 1:1), Titus (2 Cor. 7:6-14; 8:6, 23), Aquila and Priscilla (Acts 18:18-19, 26; 1 Cor. 16:19), Apollos (Acts 18:24; 1 Cor. 16:12), plus other unnamed disciples (Acts 20:1) and presbyter-bishops of the church (Acts 20:17, 28). If Romans 16 can be considered an appendix added to a copy of Romans sent to Ephesus, as maintained by some interpreters[213] (although that view seems to be rejected more and more[214]), the circle of named friends and co-workers increases (twenty-six names are listed), to whom Paul sends greetings. And if Philippians and Philemon were written at Ephesus, the names of Epaphras and Epaphroditus can also be added (Phlm. 23; Phil. 2:25).

The indications of troubles at Ephesus during Paul's lifetime are few. The most specific (1 Cor. 15:32), whether taken literally or metaphorically, indicates troubles with Roman authorities, to which Paul seems to refer elsewhere as well (2 Cor. 11:23-29). Otherwise the only other indication of troubles at Ephesus in Paul's lifetime could be in Romans 16, if that was addressed to Ephesus, where Paul warns against those who cause dissensions (16:17-18), but such persons would have been exceeded in numbers and influence by the larger circle loyal to the apostle.

Other letters in the Pauline corpus have associations with the church at Ephesus following the death of Paul. It is widely held that Ephesus was the locale of a "Pauline school" where the letters of Paul were collected and the deutero-Pauline letters were composed[215]—Ephesians, Colossians, the Pastoral Epistles, and perhaps 2 Thessalonians. The church at Ephesus is one of seven mentioned in the opening chapters of Revelation (1:11; 2:1-7), and it is addressed in the *Epistle to the Ephesians* by Ignatius in the early part of the second century. In the Apocalypse the church is commended for its stand against the Nicolaitans (Rev. 2:6) and for rejecting false apostles (2:2). In Acts the Ephesian elders are warned by Paul of both "fierce wolves" from without and false teachers from within, who will try to lead persons astray after his departure (20:29-30).

How the church at Ephesus fared at the turn of the century and in the early part of the second century will be taken up in the next chapter, based on information in the Pastoral Epistles and the writings of Ignatius. But on the basis of the writings of Paul himself, and by virtue of the likely existence of a Pauline school at Ephesus after his death, it appears that the church at Ephesus was relatively stable and had a strong core of Pauline loyalists for decades after his death. That impression will be confirmed by the evidence from the Pastoral Epistles and Ignatius.

Some Commonalities

Our attention in this chapter has been devoted to three broad areas of investigation—the churches of Palestine, the Q community, and the churches of Paul. If one were to make comparisons and contrasts among these, the contrasts would be stark on such matters as attitudes toward the law, Christology (including the use of christological titles), mission to Jews and Gentiles, church leadership (including the place of Paul within it), and so on. Whoever looks for "the beginnings of a normative tradition" and expects to find unanimity in these matters has set out on a course that leads to failure.

But there are some commonalities, and the beginnings of a normative tradition in the pre-70 era can be discerned. All three areas investigated, for example, continue the Jewish heritage of belief in the God of Israel as Creator, the Father of Jesus, and the Father of humanity. All affirm the essential humanity of Jesus, on the one hand, and his role in redemption made possible by his crucifixion and exaltation/resurrection by God. All understand that a new era has been inaugurated in consequence of the cross and resurrection, attested by the presence and power of the Holy Spirit in the lives of believers. And in each case the believers constitute communities of faith that are marked by an ethos in which the individual gives himself or herself over to others in love and service, which is inspired by and modeled on Jesus' own giving himself over. So the church at Jerusalem is characterized by sharing and mutual care (Acts 2:45); the Q community by following after Jesus in love, mercy, and generosity (Luke 6:27-36//Matt. 5:39-47); and the Pauline churches by love, building up the body of Christ, and mutual service (Rom. 12:4-8; 13:8-10; 1 Cor. 13:1-13; 14:12; Gal. 5:13-14; Phil. 1:9-11; 2:1-11; 1 Thess. 3:11-13; 4:9-10). Although these matters may seem, because of their familiarity, theological and ethical commonplaces, they ought rather to be considered remarkable achievements of communities of faith and life in their infancy. They are marks of a normative tradition that resonates elsewhere in the writings of the New Testament and other early Christian literature.

5

The Shaping of
Normative Christianity

ATTENTION WAS FOCUSED IN THE PREVIOUS CHAPTER ON THE
earliest Christian communities that came into being and flourished prior
to A.D. 70. In this chapter attention shifts to communities that, although
they may have originated prior to A.D. 70, or at least depended on pre-70
antecedents, flourished after A.D. 70 in the so-called subapostolic era—that
is, the era when early Christian literature was being produced in the name
of apostles, and before the rise of literature written in the names of non-
apostolic authors, such as Clement and Ignatius.

Three Case Studies

According to the main stream of New Testament scholarship,[1] all the
writings of the New Testament in their final form—apart from sources
within them—were produced after A.D. 70 with the exception of the authentic letters of Paul, perhaps one or more of the deutero-Pauline letters,
and perhaps the Gospel of Mark, which is sometimes placed in the late
60s, sometimes after A.D. 70.[2] But not all the writings attest their community
origins to the same degree, even though they were produced in and for
vital Christian communities. Since our interest is precisely in the nexus
between confession and community ethos, rather than in New Testament
literature and theology as such, there is warrant for being selective, and
that is to choose those instances where the nexus is highly evident within
certain New Testament documents.

Using that principle of choice, there are three bodies of literature that
are particularly important for our kind of study. The first is the Gospel of
Matthew, which sets forth a confession of faith and displays a communal
ethos to a high degree. One gets the feeling, while reading that book, that

it plays to an audience made up of Christians who are struggling with ways of living together as disciples of Jesus within a "church"—a term that appears at 16:18 and 18:17, but not in the other three Gospels. The second is the collection of three letters known as the Pastoral Epistles (1 and 2 Timothy and Titus), in which matters of faith and life in community are everywhere evident. The third is the Johannine corpus, by which I mean here the Gospel of John and the three Epistles of John (leaving the book of Revelation out of consideration), which reflects a history of faith and life over time in a given community.

In the case of the Gospel of Matthew, it is necessary to deal with issues in its setting (presumably Syria) prior to the writing of that book. In the case of the Pastoral Epistles, it is necessary to investigate the larger historical setting in their locale (presumably Ephesus) as well. Therefore those studies will attend to developments in Syria and Ephesus, although major attention will be given to an analysis of faith and life as reflected by the documents that belong to them, Matthew and the Pastorals, respectively. While there are informed estimates of the location of the Johannine community (Ephesus, Syria, or Alexandria), and arguments can be offered for each, we shall simply leave the "Johannine community" designation in place.

It can be objected that the choices made are too narrow. After all, the Gospels of Mark and Luke, the Epistle to the Hebrews, and so on were produced in and for Christian communities as well. But by way of response it can be said that the "ecclesiastical" character of the Gospel of Matthew, the Pastoral Epistles, and the Johannine writings are particularly evident and to a degree unmatched by other writings in the New Testament. Concentrating on the cases selected does not exhaust the shaping of a normative tradition. But these cases are particularly fruitful; they are sufficiently diverse; and each gives evidence of deliberate efforts at shaping confession and community ethos in communities that were becoming self-consciously Christian in the subapostolic era.

Developments in Syria

According to the Acts of the Apostles, the origins of the church in Syria can be attributed to the so-called Hellenists—that is, Greek-speaking Jewish Christians who were expelled from Jerusalem early in the 30s (8:1-4) and traveled far and wide to various destinations, including Antioch (11:19).[3] Although founded by Jewish Christians, the church at Antioch was quick to include Gentiles within its membership (11:20), and its members were soon called "Christians" by outsiders (11:26)—a nickname that eventually became a self-designation, perhaps by the time that Luke wrote Acts, but certainly by the time that Ignatius of Antioch wrote his letters in the early part of the second century (*Eph.* 11.2; *Magn.* 4.1; *Rom.* 3.2; *Pol.* 7.3).

The mission to Gentiles at Antioch became the occasion for a series of events in Jerusalem and Antioch that would have far-reaching consequences for the shaping of normative Christianity. The sources are Acts 15 and Galatians 2.[4] Although these two sources do not agree in all details, there are major points of agreement as follows:[5] (1) Certain Jewish Christians at Jerusalem—aside from James, Peter, and John—had insisted that the circumcision of Gentiles was necessary for their inclusion in the Christian community. (2) Representatives of the church at Antioch, where the circumcision of Gentiles had not been required, traveled to Jerusalem for a meeting to discuss the issue, and that group included Paul and Barnabas. (3) James, Peter, and John—the major leaders at Jerusalem—took the lead in coming to a decision, and that was that Gentiles need not be circumcised. (4) After their return to Antioch, Paul and Barnabas had a major disagreement, which ended their partnership as co-workers in mission. (5) After the clash between these two persons, Paul had virtually no further associations with the church at Antioch. Luke mentions one visit there near the end of Paul's career (Acts 18:22-23), but Paul never mentions further associations with that church in his letters.

Aside from these agreements, Acts 15 and Galatians 2 disagree on some important points. For our purposes, the following are important. (1) Although Acts is silent on the matter, Paul says that a mission to Jews was to be carried on by James, Peter, and John, and a mission to Gentiles by himself (Gal. 2:7-9). (2) According to the Acts account, an apostolic "decree" was issued that required a modified form of *kashrut* and the prohibition of idolatry and sexual immorality (15:23-29), but Paul says that the only requirement issued from the meeting was that he "remember the poor" of Jerusalem (Gal. 2:10). (3) According to Acts, the falling out between Paul and Barnabas at Antioch was due to a dispute between them over the question of taking John Mark along as a companion in their mission (15:36-41), but according to Paul the dispute was much more serious. Peter had come to Antioch (not mentioned in Acts) and had eaten with Gentiles, but he withdrew from table fellowship with them on the arrival of "certain men from James," and Barnabas joined Peter in this "hypocrisy" (Gal. 2:11-13). According to the account in Galatians 2, the split between Paul and Barnabas was only a part of the historically more significant clash between Paul and Peter.

The conflict at Antioch must have had effects on the Christian community there for some time to come. The prime issue there was not the question of the circumcision of Gentiles, for that had been decided in Paul's favor already, but the matter of table fellowship.[6] Although it has been said that there is no law in ancient Jewish sources that prevents a Jew from eating with Gentiles,[7] table fellowship with Gentiles was resisted on the grounds that gentile foods and wine were generally considered unclean.[8] It is clear from the account in Galatians that for Paul the tradition of separatism had been overcome; all who are baptized into Christ, Jew and Gentile, are united into a single body as children of God (cf. 3:26-28), and table fellowship between them would follow as a matter of course. Yet we cannot be certain that the matter of table fellowship had even been brought up at Jerusalem (to say nothing of its being settled).[9]

In any case, the party that came to Antioch "from James" demanded a two-track mission—one to Jews, another to Gentiles—without table fellowship, thereby continuing to maintain a distinction. The only way that such fellowship would be possible, according to them, was for Gentiles to adopt Jewish customs (2:14b), which shows that consequently and ultimately far more than table fellowship was involved.[10] But in the meantime, it must have appeared to those "from James" that Paul was a "gentilizer," leading Jews who believed in Christ away from the people Israel, to whom the Messiah had come, into the ways of gentile uncleanness.

What transpired at Antioch following the dispute is difficult to track. Paul must not have gained a sense of victory in the dispute, since he does not say that Peter or anyone else turned to agree with him,[11] and he must have left Antioch relatively soon. Although the church must have sided with Peter, there are no indications that Peter remained there either. It has been suggested that Jewish and gentile Christians would subsequently have held meals separately in deference to the viewpoint of James, supported by Peter.[12] That may have been so, but other circumstances were soon to be decisive for further shifts: James and Peter were martyred in the early 60s; the city of Jerusalem was destroyed by A.D. 70; and the mission to Gentiles was highly successful, while success in the mission to Jews declined. By the time Luke wrote his Acts, the issue of table fellowship between Jewish and gentile Christians was over, and so he does not mention the incident at all. He even has Peter repudiate the separation of Jew from Gentile while speaking to Cornelius (10:28).

In the post-70 era there was a growing consciousness of being "Christian" as a means of identity over against Judaism. Indications are that Antioch or its vicinity was the probable place where the Gospel of Matthew was produced (see below), and it does not appear that in that Gospel the distinction between Jew and Gentile within the community was being maintained; the primary distinction was between church and synagogue.[13]

The situation at Antioch must have been quite complex from the middle of the first century on into the second. In the previous chapter the view was accepted that Syria, if not Palestine, was the place in which the Q document was produced. It would also most likely have been the region through which the traditions of the *Gospel of Thomas* were transmitted eastward to Edessa. Moreover, as already indicated, Antioch of Syria—or its environs—was most likely the place at which the Gospel of Matthew was composed in the closing decade or two of the first century.[14] In that Gospel the apostle Peter comes to greater prominence as the prime apostle (16:13-20) than in Matthew's source (Mark 8:27-30) for the post-Easter situation (that is, in the *ekklēsia*, mentioned at Matt. 16:18).[15]

In light of the many confluences of traditions passing through Syria, it can be concluded that the evangelist who wrote the Gospel of Matthew sought to give apostolic, even dominical, warrant to one particular set of traditions and theological point of view over against others in the community who sought apostolic and dominical warrant for their own. Traditions contained in the *Gospel of Thomas* favor such a conclusion, for they press for apostolic and dominical warrant in another direction, competing with the Gospel of Matthew. Significantly, Peter and Matthew—associated with the Matthean tradition—appear together with Thomas in an incident regarding the "confession" of Jesus' identity (*Gos. Thom.* 13). The passage functions in this Gospel like Peter's confession and Jesus' response do in the Gospel of Matthew (16:13-20):

> Jesus said to his disciples, "Compare me to someone and tell me whom I am like."
> Simon Peter said to him, "You are like a righteous angel."
> Matthew said to him, "You are like a wise philosopher."
> Thomas said to him, "Master, my mouth is wholly incapable of saying whom you are like."
> Jesus said, "I am not your [sg.] master. Because you [sg.] have drunk, you [sg.] have become intoxicated from the bubbling spring which I have measured out."
> And he took him and withdrew and told him three things. When Thomas returned to his companions, they asked him, "What did Jesus say to you?"
> Thomas said to them, "If I tell you one of the things which he told me, you will pick up stones and throw them at me; a fire will come out of the stones and burn you up."[16]

In this passage Peter and Matthew, though important figures, are overshadowed in significance by Thomas, who receives revelations from Jesus that he is not to share with the others. Thomas thereby gains preeminence among the apostles over the preeminence that Peter has in the canonical Gospels, especially Matthew.[17] The prominence of Thomas is characteristic of a tradition in Syria, which is expressed later in the *Acts of Thomas* (Edessa, third century), in which Thomas is called "twin brother of Christ, apostle of the Most High and fellow-initiate into the hidden word of Christ, who dost receive his secret sayings" (*Acts Thom*. 39).[18] Elsewhere in the *Gospel of Thomas* James the righteous is elevated to leader of the disciples (logion 12). This person was the brother of Jesus and is the James of Acts 15 and Galatians 2 (the Jerusalem conference and the incident at Antioch). Although the *Gospel of Thomas* came from a date later than that of the Gospel of Matthew,[19] and from eastern Syria, it attests the existence of loyalists to James and Thomas in Syria. The heightened emphasis on Peter as the prime apostle in the Matthean community can be understood as an attempt to give apostolic authorization to the Matthean tradition and teaching.

The confluence of traditions in Syria and their divergence into two very different directions represented by the Matthean and Thomist traditions can be seen in two major ways. First, Matthew contains the Q material, and about one-third of the Q sayings have parallels in the *Gospel of Thomas*,[20] pointing to a shared tradition. But, secondly, there are a number of striking parallels between Matthew's special traditions (the so-called M material) and those in the *Gospel of Thomas*, including four parables in Matthew 13. (By way of contrast, the parallels to special Lukan traditions are few.[21]) The parallels are as follows:

Special Matthean Traditions	Traditions in Thomas	
5:14a	24	disciples as light
5:14b	32	city on a hill
6:3b	62	left hand/right hand
7:6	93	profaning the holy
10:16b	39	serpents and doves
11:28-30	90	come, my yoke is easy
13:24b-30	57	parable of the weeds
13:44	109	parable of the treasure
13:45-46	76	parable of the pearl
13:47-48	8	parable of the fishnet
15:13	40	rooting up a plant
18:20	30	Jesus with the gathered

In addition to this list, there is a clash between the sayings of Jesus in Matthew 6:2-6, 16-17 (special M) and the *Gospel of Thomas* 14. In the former, fasting, the giving of alms, and praying are to be done in secret; in the latter they are considered harmful and are to be rejected altogether.

The evidence of parallels between the *Gospel of Thomas* and Q, and also between the *Gospel of Thomas* and special Matthean traditions, speaks in favor of the view proposed here—namely, that traditions were transmitted through Antioch, and that they were taken up, selected, used, and edited by the author of the Gospel of Matthew at or near Antioch in one way, and they were taken up, selected, and transmitted by others who transported them to eastern Syria where the *Gospel of Thomas* was composed, presumably at a later date.

The author of the Gospel of Matthew sought to establish a form of Christian faith and life in Syria that was not shared by those for whom James and Thomas were the prime apostles, who sponsored, in turn, an ascetic form of Christianity that is reflected in the *Gospel of Thomas*.[22] That explains why the evangelist emphasized the primacy of Peter, who had already been a major figure in the church at Antioch. The Gospel that he produced was to give shape to a Christian community that was able to survive into the following century at Antioch. That is confirmed by the writings of Ignatius, who either made use of the Gospel of Matthew itself at several points in his writings,[23] or was at least acquainted with traditions common to the author of the Gospel of Matthew and himself,[24] and for whom Peter and Paul were regarded as apostles (*Rom.* 4.3)—Peter being the prime witness of the resurrection of Christ (*Smyrn.* 3.2), and Paul the one whom Ignatius seeks to follow in attaining to God (*Eph.* 12.2).

The Gospel of Matthew is a major resource for observing the formation of a community of faith and life in western Syria after the destruction of Jerusalem, but prior to the close of the first century.[25] Evidence within the Gospel itself indicates that the community had a strong Jewish heritage. According to the evangelist, and presumably other members of the community, the will of God is expressed through the law of Moses, as interpreted by Jesus (Matt. 5:17-20). But the community was also open to and included Gentiles, since the risen Lord had commanded his apostles to make disciples of all nations (28:19). Matthean expansions to traditions elsewhere point to the inclusion of Gentiles as well (13:38; 21:43; 22:9; and 24:14).[26]

In keeping with its Jewish heritage, the community confessed Israel's ancient credo of the oneness of God (19:17; 22:37; 23:9), who is the Father in heaven (5:16; 6:9; 16:17), the Creator and Sustainer of all things (19:4; 6:25-33). God is good (7:11; 19:17), cares for his people (6:8; 18:14), and willingly hears their prayers (6:6; 18:19; 21:22). The Scriptures of Israel reveal the will of God, although they must be interpreted, as every person of Jewish heritage would have agreed. What is disputed is not the authority of the Scriptures but their interpretation. The evangelist seems to have considered his own work to be like that of a scribe "who brings out of his treasure what is new and what is old" (13:52); that is, he draws from his tradition that which abides, the "old"—the Scriptures and the traditions about Jesus—and that which is "new"—the rendition of the old exemplified in his work and in that of any other scribe who is faithful in representing, interpreting, and applying that which he has received.[27]

In his presentation of Jesus, the evangelist makes use of the Gospel of Mark, Q, and traditions that are peculiar to his Gospel. He uses a wide range of christological titles—Christ, Lord, Son of God, Son of Man, and Son of David being the most prominent.[28] The significance of each title has been explored in detail, and various interpreters have proposed that Matthew's Christology is dominated by one of them—usually Son of God,[29] although some have contended for Son of Man,[30] Christ,[31] or Lord.[32] That debate, however, should not detract from Matthew's larger christological panorama that goes beyond his use of titles. Matthew portrays Jesus as a regal figure and the Messiah of Israel who teaches and interprets the law for his followers. He interprets the law in light of the double commandment of love for God above all things and one's neighbor as oneself: "on these two commandments depend all the law and the prophets" (22:40). That is to say, "the whole law and the prophets can be exegetically deduced from the command to love God and the neighbor, they 'hang' exegetically on these."[33] That hermeneutical principle is set over against Pharisaic interpretation of the law known to the evangelist and his community, and which is regarded as avoiding the will of God expressed through the law (cf. 23:23).

As the hermeneutical program is played out in this Gospel, it can be said that there is a radicalization of ethical commands, particularly those concerning care for one's fellow human being (cf. 5:21-48), and a downplaying of those that apply to ritual observance—those that can be fulfilled even by one who does not care about other persons (9:13; 12:7; 15:1-20; 23:23-26).[34] Jesus is able to carry on the interpretation of the law in an authoritative manner since he is the "Lord"—the title used frequently in address to him by his disciples—and because he is the obedient Son of God, who is in unity with the Father, who has delivered all things to him (11:27). He incarnates Wisdom,[35] for the imagery applied to Jesus at 11:28-30 is dependent on Sirach 51:23-30. Statements uttered by Wisdom in the latter are attributed to Jesus in the Matthean passage.

For the evangelist and his community, Jesus is also a redemptive figure, for he came to "save his people from their sins" (1:21). Although Matthew repeats the saying from the Gospel of Mark that the Son of Man came "to give his life as a ransom for many" (20:28//Mark 10:45), Matthew's redemptive Christology does not center on the cross as much as Mark's does, nor Paul's.[36] Jesus remains a majestic and authoritative figure through the accounts of the cross and resurrection. Although he could surely have escaped from his captors by calling upon God to send twelve legions of angels to rescue him (26:53), Jesus is obedient to the will of his Father

(26:42) and is intent on fulfilling the Scriptures (26:54, 56). Even in his death he yields up his spirit to God (27:50), as though he is still in control, but is obedient.

The saving benefits of Christ, in the Matthean perspective, are bestowed primarily in consequence of his resurrection, not his passion and death per se. The risen Christ appears to his disciples, declaring that "all authority in heaven and on earth" has been given to him (28:18). Although the disciples had forsaken Jesus (26:56) and, in effect, had disqualified themselves from salvation (cf. 10:33), the risen Christ commissioned them as his emissaries to make disciples in his name (28:19), which implies that they had been restored to fellowship with him. They had received forgiveness and became heirs of salvation.

At the time of writing the Gospel of Matthew, the Matthean community had already come into being. The community consisted of persons baptized in the name of the Father, Son, and Holy Spirit (28:19). It would have considered its members as people of the Messiah Jesus who had come to save them from their sins. Forgiveness of sins was asked for in the recitation of the Lord's Prayer (6:12). But forgiveness was also enacted in specific actions within the community. Matthew has amplified the text of the cup-saying in connection with the Lord's Supper, so that now the pouring out of the blood of the covenant for many is "for the forgiveness of sins" (26:28), a phrase not present in Mark's account (14:24). The implication is that in the celebration of the Lord's Supper within the community, the forgiveness of sins is bestowed on those who share in the drinking of the cup. Moreover, in the story of the healing of the paralytic (9:1-8), Matthew repeats the saying of Jesus that "the Son of man has authority on earth to forgive sins" (Mark 2:10//Matt. 9:6), but he appends to the statement that the crowds glorified God (already in Mark) his own statement that God has now given "such authority to people" to exercise on earth within the Christian community (9:8). It had of course been taught in Jewish tradition that God forgives sins. But in the case of Jesus, and then also for the church, God's forgiveness of sins is now not simply requested and proclaimed; it is actually exercised.[37] That exercise is carried out through the power given to the church to "bind and loose" on earth (18:18), that is, to declare sins forgiven and to admit persons into the fellowship, or to refrain from forgiving and even exclude persons from the community.[38]

The ethos of the Matthean community was shaped in light of its understanding of the will of God set forth in the teachings of Jesus. As persons who are forgiven—and forgiven continually on the basis of praying the Lord's Prayer, celebrating the Lord's Supper, and the practice of absolution—members of the community are to forgive others (6:12, 14-15), and that must be from one's "heart" (18:35) and without numerical limits (18:21-22).

Members are to live lives of righteousness (5:6, 20; 6:33; 13:43; 25:46), a righteousness that exceeds that of the scribes and the Pharisees (5:20), who are judged to be hypocritical (23:23a). True righteousness is a matter of doing the will of God, expressed in the double commandment of love (22:34-40), or its companion the golden rule (7:12), and attending to the "weightier matters of the law," which are justice, mercy, and faithfulness (23:23b). No one should covet status within the community (20:20-28) or seek to be addressed by titles of honor (23:8-10). On the contrary, each is to be a servant who seeks the good of others (10:24; 20:26-27; 23:11) and be generous in regard to those less fortunate (5:42; 19:21; 25:31-46). Love is to be directed not only to friends and fellow members of the community, but even to those who could be regarded as enemies (5:44). The analogy of a sound tree that bears good fruit describes the life of the true disciple (7:17; 12:33).

It is clear that there was an emphasis on discipline in the Matthean community. But it was applied in several ways, and two of them appear at first to be contradictory. On the one hand, the evangelist included two parables that hold in check a tendency to purge the community of persons considered moral failures. These are the parables of the weeds among the wheat (13:24-30, 36-43) and the great catch of fish (13:47-50). In each case the community is to understand that "evil doers" (13:41) or the "evil" ones (13:49) will be cast out at the final judgment executed by the Son of Man and his angels at the close of the age. For now and until then, however, the church will be a mixture of good and bad, a *corpus mixtum*.[39] On the other hand, the exclusion of persons judged unworthy of fellowship seems to be justified in the sequel to the parable of the marriage feast, in which the man without a wedding garment is cast out (22:11-14), and also in the treatment of the offender who will not repent, as long as the case of nonrepentance is confirmed by the presence of witnesses (18:15-18).

Yet the two thrusts are not contradictory. The evangelist recognizes the reality of sin, including judgmental attitudes (7:1), the need for patience and mercy, and at the same time the need to set limits for the sake of the well-being of the community over time. It is expected that those who belong to the community will love God and the other person, and will seek to live righteously according to all that the Lord has taught (28:20). It is recognized that some, however, cannot remain; in fact, at the final judgment it will be seen that even some who have remained in the fellowship will be shown to be false disciples (7:21-23). But the final judgment will also disclose that there are those—both in the community and outside it—who will be commended and saved on the basis of showing mercy to the hungry, thirsty, homeless, sick, and imprisoned, even though they make no claims of reward on the basis of a Christian confession (25:31-46).[40]

The shaping of a community ethos was thus obviously essential to the Matthean understanding of remaining faithful to the legacy of Jesus. Discipline and authoritative teaching were considered necessary functions within the community (18:18; 28:20). The Gospel of Matthew appears to have been itself a manual for guidance in these functions.[41] The degree to which one can speak of the existence of ecclesiastical offices in the Matthean community is debated—from the view, on one side, that the community had a strong sense of organization and authority invested in "rabbinic models of authority"[42] to the view, on the other side, that it must not have had a "teaching office" comparable to that which was developing in contemporary Judaism.[43]

What is clear is that the honorific titles of rabbi, father, and master were to be rejected (23:8-10)—which probably means that certain persons were claiming them.[44] Moreover, the titles that were in use later at Antioch (bishop, presbyter, and deacon), attested in the writings of Ignatius, were probably not yet in use either.[45] Nevertheless, the strong sense of the need to exercise authority in teaching and discipline, over against false prophets (7:15-20), and the emphasis on fidelity to the apostolic tradition represented primarily by Peter (16:17-19) point in the direction of a recognized leadership. That leadership must have been provided by charismatic figures known as scribes, prophets, and wise men (13:52; 23:34; cf. 10:41),[46] among whom no doubt was the evangelist himself, whose ways of working resembled those of a scribe.[47]

Developments in Asia Minor

Already in the previous chapter some attention was given to developments of Pauline Christianity at Ephesus. It was maintained that there was no serious threat there to the teaching and proclamation of Paul during his lifetime, and that after his death Pauline loyalists continued in Ephesus. Indeed one can speak of a Pauline school in that city in the latter part of the first century.

The Pastoral Epistles provide material that shows how a community within the Pauline field of Asia Minor, but after Paul's lifetime, came to terms with the necessity of clarity in confession and the shaping of the community's ethos in a particular way. It is taken as axiomatic here that the Pastorals are deutero-Pauline on the grounds that they differ greatly from the undisputed letters of Paul in matters of theology, language and style, and church order, and also because they lack ancient attestation as a part of the Pauline corpus.[48] They can be assigned to ca. A.D. 100, and they were probably written in Ephesus or its vicinity. Within the Pastorals themselves some twenty-eight persons are named (excluding Old Testament names, plus references to Jesus and Pontius Pilate). Of these, eighteen have a documented connection with the church at Ephesus, and the other ten may have been known there as well.[49] The "Ephesian connection" points to Ephesus or its vicinity as the place of writing. Two of the letters are addressed, and convey greetings, to persons in Ephesus (1 Tim. 1:3; 2 Tim. 4:19; cf. 1:16-18). Rather than that being a reason to assign them to a location away from Ephesus,[50] however, it could be a pseudepigraphic device used by a local author. The same could apply to the destination of the Epistle to Titus (Crete, 1:5). Although the evidence is not decisive, the tendency of scholarship to assign the Pastoral Epistles to Ephesus, or at least to Asia Minor, seems justified.[51] But even if that judgment is incorrect, and the Ephesian destination is insisted upon for the letters to Timothy, these two letters still remain as valuable sources for Christianity at Ephesus at the turn of the century.

Although the Pastoral Epistles are often regarded as rather pedestrian in their theology and are thought to be preoccupied with church order, they are in fact rich in theological texture and concerned about sound teaching in the church. Order is for the sake of teaching and defending the faith as purportedly received. Much of what has been received is of the Pauline heritage. But there is more, expressing a measure of originality in their use of the Pauline and common Christian tradition. The author of the Pastorals stresses that God is one, the Father, who has created all things good (1 Tim. 1:2; 2:5; 4:3-4; 2 Tim. 1:2; Titus 1:4, 15). The Christian does not despise the creation or flee from it. To be sure, love of wealth is a vice to avoid (1 Tim. 6:9-10; 2 Tim. 3:2); one ought to practice moderation (1 Tim. 6:8) and be generous (6:17-18). But God, who has created all things, continues to "give life to all things" (6:13) and "richly furnishes us with everything to enjoy" (6:17).

Standing in the Pauline tradition, the writer affirms that the whole human race is sinful. But there is a shift in nuance of major importance. In Paul's writings sin (singular) is a power that exercises dominion over all (Rom. 3:9; 5:12, 21; 7:14; Gal. 3:22). But in the Pastorals references are to "sins," not "sin," which persons commit (1 Tim. 5:22, 24; 2 Tim. 3:6). These sins, listed once as vices (2 Tim. 3:2-5), result from a life disoriented from serving God and from keeping the godly virtues (faith, love, purity of heart, good deeds, moderation, civic and domestic duties, contentment, generosity, respect for others, and self-control[52]). Here the author appears to be an heir of that Jewish tradition that thought of sins as caused by the "evil impulse" (*yeser ha-ra'*), which is in perpetual conflict with the "good impulse" (*yeser ha-tob*), a concept that developed in pre-Christian times (Sir. 15:11-20, particularly 15:14) and is found in other texts contemporaneous with the rise of Christianity (for example, 2 *Esdr.* 3:21; 4:30-31), as well as in rabbinic literature.[53] In any case, the Christian is summoned by the author to purity of heart (1 Tim. 1:5; 2 Tim. 2:22) and to engage in struggle toward righteousness and godliness (1 Tim. 6:11; 2 Tim. 2:22).

Humanity is in need of salvation, and that need is fulfilled by the mercy and grace of God (Titus 2:11; 3:5-7) expressed in the Christ event. Christ came into the world to save sinners (1 Tim. 1:15), and God desires all to be saved (2:4; Titus 2:11). While there is no explicit statement concerning the preexistence of the Son of God or Logos (two christological titles completely missing in the Pastorals), and some interpreters claim that the concept is therefore lacking altogether,[54] the writer does nevertheless speak of Christ's coming into the world as the appearance of the grace of God, which existed "before the ages" (before temporality, 2 Tim. 1:9-10; cf. Titus 2:11), which is functionally equivalent to the concept of preexistence. He also speaks of Christ's being "manifested in the flesh" (that is, his incarnation, 1 Tim. 3:16), and incarnation implies preexistence. The earthly life of Jesus is the result of the Christ's coming into the world (1 Tim. 1:15; 2:6; Titus 2:14), the manifestation of the Savior (2 Tim. 1:10; Titus 3:4). His death is alluded to several times (for example, at 1 Tim. 2:6; 2 Tim. 2:11; Titus 2:14). Finally, the crucified Christ has been exalted (1 Tim. 3:16; 2 Tim. 1:10; 2:12) and bears the title "Lord."[55] At one point the exalted Christ is even called "God": Christians await their "blessed hope, the appearing of the glory of our great God and Savior Jesus Christ" (Titus 2:13).[56] Although the writer makes clear distinctions elsewhere between Christ and God,[57] the distinction does not imply a separation. God and Christ are intimately related, so much so that at his parousia Christ will bear the divine glory to complete the saving work of God, and in that sense he will be "God and Savior."

The salvation of humanity, willed by God, is carried out by Christ, who is portrayed as a vigorous redemptive figure who has come to rescue humanity. In his death Christ "gave himself as a ransom [*antilytron*] for all [*hyper pantōn*]" (1 Tim. 2:6); further, "he gave himself for us [*hyper hēmōn*] in order that he might redeem [*lytrōsētai*] us from all iniquity" (Titus 2:14). Using sacrificial terminology in these places, the writer affirms that Christ has set humanity free from the consequences of sins committed—judgment and death. Christ himself has borne the divine judgment against sins for the benefit of others. As the one who has won redemption, and having been raised from death, he has "abolished death and brought life and imperishability to light" (2 Tim. 1:10). By his resurrection, death has been overcome, and that means that "life and imperishability" come into their own, into the light of day. Previously there was only perishability leading to death, but now the imperishability and life that God intends for people have been gained.

The soteriology of the Pastorals has an "objective" and "universal" character: Christ is "the Savior of all people, especially of those who believe" (1 Tim. 4:10). Although the meaning of the verse is contested,[58] the author seems to be saying that, while Christ is the Savior of all without distinction (cf. 1 Tim. 2:6), believers know him as Savior, for they have heard the gospel. The writer thereby encloses the whole of humanity within the scope of redemption, but his focus is "especially" on the community of faith as the beneficiary of salvation. But the focus is only that—a focus, not a limit.

The salvation that Christ makes possible is essentially future: life in the "heavenly kingdom" (2 Tim. 4:18). For now Christians are "heirs in hope of eternal life" (3:7; compare 1:2), expecting salvation to come (1 Tim. 4:16) and enduring until its arrival (2 Tim. 2:10, 12). Yet the writer can also speak of salvation as a present reality: God has (already) saved us (2 Tim. 1:9; Titus 3:5), and believers "take hold of" eternal life (1 Tim. 6:12, 19). The picture that emerges is that the saving work of Christ has been accomplished by Christ's death and resurrection; Christians "take hold of" the life offered in consequence of that work, of which they are heirs. They enter into that life in its fullness, the eternal kingdom, at the time of their "departure" (2 Tim. 4:6) or at the parousia of Christ (Titus 2:13), should that take place prior to one's death.

The shaping of a community ethos flows from these theological convictions. With the strong emphasis on God as Creator of all that is, and that the creation is good, the writer stresses virtues for living in a created order. An asceticism that forbids the enjoyment of foods and drink and the institution of marriage is rejected (1 Tim. 4:3; 5:23; 6:17). Marriage and having children are considered good (3:2-5; 5:10, 14; Titus 2:4). The care of the elderly by their children and grandchildren is considered a religious duty (1 Tim. 5:4). Obedience to governing authorities is expected (Titus 3:1-2). Prayers are to be offered for all, including civil authorities (1 Tim. 2:1-2). Help is to be rendered to the needy beyond the circle of believers (Titus 3:2, 8, 14). Courtesy is to be extended to all (3:2).

It has been remarked that the Pastoral Epistles set forth a "framework of bourgeois living"[59] or a "bourgeois Christianity."[60] To a degree that may be true. The virtues prescribed are not, for the most part, extraordinary; most are those that were commonly valued in Greco-Roman society as a whole.[61] But beyond the moral teaching, there is prescribed an ethos that has a distinct Christian coloration affecting the motivation and even some of the content of the ethical teaching in the Pastorals. Recalling Pauline language (Rom. 6:5), the author speaks of Christians as persons who have died with Christ (in baptism, 2 Tim. 2:11). Baptized, Christians are renewed by the gift and power of the Spirit (Titus 3:5-6). They belong to Christ and are therefore "a people of his own who are zealous for good deeds" (2:14). The self-giving of Christ in his coming into the world and in his sacrificial death is instructive on how the "godly" life is to be lived (Titus 2:11-12, 14). Moreover, since Christians live in expectation of life in the eternal kingdom, they discipline themselves in godliness (1 Tim. 4:7-8); the present days are the last days (4:1; 2 Tim. 3:1). Paul, who could exhort his readers to imitate him (1 Cor. 4:16; 11:1; Phil. 3:17), is remembered still as an example of how the life of faith is to be lived (1 Tim. 1:16; 2 Tim. 1:13; 3:10-11). In all of this there is a specifically Christian ethos that is prescribed. Baptized, renewed by the Spirit, and instructed, the Christian is to have purity of heart that issues forth in love (1 Tim. 1:5; 2 Tim. 2:22), good deeds (1 Tim. 6:18; Titus 2:7, 14; 3:8), and various other virtues, including righteousness and godliness (1 Tim. 6:11; 2 Tim. 2:22).

The community of the Pastorals was ordered more specifically than any other reflected in the New Testament writings. Ecclesiastical offices are mentioned, into which persons are inducted (1 Tim. 3:10; 4:14; 5:22; 2 Tim. 1:6), and then these persons, as office bearers, are to be respected for the sake of their work (1 Tim. 5:17). Presbyters, who form a council (a presbytery, 1 Tim. 4:14), have a "ruling" function, and some are engaged in preaching and teaching (5:17). Deacons are selected on the basis of personal qualities (3:8-13), but their duties are not spelled out. Most likely, as made clear from other sources, they served under the bishop in charitable work and temporal concerns.[62] All the ministry carried on—both the ministry of the word, and the ministry of service—is under the supervision of the bishop ("overseer").

There is some disagreement among interpreters on the relationship between bishops and presbyters in the Pastorals. While some have concluded that the two titles are equivalent,[63] as they appear to be in some other ancient sources,[64] it is striking to observe that whenever the terms are used in the Pastorals, the term *bishop* is always in the singular (1 Tim. 3:2; Titus 1:7), whereas the term *presbyter* can be in the plural (1 Tim. 5:17; Titus 1:5; cf. 1 Tim. 4:14). The bishop may well have been the leading presbyter, or perhaps came out of the presbytery, to assume the function of oversight, as various scholars have concluded.[65] In any case, the bishop has three main functions. First, working with the presbyters and deacons, the bishop supervises the life of the community as though it were an extended household (1 Tim. 3:5), caring for all matters, whether spiritual, temporal, or organizational. In all of this, he must be himself a model of Christian virtue (3:2-7; Titus 1:6-9). Second, he combats false teaching and preserves what is sound (Titus 1:9). Finally, since he must be an apt teacher (1 Tim. 3:2; Titus 1:9), we can infer that a major function of the bishop was teaching—and, with that, preaching as well (compare 1 Tim. 5:17).

Besides these offices, there are passages in the Pastorals that apply specifically to women who carry on certain functions in the community. In a section on the qualifications of deacons (1 Tim. 3:8-13) there is an aside concerning "women likewise" (3:11), and interpreters are divided on the question whether the reference is to deacons' "wives" (as in certain translations, for example, KJV, NEB, TEV, and NIV) or to women who are deacons.[66] That the passage refers to the wives of deacons can probably be excluded, since no possessive pronoun ("their") is used. But that does not mean that the term *deacon* applies to women in the Pastorals (as it surely does in Rom. 16:1), since that term seems to be limited to men (1 Tim. 3:8, 12, taken together). Perhaps the most that can be concluded is that while the title of deacon applies to males who hold that office, there are also women in diaconal service, even if they do not bear the actual title. If that is so, it means a step back from the recognition of women as deacons of an earlier era (Rom. 16:1).

Another passage speaks of women who are widows (1 Tim. 5:3-16). Those who are "true widows" can be enrolled (5:9, 11)—thus formally recognized as a distinct group—if they are at least sixty years of age and do not have children or grandchildren to support them (5:4, 8, 16). They are supported by the community (5:5, 16), and their primary functions must have been extensions of the things they were noted for on enrollment: being constant in prayer (5:5)[67] and diligent in charitable work (5:7-10) on behalf of, and at the expense of, the community. Insofar as there is a procedure for "enrollment," it is appropriate to speak of an "office" or "order" of widow,[68] which continues to be recognized in the writings of Ignatius and Polycarp of the second century, and in other sources from the third century.[69]

The writer of the Pastoral Epistles is engaged, as the community as a whole was, in a struggle with opponents who seek to turn and lead the community in new directions. These persons, considered to be false teachers, are portrayed as evil, greedy, arrogant, hypocritical, and proselytizing.[70] Their teaching is not taken up and refuted. The writer's approach is basically to attack the false teachers on moral grounds. Yet a few features of their teaching emerge.[71] They teach an ascetic way of life (1 Tim. 4:3), are engaged in speculative teaching based on an allegorical use of Scripture (1:3b-7; 4:7; Titus 1:14; 3:9), and claim that "the resurrection has taken place already" (2 Tim. 2:18). Most likely the opponents represent an early form of Gnosticism containing Jewish and Christian elements.[72] The reference to a *gnōsis* to be avoided (1 Tim. 6:20) points in the direction of an early form of Gnosticism. The allegorical use of the Old Testament by the opponents and the reference to them as the "circumcision party" (a Pauline term; cf. Gal. 2:12; Col. 4:11) indicate a Jewish element in their theological heritage and teaching.

The claim that the resurrection is past would have a Christian, even Pauline, background, in which the "already" of eschatological existence in the Pauline tradition (2 Cor. 5:17; 6:2) has been pressed further than the apostle himself was ready to go (cf. Rom. 10:9; 13:11; Phil. 2:12; 3:20; 1 Thess. 5:8-9). But it has a parallel in the gnostic *Treatise on the Resurrection* of the Nag Hammadi documents (48.31-49.24):

> The Resurrection . . . is the revelation of what is, and the transformation of things, and a transition into newness. For imperishability [descends] upon the perishable; the light flows down upon the darkness, swallowing it up. . . . Therefore, do not . . . live in conformity with the flesh . . . but flee from the divisions and fetters, and already you have the resurrection. . . . Why not consider yourself as risen and [already] brought to this?[73]

The author of the Pastorals combats the heretical teachers. On the surface, his approach is to denounce their behavior and to call upon members of the community to avoid them (1 Tim. 4:7; 6:20; Titus 3:9-10). But his primary tactic is to compose apostolic letters in the name of Paul, who can still be called forth then as an authority in the community, and to set forth a theological position that affirms the goodness of creation, the incarnation, death, and resurrection of Christ, and the futurity of salvation beyond this life, an inheritance to be gained in the "heavenly kingdom." Furthermore, and again in the name of Paul, the author seeks to create an ethos based in part on ordinary values of the Greco-Roman world and supplemented by, and motivated by, those that are drawn from the common Christian tradition. In this way the Pastoral Epistles exhibit a bold attempt to fuse theological convictions and a congruent community life together.[74]

The outcome of the controversy reflected in the Pastorals must have been the strengthening of the community against the Pauline opposition. When Ignatius wrote to the Ephesians, he—like the author of the Pastorals—called upon his readers to avoid listening to false teachers (*Eph.* 16.1—17.2) and declared that Jesus Christ is the (true) *gnōsis* of God (17.2). Gnosticism is thus still an option.[75] Yet it seems that the Gnostics have been marginalized. Although Ignatius acknowledges that false teachers had been present at Ephesus, these false teachers are now regarded as outsiders who travel about (7.1; 9.1),[76] and Ignatius commends the Ephesians for having resisted their teachings (9.1). Further, the community is not divided (8.1), and "no heresy dwells" among its members (6.2). The apostle Paul is recalled as a model (12.2), and the community is of one mind with the apostles (11.2). The bishop (Onesimus, 1.3; 6.2) and presbytery are secure

in their positions (2.2; 4.1-2; 20.2). If all that is so, the theological convictions and community ethos prescribed in the Pastoral Epistles had an
enduring effect, contributing a tributary into the broad stream of normative
Christianity.

The Johannine Community

The Johannine community is more difficult to locate in time and place than
the communities that produced the Gospel of Matthew and the Pastoral
Epistles. In regard to time, interpreters generally consider the Gospel of
John to have been completed in its present form during the last decade of
the first century A.D.[77] and the three Johannine letters a bit later, either at
the end of the century or near the beginning of the next.[78] But the history
of the Johannine community itself would have reached back to earlier times.
Behind the Gospel of John stands a span of several decades in which
traditions of and about Jesus were given their distinctive Johannine character.
It has become customary in Johannine studies to envision a series of stages
of development within the Johannine community.[79] Although differing in
details, major proponents of phases of development agree that the origins
of the Johannine community can be traced to a nucleus of Christian Jews
who remained for some time within the synagogue prior to A.D. 70. In the
course of time, however, they or their successors were expelled from worship
in the synagogue, which would have been about A.D. 85 or later when the
so-called *Eighteen Benedictions* (*Shemonah Esreh*) were revised to include a curse
upon the *minim* (heretics), which would have included Jewish Christians.
The consequence of the curse was to expel Christians from the synagogue,
and that is reflected in the Gospel of John itself (9:22; 16:2; cf. 12:42).[80]
The Gospel of John was written after this decisive split between the Johannine Christians and synagogue worship. The Epistles of John, probably
authored by one or more persons of the Johannine community other than
the author of the Gospel of John,[81] were written at a subsequent phase in
the community's life.

The geographical location of the Johannine community is regarded by
virtually all major interpreters as uncertain, some leaning toward Ephesus,[82]
others toward Syria.[83] If either of these is correct, it is necessary to think
in terms of considerable diversity within the environs of the Johannine
community. If Ephesus is the place of the writing of the Pastoral Epistles
and the Gospel and Epistles of John, or if Syria is the place of both the
Gospel of Matthew and the Gospel and Epistles of John (plus even additional
documents, such as Q and the *Gospel of Thomas*), did the Johannine community
have knowledge of the other Christian community (or communities) that
shared its own territory, and vice versa? Perhaps the statement concerning

"other sheep, that are not of this fold" of John 10:16 refers to other Christians known to the evangelist and his community.[84] In any case, one should not necessarily think of a city or geographical area as an ecclesiastical unit. If the basic unit was the house church, different expressions of Christianity could exist side by side in a given city or region.[85]

Understanding the Johannine community as having developed over time has implications for an analysis of its theological convictions, since convictions may have varied between phases or from one phase to another. At the respective phases at which the Gospel and Epistles were composed, however, there are some common confessional convictions. The God of Israel is known as the Father of Jesus (John 17:1; 1 John 1:3) and of his disciples (John 14:8; 15:16; 1 John 1:2), and apart from this God there is no other (John 17:3; 1 John 5:21).[86] The Father has sent the Son into the world (John 6:57; 1 John 4:9-10), and that was for the purpose of saving it (John 12:47; 1 John 4:14). Faith in Jesus as the one sent from God is the means of eternal life (John 3:16; 1 John 5:13). Christological titles shared in common are "the Son," "the Son of God," "the Son of the Father," "Christ," and "Savior of the world."[87] The Holy Spirit is sent from the Father by the Son (John 14:26; 1 John 4:13). Differences between the Gospel and Epistles of John exist as well, and some of them will be considered below. It is important first, however, to indicate some of the concerns evident in the Johannine community at the time of the writing of the Gospel of John.

Within the Johannine perspective, the human race exists in a state of being overcome by sin, darkness, falsehood, and death. The resolution of the human condition, leading to life that is abundant, is effected by the Father's sending of the Son into the world. That the Father sent the Son into the world is stated some forty-one times in the Fourth Gospel, and that the Son must return to the Father who sent him some twenty times.[88] The concept of Jesus as having been sent "is the most characteristic christological formula in the Fourth Gospel."[89] As the one sent from the Father, he reveals the Father (12:44-45), speaks "the words of God" (3:34; cf. 7:16), and does the will of the Father and work that the Father has assigned to him (4:34; 5:36). He returns to the Father to resume his place of honor (17:5), prepare a place for his own (14:2), send the Paraclete (16:7), and enable believers to perform works in his name through prayer (14:12-14).

The saving work of Christ is not focused primarily on Jesus' death as an atoning event. In the Johannine perspective the sending of the Son, his revelation of the Father, his passion, death, resurrection, ascension, and glorification form a soteriological continuum. His crucifixion was the means of his being "lifted up" (3:14; 8:28; 12:32-34)—that is, his return to the Father (7:33; 13:1-3; 16:28) and his glorification (12:23; 13:31). In his exalted state, the Son has authority from the Father over all humanity in order to give eternal life to those whom the Father has given him (17:2). This he gives to those who believe in him as the one sent from the Father (17:3). Salvation is thus mediated by Christ to his own. There is a "Christology of mediation" in his Gospel,[90] by which the Son bestows salvation on those who believe in him.

It has been maintained that the background of the Johannine Christology, particularly its concept of the descending and ascending of Jesus as redeemer, is the so-called Gnostic Redeemer Myth.[91] But it is unlikely that such a myth existed so early as a presupposition for Johannine Christology.[92] Although the Fourth Gospel may well reflect elements of an incipient Gnosticism in certain respects,[93] its christological and soteriological emphases can be attributed primarily to the use of traditions about Jesus combined with wisdom speculations current in Hellenistic Judaism[94] and the common stock of proclamation concerning him as sent by the Father, crucified, and exalted. Moreover, these emphases were given their distinctive character within a polemical context. Interpreters have maintained on good grounds that the Fourth Gospel had its rise in a community that responded to and addressed various groups. The major battles were over the question of Jesus' identity in relationship to God between the Johannine community, at various stages of its history, and (1) nonbelieving Jews, who had expelled Christian Jews from the synagogue, and (2) perhaps other Christian groups, which were thought to have an inadequate Christology.[95] The "dominant dispute" reflected in the Fourth Gospel is over the question of the divinity of Jesus.[96] Jesus is portrayed as one who is accused of making himself equal to God (5:18; 10:33; cf. 19:7), which can be taken as an indicator that it was precisely the status of Jesus in relationship to God that was the issue dividing Johannine Christians and Jews, and perhaps Johannine Christians and other Christians as well. The Johannine Christians were under suspicion of proclaiming and worshiping Jesus as a second God and urging others to do the same.[97]

But while the Johannine Christology could admit the application of the title "God" to Christ in doxological contexts (1:1; 20:28), it is more nuanced in others.[98] Jesus, as the Son of the Father, is one with God (10:30, 38; 14:10-11; 17:21-22) but at the same time subordinate to the Father (14:28). Christ is the revealer of the Father (12:45; 14:9) and is the one who alone mediates salvation from the Father to those who believe (14:6). Those who receive him receive the salvation he brings. As he is the mediator of creation (1:3), so he is the mediator of salvation.

In addition to its christological and soteriological emphases, the Fourth Gospel envisions a community ethos that is closely related to, and even unfolds from, these emphases. Members of the community are those who have believed in Jesus, have been baptized (3:3-8), are loved by Christ

(13:34; 14:21; 15:9, 12) and the Father (14:21), "abide" in Christ (6:56; 15:4-10), and are commanded to love one another (13:34-35; 15:12-17). Drawing upon Old Testament imagery, in which God is the shepherd of Israel (Isa. 40:11; Ezek. 34:11-24), and the Messiah is to be a king, shepherd, and teacher of divine instruction (Ezek. 37:24), Messiah Jesus is the good shepherd who gathers his flock (John 10:11-18). He and his own know one another intimately (10:14, 27). He instructs his people and gives them eternal life (10:27-28). He gives his very life for them (10:11, 15, 17), and no one can take them away from his fold (10:28-29). In another metaphor, again drawing upon Old Testament imagery (Ps. 80:9-20; Jer. 2:21), Jesus is the true vine who gives life to his people, who are his branches (15:1-8). Believers "abide" in the vine (15:4-7, 9-10) and thereby receive life in order to bear fruit (15:2, 5) and thus prove to be his disciples (15:8). The bearing of fruit is expressed in the keeping of his commandments (15:10), characterized above all by love among the members of the community for one another (15:12).

The ethos of the Johannine community is characterized primarily by love among its members, and the place for nurture and growth in love and discipleship is the fellowship of the community.[99] The presupposition of this stance is the love of God for the world, which has been revealed by God's sending of the Son (3:16-17; 12:47), and which has been exemplified particularly in the Son's giving his life for his own (10:11; 13:1). The giving of one's life for others is the supreme sign of love (15:13). As interpreters have pointed out, the emphasis in the Johannine community was on discipleship, and no interest appears regarding charisms or ecclesiastical offices.[100]

The Johannine community has been characterized as "a conventicle with gnosticizing tendencies."[101] The term *conventicle* seems apt to a point, since the Gospel of John stresses mutual love among the members of the community and a sharp demarcation of the community from the world, which is perceived as hating it (15:18-19; 17:14). Yet the expression of divine love for the world (3:16) and the longing for unity among Christians (10:16; 11:52; 17:20-23) show that labels do not apply easily. As for "gnosticizing tendencies," that characterization is apt to a degree also, but it should be understood in a particular way. Elements within the Fourth Gospel itself (such as the dualism between above and below, a Christology that all but loses sight of Jesus' humanity, and so forth) lend themselves easily to a gnosticizing tendency within the community, even though the dominant voice in the Johannine community would not necessarily endorse such.

In any case, by the time the Johannine Epistles were written, there had been a split within the community, leading to the exit of a party from the rest of the community, and these persons can be called secessionists (1

John 2:18-19). These secessionists can probably be characterized by all those things that are particularly opposed in the Epistles of John, and that are antagonistic to teachings held by a "correct" reading of the Gospel of John. They deny the incarnation and humanity of Jesus (1 John 4:2-3; 2 John 7), claim to be without sin (1 John 1:8, 10), disregard the ethical teachings ("commandments") of Jesus (1 John 2:3-4; 3:22, 24; 5:2-3), and fail to practice love (1 John 2:9-11; 3:11-18; 4:20).[102]

As indicated earlier, the author (or authors) of the Epistles of John continued central Johannine themes spelled out in the Fourth Gospel, including those of God's sending of the Son into the world to save it, the gift of eternal life for believers, and major christological titles. But there are distinctive theological claims in the Johannine Epistles that exceed those of the Gospel of John at decisive points; most of these appear in 1 John, and unless otherwise indicated, verse references are to that book. The author of 1 John claims that the confession that Jesus Christ has come in the flesh is the criterion of truth about him (4:2-3), and the death of Jesus is spoken of as the atoning event (1:7; 2:2; 4:10)—a claim that is founded on the Fourth Gospel (1:29; 10:11, 15), but is not explicitly there.

Along with other New Testament writers (Rom. 8:3; Heb. 10:18; 1 Peter 3:18), the author employs cultic, sacrificial terminology in speaking of Jesus' death as an "expiation for our sins" (*hilasmos peri tōn hamartiōn hēmōn*, 2:2; 4:10).[103] The fact that he uses this formulation with exactly the same wording on two occasions shows that it has become a standard soteriological expression of the community's confession of faith. Finally, while the gift of eternal life continues, as in the Fourth Gospel, to be the present possession of believers (5:11-13), so that they are "born of God" (3:9; 4:7; 5:4, 18) and are "God's children now" (3:2; cf. 5:1), the futurity of salvation is brought out more forcefully than in the Gospel of John.[104] On the basis of abiding in Christ, believers can have "confidence" of salvation at his coming (2:28; 3:21) and at the "day of judgment" (4:17), which is future. It is only at the appearing of Christ that believers will be like him (3:2), sharing in the fullness of salvation. These accents on incarnational Christology, the sacrificial death of Jesus as atoning, and the futurity of salvation undoubtedly address, and refute, "gnosticizing tendencies" in the teachings of the secessionists.

As the theological convictions of the Johannine community were given sharper focus by the author of 1 John, so too were the ethical teachings. The ethos of abiding in Christ and loving others in the community continues as essential to Christian identity (2:6, 27-28; 3:6, 24). But abiding in Christ and love for others have become empty slogans. The secessionists claim to have fellowship with God (1:6), say that they abide in Jesus (2:6), and consider themselves to be without sin (1:8, 10).[105] Apparently they taught that salvation, a present reality, is a matter of spiritual communion with the glorified, risen Christ, an abiding in him, a source of enlightenment (2:9), by which one becomes like him.

Over against such views, the author claims that only at Christ's parousia will believers "be like him" (3:2). In the meantime, abiding in Christ means "to walk in the same way in which he walked" (2:6)—the way of love and obedience to the Father. That means that the true disciple keeps what was taught from the beginning (2:24), observes the commandments of Jesus (3:24), and practices love (4:12-13, 16). Sin is an ever-present possibility, and even believers are sinful (1:8, 10), but Jesus has borne the consequences of divine judgment upon sin (2:2, 12), and the disciple is charged to engage in battle against sin (3:6, 9; 5:18).

The outer life of discipleship is given greater specificity than in the Fourth Gospel, in which love for others is the greatest commandment of Jesus (15:12), but is a commandment that is not given as much content as here. The love of the disciple is to reflect the love of God: "If God so loved us [in sending the Son as an expiation for our sins], we also ought to love one another" (4:11; cf. 4:19). As it is the nature of God to love, so it should be the nature of the disciple to love others (4:7, 19; cf. 3:14, 23). That takes concrete form as one does right (2:29); indeed "righteousness" has become a virtue (3:7). This includes care for the poor (3:17; cf. 3 John 5, 11), for one should not simply love in word or speech but "in deed and truth" (3:18). Sin is doing evil (5:17). As in the case of christological affirmations, the author here draws on the common stock of ethical teaching known from elsewhere in the Christian tradition, especially emphases on righteousness and the doing of good deeds, particularly for those in need.

Although the ordering of the life of the community does not match the detail of the Pastoral Epistles, in which ecclesiastical offices are rather firmly set, the self-designation of the author of 2 and 3 John as a "presbyter" (2 John 1; 3 John 1), the address of this presbyter to a trusted community leader by the name of Gaius (3 John 1), and the reference to a certain Diotrephes as a person "who likes to put himself first" (3 John 9) in opposition to the presbyter indicate that matters of authority and church order were growing concerns. The author who identified himself by the title presbyter was most likely a figure within the Johannine community who regarded himself as a guardian of the Johannine tradition, exercising authority in the community (or perhaps within a circle of congregations—that is, house churches) of Johannine tradition.[106] Otherwise titles are lacking, and personal names are used for a leader of a house church (Gaius, 3 John 1), an emissary of the presbyter (Demetrius, 3 John 12), and one who refuses to accept the authority of the presbyter (Diotrephes, 3 John 9).

The history of the Johannine community, as seen in the stages reviewed here, culminated in a split in two major directions. The fate of the secessionists was probably to end up in early Christian Gnosticism, taking the Gospel of John with them.[107] In any case, gnostic leaders were among the first to make use of it in the second century. The gnostic teachers Ptolemaeus and Heracleon both wrote expositions of it ca. A.D. 170.[108] The remainder of the Johannine community, however, probably identified with other major streams of Christianity, contributing to the broad stream of normative Christianity.[109] Evidence for the use of the Gospel of John by so-called "orthodox" Christians prior to the latter part of the second century is slim. There are parallels of words and theological concepts between the letters of Ignatius (early second century) and the Fourth Gospel,[110] leading some to conclude that Ignatius did indeed make use of the latter.[111] Yet Ignatius makes no explicit quotations of the Gospel of John. At most one can say that he was acquainted with theological ideas found in the Gospel of John, but to say that he used it as a written source before him is to go beyond the evidence.[112] The best evidence for the acceptance of the Gospel of John among the "orthodox" of the second century is its inclusion among the "four pillars" of the church's gospel (along with the other three canonical Gospels) by Irenaeus (ca. A.D. 180),[113] and its endorsement by the Muratorian Canon near the end of the second century.[114] Although not considered "orthodox," Tatian at an even earlier date (ca. A.D. 170) used the four canonical Gospels as the basis for the composition of his *Diatessaron*, which had widespread popularity even among "orthodox" circles.[115]

For our purposes, it is already instructive to limit ourselves to the stages of development that can be discerned within the Johannine community itself. At the level of writing the Gospel of John, to say nothing of the Epistles of John at this point, attempts were made to articulate a confession and to shape a community ethos in such a way that a common life of faith and behavior could be sustained. But that fusion was not to last, for the community was soon divided, and a group emphasizing an ultrahigh Christology and considering themselves enlightened and free from sin seceded from the rest of the community. The author (or authors) of the epistles of John sought to provide a new synthesis of confession and community ethos that would sustain the community, drawing upon christological and ethical resources of the common Christian tradition which would yield a more nuanced, and normative, expression of faith and life.

Some Commonalities

What was said at the end of the previous chapter could be repeated here. If one were to make comparisons and contrasts among the three communities studied here, there would be significant contrasts among them. Major differences would appear, for example, in Christology (including the use of christological titles), eschatological expectations, and church leadership (including attitudes toward ecclesiastical offices). On the other hand, there are commonalities. These include items listed previously. The God of Israel is the Creator of the world, the Father of Jesus, and the Father of humanity. The essential humanity of Jesus is affirmed (even if almost lost in the Fourth Gospel), as is his redemptive role by way of the cross and resurrection. The advent of a new era and the gift of the Spirit in the lives of believers is claimed. It is held that believers constitute communities of faith marked by an ethos in which the individual gives himself or herself over to others in love and service, which is inspired by and modeled on Jesus' own giving himself over.

Beyond these commonalities, however, there are others that are peculiar to the subapostolic age. The first is that at this stage there is the self-conscious composition of "ecclesiastical" literature. In the previous era, prior to A.D. 70, the letters of Paul were addressed to specific communities, and in them the apostle discussed rather specific issues of the moment. But the documents investigated here, though they too take up issues at hand, are more comprehensive concerning faith and life in ways that the letters of Paul are not.

Another commonality is that within the communities investigated here the apostles, now deceased, are idealized, as in the case of Paul in the Pastoral Epistles, or are those to whom the authors or sponsors of the anonymous works consider themselves loyal. The author of the Gospel of Matthew is clearly a loyalist to what is considered a Petrine tradition; the writer of the Pastorals considers himself a Pauline loyalist; and the Fourth Evangelist must have thought of himself as loyal to both Peter (21:15-23) and the beloved disciple. There is, then, the beginning of a conscious need to preserve an apostolic tradition as the authoritative tradition, which becomes explicit also in the writing of a contemporary, Clement of Rome (1 Clem. 42.1-5), and later writers.[116]

But it has to be emphasized that the claims to apostolic loyalty were not what distinguished the canonical writers and their communities from others.[117] Just as the author of the Gospel of Matthew considered himself a Petrine loyalist, so for the author of the Gospel of Thomas the apostles Thomas and James were the leading apostles, even surpassing Peter in eminence. That means that the two communities in which these Gospels were produced were actually alike in claiming loyalty to apostles (and, implicitly, apostolic warrant for their views). Yet they differed dramatically in theological and ecclesiological emphases. Gnostic interpreters of Paul and the Fourth Gospel were no less emphatic in their claims of loyalty to apostolic authority than were the authors of the Pastorals and the Johannine letters, respectively. Therefore the rise of normative Christianity, and its distinguishing itself from alternative forms, was not due simply to its appeal to apostolic tradition, important as that was. In the final analysis, theological and ecclesiological matters were decisive in the setting of limits to diversity. These matters will be taken up next.

6

The Limits to Diversity

ATTENTION WAS GIVEN IN THE PREVIOUS TWO CHAPTERS TO specific Christian communities, following a chronological order—communities of faith prior to A.D. 70 (chapter 4), and then communities that flourished after that date up to the beginning of the second century (chapter 5). If we were to continue on that course, tracing the rise of normative Christianity through the second and third centuries, and at the same time attend to simultaneous and successive developments in different geographical areas, the task would be enormous—and more than can be accomplished here. In this chapter therefore a broader approach will have to be taken, investigating a wide range of literature in light of some basic issues that had to be faced by Christian communities of all kinds in the first centuries of the common era. The dynamics at work in the formation of normative Christianity, seeking to maintain a congruence between confession and community ethos, inevitably called for the setting of limits to diversity.

The Range of Diversity

Before discussing the dynamics at work in the formation of normative Christianity, it is important to be aware of the diversity that existed in early Christianity and its environment. If Christianity had developed in one geographical area, such as Palestine, the range of diversity in culture, religious backgrounds, and socio-economic levels of peoples would have been somewhat smaller. But already within twenty years after the founding of the Jerusalem congregation, Christianity existed not only in Palestine but also in Syria, Asia Minor, Greece, Macedonia, Rome, and elsewhere. Congregations of believers existed in these far-flung places prior to the writing of the books of the New Testament and other early Christian literature.

Members of these congregations, increasingly of gentile background, brought with them a wide range of beliefs.

The core of the Christian movement at its outset was of course Jewish. But Judaism itself was highly diverse. It would be interesting and informative to know more about the backgrounds of early Jewish Christians, but we do not know the particular forms of Judaism to which the vast majority of them adhered prior to becoming Christian. Those who are known represented various traditions. Best known is Paul, who says forthrightly that he had been a Pharisee (Phil. 3:4; cf. Acts 23:6). In other cases, we are dependent mainly on three accounts by Luke in Acts. Luke says first that "a great many of the priests" became believers within the first year or two of the Christian movement (Acts 6:7). The context suggests, but does not require, that these priests resided in Jerusalem. If so, they would probably have been persons involved in cultic duties at, or in connection with, the temple.[1] The suggestion that they might have originated from the Qumran community[2] has not received much support. In any case, as priests they did not apparently affect the structure of the early community (that is, no continuing priesthood is evident).[3]

Second, Luke mentions Simon—later called Simon Magus—who was of Samaritan origin. According to the account in Acts, Simon became a believer and was baptized in response to the preaching of Philip, and later he was rebuked by Peter (8:9-24). He does not appear again in the writings of the New Testament, but he and his followers—a gnostic sect called the Simonians—are referred to in patristic and other early Christian literature,[4] although the extent to which the doctrines of the Simonians can actually be traced back to the historical Simon is questionable. Nevertheless, Simon Magus continued to have significance as a leader of a heterodox tradition; indeed, Irenaeus called Simon the one "from whom all heresies originated."[5] The Samaritan origin of still other Christians has been postulated in Johannine studies.[6] And then there is Apollos, a Jewish Christian from Alexandria, whom Paul met at Ephesus (Acts 18:24). According to the Western text of Acts 18:25, Apollos had been "instructed in his native land" and, if so, might have brought into his version of Christian faith certain aspects of Hellenistic Judaism current in Alexandria.[7] In any case, it is clear that there were differences between him and the Jewish Christian couple Priscilla and Aquila, since Luke says that "they took him and expounded to him the way of God more accurately" (Acts 18:26). He became an associate of Paul and taught in the church at Corinth. When Paul wrote to that church, there are indications that some at Corinth claimed to be followers of Apollos in distinction to Paul, but there are no indications of major theological differences between the two men (1 Cor. 1:12; 3:4-6, 22; 4:6; 16:12).

If there was diversity among Christians of Jewish (and Samaritan) background, there was even more among those of gentile origin. Some of them were "God-fearers," persons who affirmed monotheism and were acquainted with the saga and Scriptures of Israel by attending synagogues where Greek was spoken, but who did not undergo circumcision and did not observe the most particularistic aspects of the law.[8] These persons are mentioned in the writings of Josephus (*Ant.* 14.110; cf. *J.W.* 6.427; 7.45), the Acts of the Apostles (10:2, 23, 35; 13:16, 26, 50; 16:14; 17:4, 17), and in inscriptions.[9] There is probably an allusion to them at John 9:31 as well. The God-fearers were probably never a distinct group in the sense of a sect, but were persons who, having some prior knowledge of Christian presuppositions, were somewhat prepared for the Christian message and, according to Luke, many of them became Christians (Acts 17:1-4; 18:4).[10] Other Gentiles, however, came from backgrounds free of Jewish influence but affected by other traditions—particularly the popular philosophical schools, local and imported cults, the mystery religions, and syncretistic blendings of several traditions.[11] Paul, for example, speaks of the Christians at Thessalonica as having "turned to God from idols, to serve a living and true God" (1 Thess. 1:9).

Mention has been made already of Simon Magus and the Simonians, an early gnostic sect.[12] In all likelihood, it originated in Samaria during the first century A.D.[13] Diversity in early Christianity cannot be discussed without some consideration of the place of Gnosticism both in the environment of early Christianity and within certain expressions of it. The traditional view has been that Gnosticism was a second-century A.D. development within and then away from Christianity, a view that was held in early times by such writers as Eusebius and Epiphanius,[14] and that can be found in the twentieth century.[15] It has become more common today, however, to trace the origins of Gnosticism to other sources. Some have maintained that its origins are to be found in ancient Jewish circles,[16] and some would go further to speak of the locale as Palestine and Samaria[17] or centers of Hellenistic Judaism such as Alexandria.[18] But the theory of the origins of Gnosticism from a purely Jewish background has been questioned.[19] There are scholars who have maintained that its origins can be found within a much wider milieu with roots in various cultures, including gentile Hellenism, and perhaps even oriental traditions, reaching back to pre-Christian times.[20] Hans Jonas has concluded that Gnosticism can be shown to combine elements from several sources, but that the combination of all of them does not in itself explain its rise. It was, he says, a movement that "transcended ethnic and denominational boundaries."[21] Further, he says, its rise must have been "roughly contemporaneous with the infancy of Christianity (certainly not later, witness Simon Magus; possibly earlier)."[22]

The matter of origins cannot be pursued further here, but by way of summary it can be said that Gnosticism is generally regarded as having risen roughly simultaneously with Christianity, and that it had both Christian and non-Christian exponents. Its effects on Christianity can be seen in stages.[23] An "incipient Gnosticism" can be detected in the era of the New Testament and other early Christian literature (up to A.D. 125).[24] Thereafter there is the era of the great teachers and systems (mid-second and early third centuries). Finally, there are the reactions of the orthodox to them and their successors in the antiheretical writings of the second to fourth centuries.

Limiting Factors

Why is it that a normative Christianity developed, on expression of Christianity that has no specific name but is usually called "orthodoxy," "catholic" Christianity, or sometimes "ecclesiastical" Christianity? There certainly were alternatives. Eusebius provides a list of Christian sects that existed already in the second century, based on the writings of Hegesippus (ca. A.D. 100–180). These include groups both well known and obscure: Simonians, Cleobienes, Dositheans, Gorathenes, Masbotheans, Menandrianists, Marcionites, Carpocratians, Valentinians, Basilidians, and Saturnilians.[25] An even more extensive survey of Christian sects is provided in the fourth-century (ca. A.D. 375) work of Epiphanius, his *Panarion* ("medicine chest"), in which he takes up dozens of sects and refutes them.[26] But none of the sects mentioned by early Christian writers became dominant, the prototype of Christianity as a major religious tradition. The Mandaeans, who live in portions of Iran and Iraq today and consist of some fifteen thousand persons,[27] can alone be considered the continuation of ancient Gnosticism as a living religious tradition.

When we search for the reasons why one form of Christianity became dominant, it is appropriate to ask whether there is any "essence" or cluster of characteristics apart from which Christianity cannot exist. Is there anything that can be identified as that which binds together its beliefs and ethos, confession and community?

The search for the "essence of Christianity" has a history associated with major figures in nineteenth- and early twentieth-century theology, such as Friedrich Schleiermacher, Ludwig Feuerbach, Ernst Troeltsch, and Adolf von Harnack.[28] But none of these made a proposal that embraces both worldview and ethos together. Their proposals had to do primarily with worldview alone. In the case of Harnack, for example, who was perhaps the most forceful of these writers to get at the matter, the "essence" of Christianity is the gospel as Jesus proclaimed it and as expressed repeatedly in the history of the church—that is, the rule of God in the heart of the individual believer, which is attended by an assurance of God as loving Father, certainty of the infinite value of the human soul, and love for the neighbor.[29]

A more comprehensive view of Christianity, which takes both worldview and ethos into account, is that Christianity is essentially a religion of faith and love. To speak of it as "essentially" a religion of faith and love is not to speak of its "essence," nor is it to suggest that faith and love make it unique, as though other religions lack these. Nevertheless, faith and love are pervasive themes in Christianity, manifested in both its worldview and ethos. In regard to worldview, Jesus called upon his hearers to place their faith in God as heavenly Father[30] and, echoing what he considered the greatest commandment of Israel's heritage (Deut. 6:5), sought to evoke their love for God with mind and heart (Matt. 22:37// Mark 12:30// Luke 10:27). Love for God continues to be regarded as characteristic of the life of the believer in early Christianity,[31] but even more apparent is an emphasis upon faith—both in God and in Christ.[32] In regard to ethos, the commandment to love one's neighbor as oneself (Lev. 19:18) is the companion to the command to love God (Matt. 22:39//Mark 12:31//Luke 10:27) and is the central moral teaching of early Christian literature.[33] Faith, or trust, comes into the picture too, in that the believer is one who can be considered trustworthy, since he or she loves, and cares for the good of, the other.[34]

In one of his essays, Robert Wilken takes up the question of Christian identity in the first centuries of the common era. He speaks of a recognizable "continuity within early Christian life and the sense of a center among early Christians," and then adds:

> The one thing that the ancient sources make clear is that the notion of a distinct Christian identity is not a fiction in the head of a clique of bishops nor a creation of the later church. It was the common experience of men and women in the churches, and it was perceived by outsiders.[35]

He goes on to support this statement by referring to ways that pagan authors of antiquity treated Christianity. Celsus, for example, knew of the existence of various Christian sects (Gnostics, Marcionites, and so forth), for he mentions them. When he offered substantive criticism of Christianity, however, he did not refer to the sects but aimed his attack against the "great church." He "had come to know Christianity as a group of people who shared certain beliefs, observed a common way of life and . . . represented what Christianity was throughout the Roman world."[36] Wilken finds essentially the same to be the case with Galen, who also made a description of Christianity, concentrating primarily on its way of life.[37] The point to be derived from all this is that a "center" was being formed in the first two centuries that cannot be defined "solely in doctrinal terms," says Wilken:

> For it included, among other things, behavior and way of life, liturgical practice, even a sense of "belonging," of church if you will, and this sense of communal identity was present long before there were definable standards by which to measure it.[38]

If all that is so, there are several factors that marked off normative Christianity from other forms that developed in antiquity. Although there may have been others, at least six limiting factors can be seen to have been operative. Together they make up a complex in which confession of faith and community ethos are congruent, since they are grounded in faith and love. They can be stated here as affirmations for subsequent support and discussion:

1. The God of Israel can be loved and trusted as the Creator of all that is and as benevolent to humanity.
2. Jesus of Nazareth can be trusted as the one sent by God to reveal God and to redeem humanity.
3. In spite of human failure, which would disqualify one from salvation, trust in God's redemptive work in Christ is the way to salvation, which is begun in this life, but completed beyond it.
4. The person saved by faith in God's redemptive work in Christ is expected to care about, indeed love, others and be worthy of their trust.
5. Those who trust in Jesus as revealer of God and redeemer of humanity are expected to live as disciples in a community whose ethos is congruent with the legacy of his life and teaching.
6. Those who live in communities of faith belong to a fellowship that is larger than that provided by the local community, an extended fellowship.

These six affirmations are not peculiar to any one early Christian writer. They have to do with basic expressions of Christianity as found in the New Testament and in other early Christian writings coming from the late first and early second centuries, as well as in other writings of later times, which agree with their essentials. Using traditional terminology, the six affirmations have to do with theology, Christology, soteriology, ethics, and ecclesiology (both local and universal). These cohere, and they are of course expressed somewhat differently among early Christian writers. The Christology of Paul, for example, differs from that of Matthew, as do their respective ecclesiologies. Yet, taking their expressions of Christianity into account as a whole (theology, Christology, soteriology, ethics, and ecclesiology), they stand much closer together than either stands with such figures as Marcion, Valentinus, or Montanus.

The Factors at Work

No one factor contributed to the centering of normative Christianity and to the setting of limits to diversity. I am suggesting that there were several, six of which have been listed as affirmations of faith and life that seem rather clearly to have been operative. These six would have worked together symbiotically and simultaneously. But for purposes of discussion it is necessary to take them one by one. We shall follow the pattern given in the previous section.

1. *Theology.* Normative Christianity affirms that the God of Israel can be loved and trusted as the Creator of all that is and as benevolent to humanity. Traditions about Jesus show clearly that he was a child of Abraham, a Jew, and that he affirmed faith in the God of Israel, who is one, and who created the world and continues to sustain it. That God is one, the Creator, and benevolent was affirmed by early Christian writers. No evidence exists that any of the New Testament writers would have denied that affirmation. Writing near the close of the second century or at the beginning of the next, Tertullian says, "you will find no church of apostolic origin whose Christianity repudiates the Creator."[39] In context he means the God of Israel's Scriptures, who is one and who created the world.

According to early Christian writers, several of the early sects of the first and second centuries A.D. shared with traditional Judaism and normative Christianity positive affirmations concerning the God of Israel, including the Ebionites,[40] Encratites,[41] and Montanists.[42] But there were persons and their followers who maintained that Israel's God is not the highest, and that there is a benevolent God higher in divine qualities than that one. The highest God is the one revealed by Jesus, and that God is not the Creator of the world. These views were maintained and amplified by major gnostic teachers and their followers and also by Marcion, who is sometimes classified as a Gnostic, but who stands out in contrast to major gnostic teachers and gnostic movements in general.[43] While the Gnostics were not averse to the use of allegorical scriptural interpretation when convenient to do so,[44] Marcion interpreted literally those Scriptures that suited him (an abbreviated Gospel of Luke—or at least a Gospel closer to Luke's than any other[45]— and ten epistles of Paul).[46] Whereas the Gnostics generally held that there is a spark of the divine within each person, which has been created by the higher God, Marcion held that the human being was totally the work of a lesser God. And while the Gnostics (with the exception of the Valentinians) were not for the most part adept at organization, Marcion can be credited for establishing what can be labeled a church with a worldwide network, not simply a school or movement. Since there are these fundamental differences between Marcion and Gnostics in general, they will be treated separately in subsequent discussion.

Already in the first century, according to Irenaeus, Simon Magus claimed that the universe was created not by the highest God but by angels and powers.[47] He was followed in his teaching by his pupil Menander.[48] Both were of Samaritan origin and flourished in the New Testament era—Simon in Rome, where he arrived during the time of Claudius (A.D. 41–54) and remained until his death later in the first century,[49] and Menander in Antioch of Syria,[50] who probably began and ended his work slightly later. It is most likely that Simon was a Gnostic before he was a Christian (if he should be classified as a Christian at all, as Acts 8:9-13 would lead one to conclude).[51] Menander was also a pre-Christian Gnostic, and it is even more doubtful whether he became a Christian, since he claimed that he himself was the redeemer sent from on high.[52] At most, it seems, Menander can be considered a link between pre-Christian Gnosticism and Christian Gnosticism,[53] since he was the teacher of Saturninus (or Satornilus[54]) and Basilides,[55] who were gnostic leaders.

During the second century the views concerning the creation of the universe became more diverse. Saturninus, Menander's pupil in Syria, held that "the world and everything in it" came into being from angels, which had been created by the "Father unknown to all."[56] And Carpocrates of Alexandria claimed that "the world and what is in it was made by angels, who are much inferior to the unbegotten Father."[57] But there were others who went further by claiming that the world and its contents were created by a solitary second power in heaven, a demiurge, inferior to the supreme God. These include Cerinthus (Asia Minor)[58] and Apelles (Alexandria),[59] who was at one time a pupil of Marcion.

The most elaborate cosmogonies are those of the great gnostic teachers of the second century, Basilides (Alexandria) and Valentinus (Rome), for whom all things created came into being by means of the work of a series of beings (powers or aeons) that had emanated from the unknown and superior God.[60] The God of Israel's Scriptures was, in both cases, one of the beings that had emanated from the unknown God.[61] The Valentinians could also call this one the demiurge.[62] Finally, Marcion (Rome) made a very sharp distinction, even a separation, between the God who created the world (the God of the Israelite Scriptures) and the Father of Jesus Christ, a God who is greater.[63] In the case of Marcion one can speak of two Gods, although they are of course not equal.[64] Marcion attributed the origin of evil to the God who created the world, while the other is the source of goodness and is himself good.[65] The first is "a judge, fierce and warlike, the other mild and peaceable, solely kind and supremely good."[66] The one is the God of the law, the other the God of the gospel.[67]

The distinction between a higher God revealed in Christ and the lesser Creator of the universe—variously called the God of the Jews, the demiurge, an aeon or power, or a company of angels—continued in Marcionism and in gnostic communities beyond the lifetimes of the great teachers of the second century. It is referred to in the writings of Eusebius and Epiphanius of the fourth century as a currently held view by Marcionites and Gnostics in their times,[68] for example, and is found in *The Tripartite Tractate* and *The Gospel of the Egyptians* of the Nag Hammadi library.[69] The distinction may well have had its roots in Judaism prior to the rise of Christianity.[70] Philo, for example, could make a distinction between what he calls "the Most High One" and the Logos, who is "the second God" (*ho deuteros theos*) and instrumental in creation,[71] even though he continued to affirm monotheism.[72] But with Marcionism and Gnosticism the distinction was pressed. An anticosmic attitude had developed.[73] Evil, they thought, must be attributed to the stupidity and inferiority of the one who created the world.[74] Marcion, in particular, says Tertullian, "had an unhealthy interest in the problem of evil—the origins of it" and on the basis of Psalm 45:7 (where Israel's God says, "I make weal and create woe") and his own speculations concluded that the Creator was "the author of evil."[75] The gnostic attitude is expressed most succinctly in a saying in *The Gospel of Philip*, "The world came about through a mistake."[76]

The claims of normative Christianity went of course in a different direction.[77] Marcion and the Gnostics were a threat to the monotheistic tradition taught by Jesus, as recorded in the oldest gospel traditions, and by other early Christian writers of the apostolic and subapostolic eras. But their views also severed any sense of continuity with Israel and salvation history, in which the God of redemption is the God of creation. To be sure, one finds within the writings that came to be canonized some anti-worldliness (Matt. 18:7; John 8:23; 15:19; 1 Cor. 11:32; Gal. 4:3). When the Fourth Evangelist and the apostle Paul speak of the "ruler of this world" (John 12:31; 14:30; 16:11) and the "god of this world" (2 Cor. 4:4), respectively, their words border on Marcionite and gnostic terminology. But in each case the reference is to Satan—not a demiurge—who seeks to have dominion but is defeated by Christ.

Neither Marcion nor the major gnostic teachers or schools could affirm those passages that assert that one God both created the world and redeems it (John 1:10; 3:16; Acts 17:24; 2 Cor. 5:19; Heb. 1:2). Nor could they have assented to the affirmations of the fourth-century Council of Nicaea

(A.D. 325) concerning "one God" who is "Creator of all that is, seen and unseen," nor to the first article of the confession of faith of the church at Laodicea (mid-fourth century, Syria) concerning "the God of the law and the gospel, just and good," which must have been anti-Marcionite.[78]

2. *Christology.* Normative Christianity affirms that Jesus of Nazareth can be trusted as the one sent by Israel's God to reveal God and to redeem humanity. New Testament and other early Christian writers speak in two primary ways, although these are different only in degree. Either they speak of God as the one who redeems humanity through Christ—thus a "theopractic" emphasis—or they speak of Christ as the redemptive figure—thus a "christopractic" emphasis—even though Christ acts on behalf of God.[79] These shades of emphasis can be illustrated in such statements as the following: "in Christ *God* was reconciling the world to himself" (2 Cor. 5:19), which is theopractic, and "*Christ* . . . died for sins once for all . . . that he might bring us to God" (1 Peter 3:18), which has a christopractic ring to it. In theopractic statements concerning redemption, the linkage between the God of Israel and redemption is more obvious. Christ is generally portrayed more as an obedient Son and has a more passive role. But in the christopractic statements, Christ has a more active role and is portrayed as coming from above to rescue humanity and to bring humanity into a reconciled relationship with God. Normative Christianity can affirm both, although there is a tendency for earlier writers to stress the theopractic character of redemption, which preserves Jewish monotheism most clearly, while the christopractic emphasis comes to expression more in later writings, such as the Deutero-Pauline and Catholic Epistles, as christological reflection developed and liturgical and creedal language—which is primarily "second article" in focus—accentuated the role of Christ in redemption.[80] In both cases the Christ confessed is Jesus of Nazareth, a historical figure who was remembered as crucified and resurrected from the dead. In spite of all the titles of majesty (or christological titles) applied to him, Jesus was considered to have been a mortal—a human being—sharing in the finitude of humanity. That could hardly be denied, since he was crucified and died.

With the exception of the Ebionites, who affirmed the humanity of Jesus even to the point of saying that he was "the child of a normal union between a man and Mary,"[81] the tendency of early sects was to press the christopractic tradition to the point of a separation of the redeemer from the God of Israel and the denial of his humanity. According to Irenaeus and Hippolytus, the view that Christ merely appeared as a man and seemed to suffer, but actually was neither a man nor one who suffered (Docetism), was held and taught already in the first century by Simon Magus.[82] Whether the historical Simon held and taught such, there is evidence that such views were taught by the turn of the century, since the author of 1 John opposes them (4:2-3), as does Ignatius early in the second century.[83]

As the second century wore on, the separation of the Son from the God of Israel and the denial of his humanity became even more pronounced. Marcion's separation of the Son from the God of Israel has already been reviewed in the previous section. Moreover, his denial of Christ's incarnation, suffering, and death, and the corresponding claim that he merely appeared to be a human being, is well attested.[84] Cerinthus, the gnostic teacher of Asia Minor, taught that "Christ descended upon" the human Jesus at his baptism and then was "separated again from Jesus" and did not suffer in Jesus' passion.[85] Here the Christ comes not from the God of Israel but "the unknown Father" who is "the power that is over all things,"[86] and his humanity is flatly denied. Saturninus of Syria and Basilides of Alexandria taught that the Christ merely appeared to be a man.[87] Basilides claimed that Simon of Cyrene was crucified in place of the incorporeal Christ.[88] Valentinus and later Valentinians held to docetic views as well. According to Hippolytus and Irenaeus, the Italian Valentinians claimed that the Logos entered the physical body of Jesus at his baptism, but departed prior to his suffering and death. On the other hand, the Oriental Valentinians claimed that "the body of the Savior was spiritual," not fleshly.[89] In both cases the finitude, suffering, and unqualified humanity of Christ are denied. The *Gospel of Truth* within the Nag Hammadi library, which may be of Valentinian origin,[90] speaks of Christ's "fleshly form,"[91] not fleshly existence. Several other Nag Hammadi treatises present docetic views of Christ and deny his suffering and death as well, including *The Gospel of Philip, The Second Treatise of the Great Seth*, and *The Apocalypse of Peter*.[92]

The severing of Christ from the God of Israel and identifying him as the redeemer from a higher God is not simply a later stage in the unfolding of a christopractic emphasis in redemptive Christology. There is a difference in kind, not simply in degree, of christological development in such cases. Another ingredient is present—"a powerful mythic impulse"[93]—that existed independently of Christian tradition and then was combined with the latter to form gnostic Christianity.

Normative Christianity continued to affirm the humanity of Jesus. The Fourth Gospel, to be sure, portrays Jesus in ways that his humanity is virtually lost,[94] and so Gnostics could make use of it,[95] but even in that Gospel there are assertions of Jesus' humanity (particularly in its telling of his death).[96] Neither Marcion nor Gnostics could affirm that "the Logos *became* flesh" (John 1:14).[97] Even though the christopractic emphasis was dominant from at least the early part of the second century (if not already at the end of the first), so that Christology developed in intricate ways all the way up to the councils of Nicaea and Chalcedon in the fourth and fifth centuries, there exists a normative Christianity in those centuries in which the humanity of Jesus is not lost. So Ignatius speaks of Christ as one "who was truly born, both ate and drank, was truly persecuted under Pontius Pilate, was truly crucified and died."[98] Hippolytus wrote that Christ "does not refuse the conditions proper to him as a man, since he hungers and toils and thirsts in weariness, and flees in fear, and prays in trouble."[99] And Tertullian asks, "But if [Christ's] flesh is denied, how can his death be affirmed?" and if that is the case, "neither can there be assurance of the resurrection."[100]

The emphases of normative Christianity were not the result of speculation on the nature of Christ but were intricately tied into a worldview and ethos that are larger than Christology alone. A Christology reflects one's worldview and also one's community values. It also, in turn, shapes these. If one looks upon the world and assigns to it an origin from, and care by, a benevolent God in whom trust can be placed, as the Scriptures of Israel would lead one to believe, christological reflection will stress the unity of that God and his Christ, endorsing the monotheism of the Scriptures and providing a place for Christ within the larger story of Israel—that is, redemptive history. Then too if a primary value is placed on human relationships in a world that is not rejected as hopeless, but is understood as loved and redeemed by the God who created it, christological reflection will stress the commonality between Christ and humanity as a whole. If, on the other hand, one views the world as a tragic mistake in which people are trapped, and if the greatest good is release from the entrapment that envelops the world and its masses, then the alternative Christologies presented by Marcion and the Gnostics may very well be more satisfying. But such an anticosmic attitude was not Israel's legacy nor normative Christianity's sense of things.

3. *Soteriology.* Normative Christianity affirms that, in spite of human failure—which would disqualify one for salvation—trust in God's redemptive work in Christ is the way to salvation, which is begun in this life, but completed beyond it. To have salvation on any other foundation than faith is not contemplated. Even the Epistle of James, which emphasizes good works in salvation, couples the good works with the priority of faith (2:17, 24, 26). Here, as elsewhere in the New Testament,[101] good works issue forth from the life that is sound and obedient to God. Faith in God's redeeming work in Christ is the chief characteristic of normative Christianity's soteriological message and teaching.

The soteriologies of the sects, as described by the heresiologists and attested in the primary sources themselves, often rest on other foundations. Already in the first century, according to Irenaeus, the Samaritan Gnostics Simon Magus and his pupil Menander taught that salvation is obtained by *gnōsis*, which they offered those who sought it.[102] In the second century, salvation by *gnōsis* was taught by Saturninus,[103] Cerinthus,[104] and Carpocrates and his disciples.[105] According to Irenaeus and Eusebius, it was with Carpocrates and his followers that the self-designation "Gnostics" was used explicitly.[106] These particular Gnostics, known as Carpocratians, taught that Jesus "spoke in a mystery to his disciples and apostles privately, and charged them to hand these things on to the worthy and those who assented."[107] It belongs to the very character of Gnosticism that it regards *gnōsis* as "knowledge of the divine mysteries reserved for an elite,"[108] and that it sets forth a soteriological elitism.[109] If salvation is based on knowledge, it can be obtained only by the few who are capable of attaining it and are considered worthy of it by those who possess the saving knowledge and are authorized to share it.

In the great gnostic systems that developed in the second century, the soteriological elitism seen here becomes pronounced. Basilides and his followers held that salvation does not come by confessing "him who was crucified" but by knowing the secrets revealed to those who can receive them,[110] and only "one in a thousand and two in ten thousand" can know them.[111]

According to Valentinus and later Valentinians, humanity consists of three kinds of people—the pneumatics, the psychics, and the hylics. The last named (engrossed in matter) are incapable of salvation. The psychics (Christians other than Valentinian Gnostics) have imperfect knowledge but by faith and good works can attain "the place of the 'Middle,'" a realm of the demiurge. But the pneumatics ("spiritual ones"—that is, the Valentinians themselves) receive the perfect, saving *gnōsis* and by means of it enter the pleroma.[112] Good works are not necessary; in fact, pneumatics will be saved regardless of what kind of conduct they have, for they are spiritual by nature and cannot perish.[113] The knowledge that saves was revealed by the Savior himself to only a few, since most are not capable of receiving it.[114] In the opinion of Theodotus, a Valentinian, the *gnōsis* by which a few are saved is superior to baptism for the many as a means of salvation.[115] Nag Hammadi texts attributed to Valentinianism, such as *The Gospel of Truth* and *The Gospel of Philip*,[116] speak of the saving power that *gnōsis* brings to the few as well.[117] *The Tripartite Tractate* continues the Valentinian threefold distinction among people.[118]

Salvation by *gnōsis* is found in other Nag Hammadi sources, and in these too salvation comes only to the few who are worthy and able to receive the enlightenment that *gnōsis* brings. In the *Apocryphon of James* the risen Christ declares to his disciples that "unless you receive [the kingdom of heaven] through knowledge, you will not be able to find it."[119] In the *Apocryphon of John* the risen Christ declares to John, son of Zebedee, that the latter is to write down and give teachings revealed "secretly" to his "fellow spirits," for, he says, "this is the mystery of the immovable race."[120] In *The Sophia of Jesus Christ* he says to his disciples, "whoever is worthy of knowledge will receive it."[121] In the *Apocalypse of Peter* the Savior says to the apostle: "Do not tell [the mysteries revealed] to the sons of this age."[122] And in *The Testimony of Truth* it is said that the "foolish" call themselves "Christians," but they are ignorant; "when man comes to know himself and God who is over the truth, he will be saved."[123]

It may be going too far to say that for all Gnostics salvation is "by *gnōsis* alone." Carpocrates, for example, taught that it is "through faith and love" that people are saved, according to Irenaeus. But what is given with one hand is taken back by the other, since the passage falls within a context where it is said that the mysteries of Jesus are to be handed on only to those who are considered worthy to receive them.[124] In *The Apocryphon of James* it is said that "life" comes from faith, love, and works, and that salvation is the result of doing the will of God.[125] But of course these are the virtues of persons who have received the "secrets" revealed to Peter and James; in fact only a few will be saved.[126] Other statements concerning faith can be found as well. Basilides, for example, considers his followers to be believers in the Nous (also called Christ), who liberates them from the powers that created the world.[127] In the Nag Hammadi literature there are emphases on faith in the resurrection, in God, or in the truth.[128] In view of such statements on faith, it may be impossible to find evidence for salvation "by *gnōsis* alone" among the Gnostics. Yet it is inconceivable that salvation would be possible in gnostic thought without it. The same applies to Marcion, whose theology contains a rich variety of Christian themes. Irenaeus reports that, according to Marcion, "there will be salvation only for souls which have learned his doctrine."[129]

An emphasis on *gnōsis* should not in itself be thought of as that which divides Marcion and the Gnostics from normative Christianity, since a similar emphasis is found already in the Old Testament and other literature of Jewish origin and also in the New Testament. According to the wisdom tradition of Israel, knowledge from or about God is to be acquired by the person who seeks to follow the paths of righteousness in fidelity to God and God's will (Prov. 2:5-10; 9:10; 22:17-19; Eccl. 2:26), and the same idea can be found in Hellenistic Judaism and the writings of Qumran.[130] A Q saying of Jesus, which has parallels outside the canonical Gospels,[131] and can probably be considered authentic,[132] speaks of *gnōsis* as salutary for Jesus' followers in discerning the will of God (Luke 11:52//Matt. 23:13).[133] Paul commends members of the church at Rome for being "filled with all knowledge (*gnōsis*)" and those at Corinth as enriched with "all knowledge (*gnōsis*)" (Rom. 15:14; 1 Cor. 1:5). Knowledge (*gnōsis*) is also listed as one of the gifts of the Spirit (1 Cor. 12:8).[134] The writer of Colossians speaks of "the knowledge (*epignōsis*) of God's mystery (*mystērion*)" (2:2). The writer of 2 Peter speaks of supplementing "faith with virtue, and virtue with knowledge (*gnōsis*)" (1:5).

Yet in each case it would be going too far to say that *gnōsis* means anything more than knowledge that is available for the person who has faith and pursues greater understanding; in no case is it a prerequisite for salvation. In fact, *gnōsis* was considered a problem by Paul in his dealings with the church at Corinth. His correspondence shows that there were persons within the Corinthian congregation who boasted of their *gnōsis* (1 Cor. 8:1, 10), claimed that all things were permitted to them (1 Cor. 10:23), and looked down upon those they considered weak (1 Cor. 8:10-11). Such persons were probably from upper-class backgrounds with a high level of sophistication.[135]

In any case, "the gnostic understanding of liberty seems to have corrupted the Pauline congregation."[136] Paul argued that love is greater than knowledge (1 Cor. 8:1; 13:2, 8), which is also maintained in the Epistle to the Ephesians (3:19). Even in Colossians, which speaks of "the knowledge of God's mystery," the "mystery" is none other than "Christ, in whom are hid all the treasures of wisdom and knowledge" (2:3). The context in which this terminology appears concerns growth in love and understanding for those who are established in the faith and are rooted in Christ (2:1-7).[137] This Christ is the crucified one who has reconciled all things to himself "by the blood of his cross" (1:20)—that is, "in his body of flesh by his death" (1:22)—affirmations that the Gnostics and Marcion would find deplorable. As indicted in the previous chapter, *gnōsis* was also considered a threat to the community in which the Pastoral Epistles were written (1 Tim. 6:20).

4. *Ethics.* Normative Christianity affirms that the person saved by faith in God's redemptive work in Christ is expected to care about, indeed love, others and be worthy of their trust. Normative Christianity expresses norms for living. The sources for these norms include the moral tradition of the Old Testament and Judaism, the teaching and example of Jesus, and aspects of moral teaching in pagan Hellenism.[138] Although much more could be said, out of Israel's heritage came the Ten Commandments (Exod. 20:2-17; Mark 10:19; Rom. 13:9), the double commandment of love (Deut. 6:4-5 and Lev. 19:18; Mark 12:29-31 par.; cf. Rom. 13:8-10; Gal. 5:14), and a host of teachings concerning responsibility to others and acting mercifully. The traditions contained in the canonical Gospels are undoubtedly correct in affirming that Jesus picked up and sustained these major teachings of Israel's heritage, and the canonical Gospels transmitted them in any case to early Christian communities. Further, Jesus' life of self-giving service to others became a model for Christian conduct in normative Christianity

(Mark 10:42-45 par.; John 13:15; Phil. 2:1-11; Heb. 12:1-2; 1 Peter 2:21). Finally, aspects of pagan Hellenistic ethics appear in exhortations to live in harmony with traditional virtues and codes of behavior (Rom. 13:1-7; Phil. 4:8-9; Eph. 5:22—6:9; Col. 3:18—4:1; 1 Peter 2:13—3:7). But one need not confine one's attention to familiar Christian texts to discern features of early Christian ethics. Even pagan observers and critics of Christianity, such as Celsus and Lucian, were impressed by the way of life that Christians practiced, particularly their effectiveness in providing material help for persons in need.[139] Beyond that, the Christian community provided a sense of belonging, a place of human warmth.[140]

Prominent in the writings of the heresiologists is the claim that the various sects and their teachers of the first three centuries either disregarded ethical norms or actually promoted immorality. How much of that can be believed is, of course, an open question.[141] One way to discredit the sects is to accuse them of immorality, especially in regard to sexual conduct, on the basis of the old principle that a "tree is known by its fruit" (Matt. 12:33). Yet there are indications that the testimony of the heresiologists is at least in some cases accurate.

Regarding the early Gnostics, Simon Magus and his pupil Menander, both are described in second-century sources as magicians and tricksters,[142] which must finally account for the appellation Magus ("magician") in the case of Simon. Simon and his followers are also accused by the second-century writers Irenaeus and Hippolytus of sexual promiscuity,[143] although Justin says that they might not be guilty of that charge.[144] The Nicolaitans, whose origins can be traced to the first century (cf. Rev. 2:6, 14-15), are also charged with libertine conduct by Irenaeus and Hippolytus,[145] which could be based on the statements in the book of Revelation rather than observation, however, since there they are charged with the same offenses as in the writings of the heresiologists—eating food sacrificed to idols and practicing sexual immorality.

In the second century and later, sexual misconduct continued to be an issue. The Carpocratians and the Gnostics who followed Basilides were said to have been promiscuous.[146] On the other hand, Basilides's fellow pupil, Saturninus, and also Marcion taught sexual abstinence altogether.[147] The information on the Valentinians is mixed. Irenaeus speaks of at least one wing of Valentinians that was libertine,[148] but there is little evidence of it in other important sources.[149] In fact, The Gospel of Philip, which may be Valentinian, affirms marriage.[150] Yet even that document generally reflects an ethic of indifference:[151] "In this world there is good and evil. Its good things are not good, and its evil things not evil."[152]

The sources take up other issues of human conduct besides sexual matters. It is said of Carpocrates and his followers that good and evil are a matter of one's own opinion.[153] Marcion and his churches, on the other hand, taught universal love, including love for one's enemies, and unlimited forgiveness of those who have done wrong.[154] Moreover, certain Nag Hammadi texts have a moral concern. Two of these are thought to be of Valentinian origin.[155] These are *The Gospel of Truth*, in which readers are admonished to comfort the sick, feed the hungry, and give rest to the weary,[156] and the *Tripartite Tractate*, in which the "pneumatics" are described as those who understand (and presumably do) that which is good for the church.[157] Another Nag Hammadi document, which is judged not to be of gnostic origin,[158] consists of wisdom sayings with strong ethical and ascetic teaching, *The Sentences of Sextus*.

Although it would clearly be incorrect to say that the Gnostics gave no thought to ethics, and certainly wrong to say that they promoted either outright libertinism or vigorous asceticism—with no moderate views between them[159]—the contrasts with normative Christianity are striking. Even if the heresiologists were extreme in their caricatures of gnostic behavior, there is precious little in gnostic sources themselves to refute them. Moral exhortation is all but lacking altogether. Many pages of the collection of Nag Hammadi texts can be considered to be of gnostic origin, but the amount of exhortation in them to care for others and to be trustworthy could be condensed into a very precious few, perhaps a page or two at most.

5. *The Church as Community*.   Normative Christianity affirms that those who trust Jesus as revealer of God and redeemer of humanity are expected to live as disciples in a community whose ethos is congruent with the legacy of his life and teaching. Normative Christianity, as we see it emerge in the early centuries is, for the most part, communal. Traditions about Jesus hold that he had disciples who formed a fellowship with him and with one another, and there is no reason to doubt the historicity of that claim.[160] The writings of the New Testament arise out of, or are addressed to, communities of faith. The same is true of writings after the New Testament, that stand in the normative tradition. The various communities of faith differed from one another from the very beginning in certain respects, such as in language, the ethnic composition of members, and matters of structure and leadership. Their respective ecclesiologies therefore differed as well. Nevertheless, a communal character and a care for the well-being of the community of faith typify expressions of normative Christianity.

The normative and later orthodox tradition was the most inclusive, or comprehensive, in its ability to embrace diversity. The terms *normative* and *orthodox* may sound narrow and exclusivistic. But historically the normative-orthodox stream of tradition has been the most responsive to changes, when needed, and most able to hold people together who differ theologically and in piety—at least within some widely set limits.[161] It is the sects that have insisted on the separation of the "right minded" from others, who are considered hopelessly ignorant or in error.[162]

Certain movements and sects that arose in the first century, and can be identified by references to them in ancient sources, were by and large of relatively short duration. When Origen mentions the followers of Simon Magus in his *Contra Celsum* (ca. A.D. 246–248), he estimates that "one cannot find thirty all told in the world, and perhaps this number is too high."[163] Followers of Menander existed when Justin wrote his *First Apology* (ca. A.D. 155), though not many.[164] By the time of Epiphanius (fourth century) it could be said that "his sect has mostly come to an end."[165] All that is not surprising, because Simon and Menander, both miracle workers, made claims for themselves of such a kind that once they had died their followers had little reason to continue. Simon was regarded by followers as a god in his lifetime,[166] and Menander acclaimed himself a savior, into whom his disciples were baptized to gain immortality.[167] The intensity of devotion to these men and their works could not be transferred to any successors; in fact, there could be no true successors.[168] The Nicolaitans also, whose origins are traced to the first century by heresiologists[169] (and the references in Rev. 2:6, 14-15 confirm), were said by Eusebius to be a "very short-lived sect" that apparently had gone out of existence by the time he wrote about them (early fourth century).[170]

Marcion and the gnostic leaders and movements of the second century and later are of particular interest in ecclesiological developments. Marcion's followers called themselves "Christians";[171] they constituted congregations similar to any others;[172] and they called their buildings churches.[173] They had clerical offices, including those of bishop, presbyter, and deacon.[174] Like other Christians, some of the Marcionites suffered martyrdom.[175] They practiced baptism and celebrated the Lord's Supper.[176] But in these rites there were distinctive practices. According to Epiphanius, baptism was administered to a person in Marcionite churches as many as three times, "and more to anyone who wishes,"[177] so that one could be rebaptized after transgressions. Tertullian, writing earlier, says that baptism was administered only to the person who was a "virgin or widowed or unmarried, or has purchased baptism by divorce."[178] Marcion considered marriage destructive and advocated celibacy.[179] Wine was replaced by water in celebrations of the Lord's Supper.[180] Widely attested in the ancient sources is the claim that, for Marcion, salvation is for souls only, not bodies,[181] and only those who have learned his doctrine will be saved.[182] The result is that the ideal of a Marcionite community is one in which a member lives an ascetic, celibate life, given to the discipline and teaching of the Christian tradition as interpreted by Marcion and his authoritative clerical successors.

Marcionism continued as a movement at least to the end of the third century in the west and for a couple more centuries in the east,[183] but finally disappeared. Its confession of the higher, unknown God, who is above the God of creation, and its consequent teaching of the salvation of the soul alone were congruent. But that was not conducive to the formation of communities of faith that would endure. In spite of communal forms of existence, Marcionism was finally individualistic and anticorporeal. Here an antibody attitude turned out to be anticorporeal in the final analysis. Furthermore, a religious tradition that exalts celibacy needs another larger, compatible community from which to recruit members. That would explain why Marcionite churches existed primarily in the vicinity of normative Christian churches, for it was from the latter, rather than from the general populace, that Marcionites drew most of their adherents.[184] But since the churches of the normative-orthodox tradition judged the Marcionite churches not to be legitimate heirs of apostolic tradition, and their numbers and influence grew in the Constantinian era, the growth and even survival of Marcionite churches became ever more difficult.

Major gnostic teachers of the second and later centuries were, like Marcion, persons with a following. Some of the earlier leaders were not particularly successful. Cerinthus, although an important early Gnostic in Asia Minor, does not seem to have been the founder of a school or community. Carpocrates of Alexandria, on the other hand, had disciples and successors known as Carpocratians. But when Eusebius wrote his history (ca. A.D. 323), he implied that the sect had died out.[185]

Most successful were Basilides and Valentinus and their followers. Basilides, who was never excommunicated from the church at Alexandria, had a following there that continued to flourish in the days of Epiphanius (fourth century).[186] Yet, according to Irenaeus, Basilidean Gnostics were to be "invisible and unknown to all," and they were to conceal their secrets in silence.[187] The attitude of these Gnostics was elitist to the extreme, since they held that only one in a thousand or two in ten thousand are capable of knowing the secrets.[188]

The Valentinians can also be regarded as having been elitist, since they held that only the "pneumatics" could be capable of salvation in its fullest sense.[189] Non-Valentinian Christians, classified as "psychics,"[190] could receive only a semblance of salvation, even though they believed in Christ. The stress on *gnōsis* as the means of salvation—and the insistence that most persons are not capable of receiving it[191]—is an attitude that gives shape to a community that is exclusive and composed of persons who are primarily concerned about the cultivation of their own personal spirituality. Yet, for all the individualism that Valentinianism shared with other gnostic sects, one can speak of a Valentinian ecclesiology.[192] According to various sources considered Valentinian, certain Valentinian communities had discernible structures for the catechetical instruction of initiates,[193] baptism with the use of trinitarian formulas,[194] Eucharists,[195] and authoritative scriptural interpretation.[196]

Gnostic texts discovered at Nag Hammadi generally reflect the individualism that is evident in the writings of the heresiologists on Gnosticism. According to *The Gospel of Truth*, a Valentinian work, the Father loves the perfect and worthy.[197] Even though the *Tripartite Tractate* abolishes distinctions between the sexes, socio-economic classes, Jew and Gentile, and angels and human beings,[198] it nevertheless preserves the Valentinian distinction between three types of humanity—the pneumatics, the psychics, and the hylics (or materialists).[199] In the *Sophia of Jesus Christ* the risen Christ says that only "the worthy" shall receive *gnōsis*.[200] And in the *Gospel of Thomas*— which may or may not be of gnostic origin, but was discovered at Nag Hammadi among gnostic texts—he declares, "Blessed are the solitary and elect, for you will find the kingdom. For you are from it, and to it you will return."[201]

One gnostic document from Nag Hammadi of particular importance for gnostic ecclesiology is the tractate called *The Interpretation of Knowledge*.[202] The document appears to address a gnostic Christian community in which "pneumatics" and ordinary members are in conflict.[203] The former have the gifts of prophecy and speaking the word.[204] Into this situation the author tells the pneumatics that to despise the others is to be ignorant,[205] and tells the ordinary members that they too have a place within the community and should be thankful that they do not exist outside the body (*sōma*).[206] More than that, however, the author picks up the Pauline concept of the church as the "body of Christ," insisting that each part of the body has its own function, and that all members ought to be working together.[207] Each should enjoy the plentitude of gifts that has been given to others,[208] and each should share the gifts each has been given.[209] Nevertheless, the document is hardly egalitarian, for some persons in the community are thought to have greater gifts, and hence more prominent positions, than others.[210] In making a distinction in metaphors between "roots" and the "fruits" they produce, the author is probably making a distinction between "pneumatic" and "psychic" gnostic Christians within the community.[211]

Although this document has been called a gnostic church order,[212] it obviously shares much in common with the traditions of normative Christianity—including teachings of Jesus in the canonical Gospel of Matthew and passages in several Pauline and deutero-Pauline letters (Romans, 1 Corinthians, Ephesians, Philippians, and Colossians)[213]—and may not be regarded as a typical expression of gnostic Christianity as known from other sources. Generally it can be said that gnostic texts were not addressed to communities for building up a common corporate life, but were intended for individuals in meditation.[214] In commenting on the *Sitz im Leben* of the gnostic writings found among the Nag Hammadi texts, Frederik Wisse has written:

> [These texts] do not reflect the normative beliefs of a structured community, nor were they designed to function as the holy books of a sect or sects. They are the true product of heterodoxy, i.e. a syncretistic situation conducive to speculative thought and without hierarchical control. As such we are dealing with a literary rather than a sectarian phenomenon.[215]

Furthermore, the very nature of Gnosticism—with its emphases on self-realization, spiritual freedom, and salvation by the *gnōsis* available to the elite—did not favor, and even worked against, the establishment of communities of mutual care among members.[216] In his assessment concerning the disappearance of gnostic communities from history (but making allowances for the Manichaeans), Kurt Rudolph has written that "they did not succeed in becoming broad mass movements; for this they were too narrow-mindedly esoteric and, above all, hostile to the world."[217]

6. *The Church as Extended Fellowship.* Normative Christianity affirms that those who live in communities of faith belong to a fellowship that is larger than that provided by the local community. Naturally this outlook would not have been evident in the very beginning of the earliest Jerusalem community—and possibly not in the Q community, of which we know so little. But even in the Q community there may well have been a sense of a larger, extended fellowship by virtue of its interaction with itinerant missionaries from other communities.[218] In any case, according to Acts, Christian communities arose in Palestine, Syria, Asia Minor, Rome, and elsewhere fairly quickly, and there was a sense of their belonging to a wider fellowship. So Luke speaks of "the church throughout all Judea and Galilee and Samaria" in the singular (Acts 9:31), as though there were only one Palestinian church. The church at Jerusalem continued to exert leadership, and therefore interact with other communities of faith, as long as the "pillar apostles" (Peter, James, and John) were there (Gal. 2:9).

What is striking is that the term *ekklēsia*, which would normally designate a local gathering, was also applied to the church in its entirety. How soon that happened is impossible to know, but the letters of Paul attest its usage in the middle of the first century (1 Cor. 12:28; 15:9; Gal. 1:13; Phil. 3:6). Moreover, there was an interconnectedness, a networking, between the congregations, between apostles and congregations, and between ordinary members within different congregations, as the lists of greetings in Paul's letters show. New Testament writings tell of visits by members of one community to another, the sending of financial aid from one to another, and intercessory prayer for the well-being of communities other than one's own.[219] The practice of extending hospitality is noticeably present in the writings of the New Testament, giving witness to "the presence of God or Christ in ordinary exchanges between human guests and hosts."[220]

The amount of documentation regarding mutual care and interchange among the communities of faith is impressive. There are few analogies in antiquity, if any at all, to the amount of correspondence flowing about among the early Christian communities.[221] This in itself shows how members of these communities had a sense of belonging to a fellowship extending beyond the local community, and how there was a sense of mutual accountability among the communities themselves. The correspondence includes the letters of Paul, the deutero-Pauline letters, the Catholic Epistles, and the epistolary materials in other books of the New Testament (Acts 15:23-29; Rev. 2:1—3:22), the letters of Clement, Ignatius, Barnabas, and Polycarp in early Christian literature, and many items of correspondence quoted or referred to in the *Ecclesiastical History* of Eusebius. And the list could go on. Generally it can be said that religious associations and cult groups in antiquity had an "inward focus," while the Christian communities had an "international scope."[222] That view concerning early Christianity can be confirmed by the sheer volume of known correspondence alone.

The closest analogy to the networking evident in these sources would be among the churches of Marcion. Justin, Marcion's contemporary, wrote (ca. A.D. 155) that Marcion had followers among "every race" of humanity.[223] Tertullian refers to the churches of Marcion in his day (ca. A.D. 200), saying that they are "of late arrival" (recent) and "having for founder either Marcion or someone from Marcion's hive." He adds that "wasps make combs, and Marcionites make churches."[224] He also declared that Marcion's heretical teaching "has filled the whole world."[225] In the fourth century Epiphanius says that Marcionite churches are found at that time in Rome, other parts of Italy, Egypt, Palestine, Arabia, Syria, Cyprus, Boeotian Thebes (within Greece), Persia, and other places.[226] But one should not think of them as constituting a monolithic fellowship. Eusebius, quoting from a late second-century document by a certain Rhodo, a disciple of Tatian, says that Marcion's followers were split into various groups and describes the teachings of three irreconcilable positions.[227]

Marcionite churches continued to exist until sometime into the fifth century in some areas, but had lost cohesion and the ability to sustain one another sometime earlier.[228] Among the Gnostics, various founders, leaders, and teachers moved from place to place, and later on the Manichaeans had a collection of letters by Mani, now lost.[229] Nevertheless, it can be said that there is no literary or archaeological evidence to suggest that there were regular, significant links among gnostic or Marcionite communities.[230]

The heresiologists no doubt go too far in claiming that the Gnostics were constantly feuding among themselves and broke up into separate groups.[231] But the Nag Hammadi texts provide evidence that there were polemics among them. The gnostic authors of both *The Testimony of Truth* and the *Valentinian Exposition* launch attacks upon other gnostic groups.[232] One document, which includes the extension of greetings "in brotherly love," thus showing a sense of solidarity among communities, is *The Treatise of the Resurrection*.[233] But in general it can be said that Gnosticism, with its emphasis on self-realization and freedom, did not foster networks of mutual interest, much less accountability, between communities. This can be said even about the most ecclesiological Gnostics, the Valentinians: "It appears that the various Valentinian off-shoots were localized and lacked associational links to a regional or universal community."[234]

Similar judgments can be made concerning communities of so-called Jewish Christianity. Justin, in the middle of the second century, refers to Jewish Christians who, though "they place their hope in Christ," practice circumcision, observe the Mosaic law, and refuse to have conversations and meals with gentile Christians.[235] This version of Christianity must have originated in the first century with James the Just (brother of Jesus) in Jerusalem—who was opposed to table fellowship between Jewish and gentile Christians (Gal. 2:12)—and other like-minded Jewish Christians. Later in the second century, by the time of Irenaeus and Hippolytus, the term *Ebionites* was applied to those who continued their separatism.[236] But by the time that Eusebius wrote his history, in the early fourth century, the Ebionites were no longer a major tradition within Christianity. He speaks of them in one place as though they have ceased to exist,[237] but in another as though they continue to do so.[238] The historical destiny of the Ebionites is elusive. It is possible that they lost their separate identity and entered into the mainstream of an overwhelmingly gentile church in the post-Constantinian era. On the other hand, remnants may have existed as late as the rise of Islam and, if so, may have been absorbed into it.[239] In any case, the Ebionite emphasis on Jewish-gentile separation, plus the view of at least certain Ebionites that those among themselves who fulfill the law of Moses "become Christs,"[240] could not of course be compatible with the normative tradition that was able to embrace Jew and Gentile in one fellowship. Even the most "Jewish" of documents in that tradition—such as the Gospel of Matthew, the Epistle of James, and the *Epistle of Barnabas*—had moderate attitudes by comparison to those of the Ebionites.

The Effects

Besides the six factors discussed here, there may well have been others at work in the development of a normative tradition. Nevertheless, the development of a normative tradition can be discerned, which took seriously a complex of factors having to do with beliefs and the formation of communities and the ethos of each.

The diversity of early Christianity has been duly recognized in contemporary scholarship, and rightly so. The study of the New Testament alone yields a picture of significant diversity. Beyond that, the study of early church history into the second and third centuries shows even greater diversity. Consensus on the present canon of the New Testament, for example, was late in coming. Although the four Gospels, Acts, and the letters of Paul (including the deutero-Paulines) seem to have had a secure place as authoritative writings in major geographical areas and their churches by A.D. 200, it was not until the fourth century that the historic consensus of the inclusion of other books, and the exclusion of others, can be discerned. Still in the second century there were additional books in use as authoritative in certain churches,[241] while the Marcionite churches excluded all but an abbreviated Gospel of Luke and ten epistles of Paul.

Yet, having granted the diversity that existed, a normative tradition developed, and that tradition was contended for by theological and ecclesiastical leaders within communities of faith located in various geographical areas. One can see the beginnings of the process early on. While it can be said that there was "substantial diversity within the early Christian religion, probably going back to a time just after Jesus' death in about the year 30,"[242] the beginnings of normative Christianity can be traced to very early times too, such as when the apostle Paul contended for norms in controversies with his opponents[243]—norms that had to do with how believers are to confess the faith and live together in communities of faith. Moreover, the roles of other apostles, such as Peter and James—for all their differences with Paul and each other—and the writings of the New Testament as a whole provide ample testimony of a struggle for norms of faith and community ethos in the midst of diversity, which was broad indeed, but which also had recognizable limits in communities far and wide.

The effect of it all was the shaping of a normative tradition that provided the basis for the emergence of orthodoxy. One cannot exclude from consideration the presence of struggles for power between parties and personalities in the shaping of that tradition. But the penchant for leaving the matter at that in some quarters of modern scholarship is reductionistic. The primary struggle was the struggle for the truth of the gospel (right confession of faith) and community life congruent with it. Inevitably the normative-orthodox tradition and its alternatives had to go their separate ways.

7

Normative Christianity and the Legacy of Jesus

AS INDICATED IN THE OPENING CHAPTER, THE TERM *normative Christianity* has liabilities. Above all, it could be misunderstood to mean a rather narrow expression of Christian faith and life. As used in this discussion, however, it points instead to a rather broad stream of Christian traditions that coexisted prior to orthodoxy, and which together constituted major foundations for the latter. Like the finalized canon of the New Testament, normative Christianity recognizes and preserves different expressions of Christian faith, while acknowledging that there are limits to acceptable diversity.

The term *normative Christianity*, as used in this book, embraces the totality of what is found in the canonical (= normative) writings gathered in the New Testament and other expressions of Christian faith, literary or otherwise, that are congruent with the canonical writings. It is not necessary to debate whether the canonical writings shaped normative Christianity, or whether normative Christianity produced the canon. It is sufficient to say that the canonical writings were produced by exponents of normative Christianity; that these writings continued to have a major, authoritative influence in communities of faith beyond the times and places for which they were written; and that, over time, they were adopted by orthodox communities of faith as canonical.

The question that remains is the degree to which the normative tradition reflects the legacy of Jesus adequately. If all traditions in early Christianity are but alternative interpretations of Jesus, the so-called normative tradition is relativized. It can be judged simply as the position expressed by the "winners" in early Christian controversies who stamped out other expressions, which might have been equally valid, and the loss of which has led to an impoverishment of both Christianity itself and our knowledge of the vitality and variety of early Christianity.

The problem of judging the adequacy of normative Christianity to reflect, or to continue appropriately, the legacy of Jesus is extremely difficult, for both historical and theological judgments enter into consideration. Apart from the question whether Jesus intended to leave a lasting legacy—a church, a school of disciples, a band of prophets, a renewal movement in Israel, or whatever—there is the question of how the earliest followers of Jesus interpreted his significance after his death and resurrection. At this point the question can be divided into two parts: first, the legacy of Jesus' historical ministry, as it can be critically discerned; and second, the expression of that legacy by Jesus' earliest followers in the post-Easter situation.

Jesus and His Legacy

There are clear lines of continuity between the words and deeds of the earthly Jesus and core affirmations of normative Christianity. The most obvious is the affirmation that God—the God of Israel and the whole world—is Creator and is benevolent to humanity, and that God is to be loved and trusted. This needs no further discussion beyond what has been provided in the previous chapter. It is evident that the affirmation was shared by Jesus and exponents of normative Christianity, whereas it was denied by Marcion and in general by Gnostics. Moreover, there is a large measure of continuity in terms of ethics, particularly in regard to the love commandment, which surely goes back in some form to Jesus, since it has attestation in both synoptic and Johannine traditions (Matt. 22:34-40//Mark 12:28-34//Luke 10:25-28; John 15:12),[1] and which has a prominent place in early Christian ethical teaching in the normative tradition.[2]

Other matters are more complicated since they have to do with specifically Christian themes—Christology, soteriology, and ecclesiology. Moreover, the Gospels are our only sources for investigating Jesus' understanding of his person and mission, and they were written after considerable reflection on these topics had taken place already. The traditions within the Gospels have been colored by post-Easter concerns. Nevertheless, some things can be said with a high degree of certainty.

For normative Christianity, Jesus of Nazareth was sent by God to reveal God and to redeem humanity. But can such an interpretation of Jesus be shown to be rooted in Jesus' own ministry? There can be little doubt but that Jesus, at least from the time of his baptism by John, had a sense of being called by God for a mission to Israel. That included his proclamation of the kingdom of God as present reality and future hope.[3] Moreover, it can be said that Jesus had a distinct, even unique, sense of an intimate relationship to God, using the term *abba* in reference to him.[4] Although it is certainly not likely that Jesus thought of his teaching and activities as the sole means of revelation of God and God's will, he taught with a sense of authority not derived from his learning or dexterity in scriptural interpretation, but from his sense of intimacy with God and God's will.[5] Therein lies the basis for later christological affirmations concerning Jesus as the unique Son of God, who had been sent into the world.

The question of a messianic consciousness—which has often been denied in previous scholarship,[6] but which has been taken up again as a possibility[7]—is more problematic. The same is true in regard to the question whether Jesus considered his mission as redemptive. These questions are usually tied up with still another question, and that is whether Jesus anticipated his own death and resurrection and, if so, how he would have understood them.[8] Yet that issue can be set aside for the moment. Whatever else can be said, Jesus declared forgiveness of sins and salvation from God to those who were considered by contemporaries as unworthy of either.[9] By doing so, Jesus engaged in a redemptive mission in his earthly ministry. He was of course answerable to God for his words and actions, but was apparently confident that he acted with authority, expecting vindication. Further, although it is unlikely that he spoke of himself expressly as the Messiah of Israel, it can be said that he identified with a redefined messianic role in his words and deeds.[10] Jesus was not simply a prophet of the coming kingdom, for he revealed the nature of the messianic kingdom by his words and by his actions, acting out the role of one who embodies the features of life in the messianic kingdom and thereby representing it proleptically to his contemporaries. He showed himself to those who would believe as one who was destined to have a leading role, and therefore preeminence, in the kingdom to come. In this way he so identified with a redefined messianic role that the line of demarcation was worn away and even crossed. He was, in his own way, a redemptive, messianic figure. He went on to accept crucifixion on the basis of the charge of being the Messiah, a charge that he did not reject.

It is only a very small step from all this for Jesus' disciples to understand later that his death and resurrection, considered to be in accord with the will of God, constituted a decisive redemptive event. For after his death and resurrection his followers experienced both his presence among them and newness of life through the presence and power of the Spirit.[11] Jesus, who had assumed the burden of others in his earthly ministry, had assumed the burden of all persons once and for all by means of an atoning death, for his resurrection and the pouring out of the Spirit mark the beginning of a new age, which has universal, cosmic dimensions. The ways in which the cross and resurrection were to be interpreted varied in later stages of development in various communities. But the affirmation that Jesus was the revealer of God and the redeemer of humanity, so prominent in normative Christianity, can be seen to have been anticipated in the words and deeds of Jesus.

The means of appropriating the redemptive benefits of Christ in normative Christianity is faith, not *gnōsis*. In the post-Easter situation such faith is a response to the proclamation of the gospel of Jesus' death and resurrection (Paul; cf. Rom. 10:9, 17) or belief in Jesus (John 3:16, 36; 5:24; 2 Tim. 3:15; 1 Peter 1:5, 9). The same cannot of course be said for saving faith in the ministry of the earthly Jesus. Yet the line of continuity in the appropriation of salvation in both the pre-Easter and post-Easter situations is faith, not *gnōsis*. Healing narratives in the traditions of Mark, reproduced by Matthew and Luke (Mark 5:34//Matt. 9:22//Luke 8:48; Mark 10:52//Luke 18:42), and another such narrative in a tradition peculiar to Luke (17:19) speak of healing in soteriological language: "your faith has saved you." But faith is also the response among those to whom the forgiveness of sins is declared effective, as attested by the word of Jesus (Luke 7:50) or by implication in the action of the one whose sins are forgiven (Mark 2:10-12//Matt. 9:6-8//Luke 5:24-26).

Finally, in the tradition of normative Christianity, believers have a sense of belonging to a community of faith and even a larger fellowship beyond the local community. That was a feature shared by Marcionite Christianity as well, and perhaps by some gnostic groups, but in any case it is a feature of normative Christianity. The question here is not whether the sense of belonging was unique to normative Christianity, but whether it continues the legacy of the earthly ministry of Jesus. As indicated in the previous chapter, traditions about Jesus hold that he had disciples who formed a fellowship with him and with one another, and there is no reason to doubt the historicity of that claim. Furthermore, the Gospel traditions, both synoptic and Johannine, relate that the fellowship around Jesus was to have a certain quality that can be characterized as familial, in which all are brothers and sisters (Matt. 5:22-28; 18:15; 23:8; 12:46-50//Mark 3:31-35//Luke 8:19-21), and none is to seek supremacy over the others but should be their servant (Matt. 20:20-28//Mark 10:35-45//Luke 22:24-27).

What is distinctive here, as well as in normative Christianity later, is that the elitism of various gnostic groups is ruled out. The shaping of an ethos for community life in normative Christianity thus has its antecedents in the earthly ministry of Jesus. The sense of belonging to a larger fellowship beyond the immediate community, however, must be credited to post-Easter developments as Christianity spread outward geographically and as members of the various communities became aware of their indebtedness to missionary activities and exchanged communications.

It can be argued that the picture of Jesus and his legacy sketched here, like so many others in contemporary scholarship, is "myopic" because it is founded almost entirely on a narrow set of documents, the Synoptic Gospels in particular. The problem with the use of the Synoptic Gospels to the exclusion of other materials now available—the Nag Hammadi tractates, for example—is that the documents used are one-sidedly confessional; they make use of traditions about Jesus that are "in accord with a given 'cover story' of faith; that is to say, in accord with a given community image of Jesus." What is needed is a study of "the Jesus tradition as a whole."[12]

That authentic traditions about Jesus can be found in sources outside the canonical Gospels goes without saying; that has been claimed again and again to nearly everyone's satisfaction, such as in the case of certain sayings and parables in the *Gospel of Thomas*.[13] But even when that is granted, it is necessary to insist that every other available source has a "cover story" too. In the writings of Marcion and the Gnostics alike, Christ is severed from the God of Israel, the material world, and bodily, fleshly existence. When that is done, one must dispense with the following affirmations of normative Christianity: (1) that the story of Jesus continues the story of the God and people of Israel; (2) that Christ shared human existence in a material matrix, in which he healed the sick and had fellowship with outcasts; and (3) that he experienced human limitations, suffering, and death. Are these affirmations within normative Christianity to be regarded as having no foundations in the historical ministry of Jesus, as that was remembered by his earliest followers? These affirmations are present in sources judged to come from the earliest times—the Gospel of Mark, the Q material, traditions peculiar to Matthew and Luke, and the Gospel of John. Moreover, the most undisputedly historical datum available concerning Jesus of Nazareth is that he was crucified under Pontius Pilate.[14] Whatever picture one constructs of Jesus must come to terms with that datum and a plausible reason for it. That datum is a major ingredient in the "cover story" of the Synoptic Gospels. Theology aside, at that point the Synoptic Gospels have the story right from a purely historical point of view.

Earliest Christianity and Normative Christianity

The second line of investigation concerning the question of the adequacy of the normative tradition in reflecting, and indeed continuing, the legacy of Jesus is to ask whether it maintained what was essential in the proclamation of the earliest interpreters of Jesus' significance. Among the earliest traditions that interpret his significance are those that present Jesus as a redemptive figure who had been crucified and raised from the dead. Included here is the creedal formula of 1 Corinthians 15:3-7, which Paul must have received from Peter and James (both are mentioned in the formula itself, 15:5, 7) on his first visit to Jerusalem in the early to mid-30s (Gal. 1:18-20).[15] To this can be added a number of other creedal and hymnic passages, which are generally considered to be of early origin, and which contain recitations of Jesus' death, resurrection, or both (Rom. 1:3-4; 4:25; 10:9; Gal. 1:4; Phil. 2:6-11; Col. 1:15-20; 1 Tim. 3:16; and 1 Peter 3:18).

In addition to these, critical scholarship has suggested that there are other passages that reflect early proclamation without reference to the cross and resurrection. If so, these would represent interpretations of Jesus that differ from the so-called kerygmatic interpretation of Jesus as a redemptive figure who had been crucified and raised from the dead. These include passages embedded in New Testament documents that focus on Jesus as future redeemer. Among them are Peter's sermon in Acts 3:12-26, which John A. T. Robinson held as containing "the most primitive Christology of all,"[16] in which Peter speaks of God's future sending of "the Messiah appointed for you, that is, Jesus, who must remain in heaven until the time of universal restoration that God announced long ago" (3:20-21). In the meantime, Jesus is but the "Christ-elect."[17] In addition, there is the old Aramaic petition *maranatha* (actually two words, *marana tha*, "our Lord, come") in 1 Corinthians 16:22 and *Didache* 10.6 (plus the Greek version at Rev. 22:20), which seems to look to the future coming of the Lord (Jesus) for redemption.[18] And finally, it has been maintained that the tradition of Jesus as future redeemer appears in the Q material, where Jesus as the Son of man is "the redeemer of the future."[19]

If there was a very primitive interpretation of the significance of Jesus that focused solely on the future, rather than on the past or present, as the time of his redemptive work, it must have faded quickly, since it was not represented by any later form of Christianity that is known. But the thesis itself does not hold up. It is unlikely that the speech of Peter in Acts 3:12-26 represents early Christian proclamation or Christology.[20] But even if it does, while it looks to the future for the completion of God's redemptive work (as does normative Christianity as a whole), that future has the cross and resurrection as its presupposition. There are explicit references within it to Christ's suffering (3:18), crucifixion (3:13, 15), resurrection (3:15), and glorification (3:13). In the *maranatha* petition, the words are directed to Jesus, not God, which presupposes that he is the crucified and risen Lord now enthroned in heaven and capable of hearing and responding to the cry of those who call upon him. The petition could hardly have been uttered without the recollection of Jesus' cross and resurrection.

8. The documents from this find are collected and translated in *The Nag Hammadi library in English*, ed. James M. Robinson, 3d ed. (San Francisco: Harper & Row, 1988).

9. On the meaning of the term *canon*, see especially the article by Hermann W. eyer, "Kanōn," *TDNT* 3:596–602.

10. The story of the canonization process has been told many times. Some of e major works are by Wilhelm Schneemelcher, "The History of the New Testament non," in *New Testament Apocrypha*, ed. Edgar Hennecke and W. Schneemelcher, ols. (Philadelphia: Westminster Press, 1963–65), 1:28–60; Werner G. Kümmel, oduction to the New Testament, rev. ed. (Nashville: Abingdon Press, 1975), 475–510; rry Y. Gamble, *The New Testament Canon: Its Making and Meaning* (Philadelphia: tress Press, 1985); and Bruce M. Metzger, *The Canon of the New Testament: Its Origins, lopment, and Significance* (Oxford: Clarendon Press, 1987).

1. On the date of *1 Clement*, see Michael W. Holmes, "Introduction [to First ment]," in *The Apostolic Fathers*, trans. J. B. Lightfoot and J. R. Harmer, 2d ed., nd rev. Michael W. Holmes (Grand Rapids, Mich.: Baker Book House, 1989),

. A date of ca. A.D. 100 is maintained by several scholars. For review of arship and conclusion, see Arland J. Hultgren, *1 and 2 Timothy, Titus*, ACNT neapolis: Augsburg, 1984), 19–31. A later date (ca. A.D. 120–160) is proposed elmut Koester, *Introduction to the New Testament*, 2 vols. (Philadelphia: Fortress 1982), 2:305.

The date of 2 Peter is often put at A.D. 125–150. Cf. Kümmel, *Introduction* 434; and Koester, *Introduction to NT*, 2:297. On its social, cultural, and religious nment, see Tord Fornberg, *An Early Church in a Pluralistic Society: A Study of 2* onBNT 9 (Lund: Carl Bloms Boktryckeri, 1977).

Sometimes the term is applied anachronistically and too broadly, as in the y Walter Bauer, *Orthodoxy and Heresy in Earliest Christianity* (Philadelphia: Press, 1971), who says summarily that in his book "'orthodoxy' and 'heresy' r to what one customarily and usually understands them to mean" (pp. xxii–

f. William Henn, "Orthodoxy," *The New Dictionary of Theology*, ed. Joseph nchak et al. (Wilmington, Del.: Michael Glazier, 1987), 731–33. He in- hat the term *orthodoxy*, not found in the New Testament and Apostolic ppears "in the writings of Eusebius of Caesarea (d. 339), Julius I (d. 359), s (d. 373), and Basil (d. 379), and was used by the Councils of Ephesus Chalcedon (451). Then gradually orthodoxy came to mean not simply rine but the traditional and universal doctrine of the church as defined ion to heterodoxy or heresy" (p. 732).

course the term *heresy* is itself difficult to define. On its various meanings w Testament and the early church to Origen, see Heinrich Schleier, DNT 1:182–84. Later formulations generally distinguish it from apostasy, ignorance. It is the willful, explicit denial of central Christian beliefs Christian community, according to Thomas Aquinas, *De malo* 8.1–7. In heologica, Part II (Second Part), Question 11, Aquinas speaks of heresy

Finally, as indicated in chapter 4, the Q material has allusions to the rejection of the Son of Man (Luke 9:58//Matt. 8:20) and his crucifixion (Luke 19:12//Matt. 25:14), and the Q saying that one must bear one's own cross and follow Jesus to be a disciple (Luke 14:27//Matt. 10:38) presupposes the cross of Jesus. In addition Q contains allusions to Jesus' resurrection (Luke 22:28-30//Matt. 19:28) and his parousia (Luke 12:40//Matt. 24:44). In sum, there are allusions in Q to Jesus' rejection, death, resurrection, and coming again—the main points of the common Christian tradition, which normative Christianity maintained. These considerations undermine the claim for a primitive Christian tradition or Christology of Jesus as future redeemer apart from the tradition of Jesus as crucified and raised.

Of course there were other early traditions about Jesus that did not interpret him as a redemptive figure who had been crucified and raised. These can be classified form critically as parables, conflict stories, miracle stories, legends, wisdom sayings, and so on. On the basis of the investigation of each unit, many of these traditions can be traced back in points of origin to the very beginnings of Christianity. Some, such as certain parables and wisdom sayings, can be attributed to Jesus. Even others, such as certain miracle stories and conflict stories, can be traced back to the compositional activities of storytellers who remembered the deeds, words, and debates of the earthly Jesus—or received such remembrances.

These traditions were incorporated into the Gospels, both canonical and extracanonical. Collections of Jesus' wisdom sayings and miracle stories— whether authentic or not—came to have a life of their own, as several apocryphal Gospels attest. But in the case of the canonical Gospels, such traditions, and still others, were incorporated within narratives that con- cluded with accounts of Jesus' passion, death, and resurrection. It is correct to say with Helmut Koester that the Gospel tradition portraying Jesus as crucified and raised "became the central criterion of faith for the 'canonical' writers"[21]—that is, those who represented normative Christianity. There are reasons why that should have been so. At least three can be cited here.

First, it was the tradition that was "of first importance" to major figures in early Christianity, such as Paul, Peter, and James (cf. 1 Cor. 15:3). The fact that that tradition was central to early apostolic proclamation and teaching gave it a rather "canonical" or "normative" role early on and in a number of communities.

Second, the account of Jesus' death and resurrection could be presented not only in kerygmatic creedal statements but also in story form. In this regard, this type of tradition had a decisive advantage over the others. Collections of Jesus' teachings and collections of stories about him could exist on their own, as certain apocryphal Gospels show, but they were not likely to accommodate or absorb other types of traditions. But the story of

Jesus crucified and raised can be preceded by accounts of his teaching and deeds. In fact, the rehearsal of accounts of the cross and resurrection begs for more information about this figure who was crucified and raised. Therefore the Q material could be absorbed by Matthew and Luke, and all four canonical Gospels could incorporate traditions of Jesus' teaching and deeds within their narratives.

But, finally, there is another reason, and that is of a different kind, why the tradition of Jesus as crucified and raised would become ascendant in the earliest communities of faith and then in normative Christianity. That is that this tradition carried with it the message that through these events an eschatological event with saving effect had occurred. Of the various types of tradition, this one alone finally addresses the human predicament, in which it is necessary not only to *know* something—of God, Jesus, the world, and the self—but to have something *done* to resolve it. The traditions of Jesus as teacher of wisdom (or of *gnōsis*) can lead one along the path of understanding, and that was the way of salvation for Gnostics. But for the normative Christian tradition there was a different interpretation of the significance of Jesus. For the earliest faith community, which included disciples of the earthly Jesus, Jesus' death and resurrection would have been not only the most memorable event of his fate, but also the event that marked the turn of the ages, beginning a new era in which sin and death had been surpassed, and righteousness and life were gifts of God through the Spirit.

The message of the saving effects of Jesus' death and resurrection became the central affirmation of the earliest creedal formulas, the basis for proclamation, and the motive and framework for the production of the narratives presented in the canonical Gospels. Moreover, the proclamation of Jesus' death and resurrection was the basis not only for literary production, but also for the creation of communities of faith, each having an ethos shaped by the rendition of such proclamation and by teaching related to it. The combination of what was to be believed and how a community was to live in conformity with that belief—both sound belief and sound ethos—led to the rise of normative Christianity.[22] In all this it can be said that normative Christianity continued and furthered the legacy of Jesus as represented by his earliest interpreters.

Notes

1. Normative Christianity a[s] Problem and Issue

1. An example is the use of the term *orthodoxy* in E[usebius?] 3.25.7; 4.23.2; 4.23.8; and 6.18.1. The date of this work

2. George Foot Moore, *Judaism in the First Centuries of* [the Christian Era] *the Tannaim*, 3 vols. (Cambridge, Mass.: Harvard Univ. [Press])

3. Two examples may suffice: E. P. Sanders, *Paul an[d Palestinian Judaism: A Com]parison of Patterns of Religion* (Philadelphia: Fortress Pres[s]; Charlesworth, "Introduction for the General Reader," i[n The Old Testament Pseude]*rapha*, ed. J. H. Charlesworth, 2 vols. (Garden City, [N.Y.: Doubleday]) 1:xxix.

4. Ernst Troeltsch, *The Absoluteness of Christianity a[nd the History of Religions]* [Rich]mond: John Knox Press, 1971), 85.

5. Three major works in particular illustrate the[se efforts: James D. G. Dunn,] *Unity and Diversity in the New Testament: An Inquiry into [the Character of Earliest Christianity,]* 2d ed. (Philadelphia: Trinity Press International, 19[90); Leonhard Goppelt, Theology] *of the New Testament*, 2 vols. (Grand Rapids, Mich.: [Eerdmans, 1981–82),] esp. vol. 2, *The Variety and Unity of the Apostolic Wi[tness to Christ; and E. Earle Ellis, The]* *Variety and Unity in New Testament Thought* (Oxfor[d: Oxford Univ. Press, 1991).]

6. Attempts are made by Dunn, Goppelt, and [Ellis (see the previous note), and] also by others, such as Werner G. Kümmel, *The T[heology of the New Testament according] to Its Main Witnesses, Jesus-Paul-John* (Nashville: A[bingdon Press, 1973), and by] the authors of essays in *Die Mitte des Neuen Testam[ents: Einheit und Vielfalt neutestamentlicher]* *Theologie: Festschrift für Eduard Schweizer zum siebz[igsten Geburtstag,* ed.] Hans Weder (Göttingen: Vandenhoeck & Ru[precht, 1983).]

7. Cf. Paul J. Achtemeier, *The Quest for Un[ity in the New Testament Church: A Study]* *in Paul and Acts* (Philadelphia: Fortress Press, [1987).]

as a corruption of the dogmas of the Christian faith. The subject is treated at length by Karl Rahner, *On Heresy*, QD 11 (New York: Herder & Herder, 1964). The range of meanings is documented by David Christie-Murray, *A History of Heresy* (New York: Oxford Univ. Press, 1989), 1–12.

17. For references, see note 1, above.

18. The term is used for second- and third-century churches that anticipated orthodoxy, by Bentley Layton, "General Introduction," in his *The Gnostic Scriptures* (Garden City, N.Y.: Doubleday, 1987), xx–xxiii.

19. The term has been popularized particularly by Ernst Käsemann, "Ministry and Community in the New Testament," in his *Essays on New Testament Themes*, SBT 41 (Naperville, Ill.: Alec. R. Allenson, 1964), 91; idem, "Paul and Early Catholicism," in his *New Testament Questions of Today* (Philadelphia: Fortress Press, 1969), 236–51. The concept is discussed further by Stephen Neill and Tom Wright, *The Interpretation of the New Testament 1861–1986*, 2d ed. (New York: Oxford Univ. Press, 1988), 200–204; and Dunn, *Unity and Diversity*, 341–66. The term *emergent catholicism* was proposed by Norman Perrin, *The New Testament: An Introduction* (New York: Harcourt Brace Jovanovich, 1974), 61.

20. For a positive evaluation of early catholicism by one who claims that it was a legitimate development of early Christianity, see Reginald H. Fuller, "Early Catholicism: An Anglican Reaction to a German Debate," in *Die Mitte des Neuen Testaments*, ed. Luz and Weder, 34–41.

21. The term appears in Johannes Weiss, *Earliest Christianity: A History of the Period A.D. 30–150*, 2 vols. (New York: Harper & Row, 1959), 2:731, 735; Bauer, *Orthodoxy and Heresy*, 229; and in the essay by Käsemann, "Paul and Early Catholicism," 237. It is also used by Georg Strecker, "On the Problem of Jewish Christianity," an appendix to Bauer, *Orthodoxy and Heresy*, 285; Dunn, *Unity and Diversity*, 385; Raymond E. Brown, *The Community of the Beloved Disciple* (New York: Paulist Press, 1979), 155–64, 167; and Petr Pokorný, *The Genesis of Christology: Foundations for a Theology of the New Testament* (Edinburgh: T. & T. Clark, 1987), 13.

22. Cf. the comment of Dunn, *Unity and Diversity*, 373: "there was no single normative form of Christianity in the first century." In context, of course, his statement is correct, for wide diversity in faith is evident, which his book demonstrates. Yet he contends that there is a "unifying strand" and an "integrating centre" within the diversity, and he calls that "the unity between the historical Jesus and the exalted Christ" (p. 369). Cf. also the comment of John and Kathleen Court, *The New Testament World* (Cambridge: Cambridge Univ. Press, 1990), 369: "the New Testament age cannot be regarded as any kind of golden age, in which all was basic, simple, normative, united, and agreed."

23. The term has been used before. It is used to describe the tradition and message represented in creedal formulas and early Christian literature by W. H. C. Frend, *The Rise of Christianity* (Philadelphia: Fortress Press, 1984), 134–39.

24. Court, *The New Testament World*, 362.

25. Elaine H. Pagels, *The Gnostic Gospels* (New York: Random House, 1979), xxxvi.

26. Ibid., 27; cf. also p. 118.

27. Ibid., 149; cf. also p. 118.

28. John Dart, *The Jesus of Heresy and History: The Discovery and Meaning of the Nag Hammadi Gnostic Library* (San Francisco: Harper & Row, 1986), xvi.

29. Burton L. Mack, "All the Extra Jesuses: Christian Origins in the Light of the Extra-Canonical Gospels," *Semeia* 49 (1990): 169. This viewpoint is amplified in Mack's *The Lost Gospel: The Book of Q and Christian Origins* (San Francisco: Harper-SanFrancisco, 1993), 227–36.

30. Helmut Koester, "Epilogue: Current Issues in New Testament Scholarship," in *The Future of Early Christianity: Essays in Honor of Helmut Koester*, ed. Birger A. Pearson (Minneapolis: Fortress Press, 1991), 472.

31. Ignatius, *Magn.* 6.1; quoted from *The Apostolic Fathers*, trans. Kirsopp Lake, 2 vols., LCL (New York: G. P. Putnam's Sons, 1912–13), 1:201–3.

32. Cf. *1 Clem.* 44.1–3; Ignatius, *Eph.* 20.2; *Magn.* 7.1; *Trall.* 2.2; *Phld.* 3.2; 7.2; *Smyrn.* 8.1–2; and Irenaeus, *Adv. Haer.* 4.26.2.

2. Before Orthodoxy: Four Approaches

1. *1 Clem.* 42.1–4; quoted from *The Apostolic Fathers*, trans. Kirsopp Lake, 2 vols., LCL (New York: G. P. Putnam's Sons, 1912–13), 1:79–81.

2. Eusebius, *Hist. eccl.* 3.32.8; quoted from Eusebius, *The History of the Church from Christ to Constantine*, trans. G. A. Williamson (Minneapolis: Augsburg, 1975), 143.

3. Tertullian, *Adv. Marc.* 4.7, writes: "the truth must of necessity precede the false, and proceed from those from whom its tradition began" (i.e., the apostles); and, "In my statement of case against all heresies my custom is to mark out a short cut on the evidence of dating, claiming that our rule of faith came first and that all heresy is of more recent emergence" (5.19); quoted from *Tertullian Adversus Marcionem*, ed. and trans. Ernest Evans, 2 vols. (Oxford: Clarendon Press, 1972), 2:273; 2:629–31. Similar statements are made in Tertullian, *De Praesc. Haer.* 31.

4. Walter Bauer, *Orthodoxy and Heresy in Earliest Christianity* (Philadelphia: Fortress Press, 1971).

5. Ibid., xxii.

6. Ibid., 229.

7. Ibid., 21, 53, 229 (regarding the triumph of orthodoxy in Edessa, Alexandria, Asia Minor, Macedonia, and Antioch).

8. Ibid., xxii–xxiii.

9. Ibid., xxv.

10. Ibid., xxiv.

11. Ibid., 21–22.

12. Ibid., 20–21.

13. Ibid., 17.

14. Ibid., 43.

15. Ibid., 50–53.

16. Ibid., 53–54, 59.

17. Ibid., 63, 69.

18. Ibid., 70.

19. Ibid., 79–80.

20. Ibid., 75.

21. Ibid., 102.

22. Ibid., 240.

23. Ibid., 230–31.

24. An extensive survey of reviews and criticisms of Bauer's work by Georg Strecker, "The Reception of the Book," appears as an appendix to Bauer's *Orthodoxy and Heresy*, 286–316. Three other studies of particular importance are by Daniel J. Harrington, "The Reception of Walter Bauer's *Orthodoxy and Heresy in Earliest Christianity* during the Last Decade," *HTR* 73 (1980): 289–98; Thomas A. Robinson, *The Bauer Thesis Examined: The Geography of Heresy in the Early Christian Community*, SBEC 11 (Lewiston, N.Y.: Edwin Mellen Press, 1988); and Michael Desjardins, "Bauer and Beyond: On Recent Scholarly Discussions of *Hairesis* in the Early Christian Era," *SC* 8 (1991): 65–82.

25. Tertullian, *Adv. Marc.* 1.1; Epiphanius, *Panarion* 42.1.1–42.2.8. That Marcion shared the faith of the "great church" prior to maintaining his own version of Christianity is maintained by Adolf von Harnack, *Marcion: The Gospel of the Alien God* (Durham, N.C.: Labyrinth Press, 1990), 16–18.

26. Cf. James McCue, "Bauer's *Rechtgläubigkeit und Ketzerei*," in *Orthodoxy and Heterodoxy*, ed. Johann-Baptist Metz and Edward Schillebeeckx (Edinburgh: T. & T. Clark, 1987), 30.

27. L. W. Barnard, "The Origins and Emergence of the Church in Edessa during the First Two Centuries A.D.," *VC* 22 (1968): 161–75.

28. Ibid., 173; and Helmut Koester, "GNOMAI DIAPHOROI; The Origin and Nature of Diversification in the History of Early Christianity," in *Trajectories through Early Christianity* by James M. Robinson and Helmut Koester (Philadelphia: Fortress Press, 1971), 128–29.

29. Günther Bornkamm, "The Acts of Thomas," in *New Testament Apocrypha*, ed. Edgar Hennecke and Wilhelm Schneemelcher, 2 vols. (Philadelphia: Westminster Press, 1963–64), 2:425–42; and A. F. J. Klijn, *The Acts of Thomas: Introduction, Text, Commentary*, NovTSup 5 (Leiden: E. J. Brill, 1962), 30–33.

30. Egypt or Syria is proposed by Bertil Gärtner, *The Theology of the Gospel According to Thomas* (New York: Harper & Bros., 1961), 272.

31. Henri-Charles Puech, "Gnostic Gospels and Related Documents," in *NT Apocrypha*, ed. Hennecke-Schneemelcher, 1:287; W. C. van Unnik, *Newly Discovered Gnostic Writings: A Preliminary Survey of the Nag Hammadi Find*, SBT 30 (Naperville, Ill.: Alec R. Allenson, 1960), 49–50; Oscar Cullmann, "The Gospel of Thomas and the Problem of the Age of the Tradition Contained Therein," *Int* 16 (1962): 427; W. H. C. Frend, "The Gospel of Thomas: Is Rehabilitation Possible?" *JTS* 18 (1967): 13–26; Helmut Koester, *Introduction to the New Testament*, 2 vols. (Philadelphia: Fortress Press, 1982), 2:152; Michael Desjardins, "Where Was the Gospel of Thomas Written?" *TJT* 8 (1992): 121–33; and Ron Cameron, "Thomas, Gospel of," *ABD* 6:535–36. Desjardins suggests that, since it was written in Greek, Antioch of Syria is the most likely place of composition. Cameron, on the other hand, suggests Edessa or another city in the same geographical provenance.

32. Koester, *Introduction to the NT*, 2:152; Stevan Davies, *The Gospel of Thomas and Christian Wisdom* (New York: Seabury Press, 1983), 3; and Ron Cameron, *The Other Gospels: Non-Canonical Gospel Texts* (Philadelphia: Westminster Press, 1982), 25; idem, "Thomas, Gospel of," 6:535–36.

33. A. Guillaumont et al., *The Gospel According to Thomas* (New York: Harper & Bros., 1959), vi ("produced about 140 A.D."); Puech, "Gnostic Gospels," 1:305 ("about 140, or perhaps even a little later"); Cullmann, "The Gospel of Thomas," 427 ("around the middle of the second century A.D."); Gilles Quispel, "The *Gospel of Thomas* Revisited," in *Colloque international sur les textes de Nag Hammadi*, ed. Bernard Barc (Quebec: Les Presses de l'Université Laval, 1981), 223–27, 237 (ca. 140); R. McL. Wilson, *Studies in the Gospel of Thomas* (London: A. R. Mowbray & Co., 1960), 7–8, 146–47; Gärtner, *Theology*, 271; Frend, "The Gospel of Thomas," 23–25; and Michael Fieger, *Das Thomasevangelium: Einleitung, Kommentar, und Systematik*, NTAbh 22 (Münster: Aschendorff Verlag, 1991), 4, 7. The last four place the composition of the document in the middle of the second century as well (without giving a more precise date). In his Presidential address at the 1993 meeting of the Studiorum Novi Testamenti Societas, Martin Hengel stated that attempts to fix earlier dates for the *Gospel of Thomas* are unconvincing. The address will be published as "Aufgaben der neutestamentlichen Wissenschaft," *NTS* 40/3 (1994).

34. Frend, "The Gospel of Thomas," 25; Barnard, "Origins and Emergence of the Church in Edessa," 173.

35. Cf. Gilles Quispel, "The Gospel of Thomas and the New Testament," *VC* 11 (1957): 205.

36. H. J. W. Drijvers, "Edessa und das jüdische Christentum," *VC* 24 (1970): 4–33.

37. Colin H. Roberts, *Manuscript, Society and Belief in Early Christian Egypt* (London: Oxford Univ. Press, 1979), 12–14. The significance of this and other matters related to Christian origins in Egypt is discussed by Birger A. Pearson, "Earliest Christianity in Egypt: Some Observations," in *The Roots of Egyptian Christianity*, ed. Birger A. Pearson and James E. Goehring (Philadelphia: Fortress Press, 1986), 132–59; and C. Wilfred Griggs, *Early Egyptian Christianity: From Its Origins to 451 C.E.*, CS 2 (Leiden: E. J. Brill, 1990), 24–28.

38. James F. McCue, "Orthodoxy and Heresy: Walter Bauer and the Valentinians," *VC* 33 (1979): 118–30; and Birger A. Pearson, "Gnosticism in Early Egyptian Christianity," in his *Gnosticism, Judaism, and Egyptian Christianity* (Minneapolis: Fortress Press, 1990), 194–213.

39. Hans Lietzmann, "Notizen," *ZNW* 20 (1921): 175–76; Bauer, *Orthodoxy and Heresy*, 58; Manfred Hornschuh, *Studien zur Epistula Apostolorum*, PTS 5 (Berlin: De Gruyter, 1965), 99–119; Koester, *Introduction to the NT*, 2:237; Cameron, *The Other Gospels*, 133. The history of scholarship is summarized by Julian V. Hills, *Tradition and Composition in the Epistula Apostolorum*, HDR 24 (Minneapolis: Fortress Press, 1990), 1–9; he assigns it to Asia Minor, Egypt, or Syria (pp. 9 and 172).

40. The date of A.D. 120 is assigned to it by Hornschuh, *Studien*, 99–119; Lietzmann, "Notizen," 174, placed it about A.D. 140; the first half of the second century is the date assigned by Hugo Duensing, "Epistula Apostolorum," in *NT*

Apocrypha, ed. Hennecke-Schneemelcher, 1:191. The middle of the second century is the date assigned by Hills, *Tradition and Composition*, 9 and 172. Bauer, *Orthodoxy and Heresy*, 58, assigns it to A.D. 180; and Cameron, *The Other Gospels*, 133, assigns it to the middle or late second century. The second half of that century is the date proposed by Helmut Koester, *Ancient Christian Gospels: Their History and Development* (Philadelphia: Trinity Press International, 1990), 312.

41. Cf. Griggs, *Early Egyptian Christianity*, 32–33.

42. Cf. McCue, "Orthodoxy and Heresy," 127, 130; and Pearson, "Gnosticism in Early Egyptian Christianity," 208.

43. That Ignatius may have had difficulties at Antioch with "a group opposed to his authority" (but not necessarily his theology) is discussed briefly by William R. Schoedel, *Ignatius of Antioch*, Hermeneia (Philadelphia: Fortress Press, 1985), 10–11; in more detail, idem, "Theological Norms and Social Perspectives in Ignatius of Antioch," in *Jewish and Christian Self-Definition*, ed. E. P. Sanders et al., 3 vols. (Philadelphia: Fortress Press, 1980–82), 1:36–44.

44. Justin, *Apology* 1.26.4; Hippolytus, *Ref.* 7.16.

45. Bauer, *Orthodoxy and Heresy*, 63–64.

46. Eusebius, *Hist. eccl.* 3.22.1; 3.36.15. The names of the first three are Euodius, Ignatius, and Heros.

47. Cf. Rudolf Bultmann, *Theology of the New Testament*, 2 vols. (New York: Charles Scribner's Sons, 1951–55), 2:191–99; idem, "Ignatius and Paul," in *Existence and Faith: Shorter Writings of Rudolf Bultmann*, ed. Schubert M. Ogden (New York: Meridian Books, 1960), 267–77; and Koester, "GNOMAI DIAPHOROI," 122–23.

48. On at least three occasions Ignatius alludes to Gospel traditions found only in Matthew: *Smyrn.* 1.1 (Matt. 3:15); *Pol.* 2.2 (Matt. 10:16); and *Eph.* 19.2–3 (Matt. 2:1-12).

49. Werner G. Kümmel, *Introduction to the New Testament*, rev. ed. (Nashville: Abingdon Press, 1975), 119; Jack D. Kingsbury, *Matthew*, 2d ed., PC (Philadelphia: Fortress Press, 1986), 106; and Koester, *Introduction to the NT*, 2:172.

50. Raymond E. Brown et al., *Peter in the New Testament* (Minneapolis: Augsburg, 1973), 75–107.

51. Kümmel, *Introduction to the NT*, 480–81, reviews the evidence and scholarly discussion.

52. The date and place of composition, as well as the theology of the Pastoral Epistles, are dealt with in Arland J. Hultgren, *1 and 2 Timothy, Titus*, ACNT (Minneapolis: Augsburg, 1984), 19–38.

53. Justin, *Apology* 1.26; 1.56.

54. Bauer, *Orthodoxy and Heresy*, xxiii.

55. The full datum is H. E. W. Turner, *The Pattern of Christian Truth: A Study in Relations between Orthodoxy and Heresy in the Early Church*, Bampton Lectures 1954 (London: A. R. Mowbray, 1954).

56. Ibid., 39–94.

57. Ibid., 9.

58. Ibid.

59. Ibid., 10.

60. Ibid., 26.

61. Ibid.

62. Ibid., 26–30.

63. Ibid., 31–34.

64. Ibid., 474. Cf. pp. 28, 389.

65. Ibid., 476.

66. Ibid., 101.

67. Ibid., 478, 498; cf. p. 34.

68. Ibid., 478.

69. Ibid., 479.

70. The book contains eight essays; four had been published elsewhere, 1964–1971. The full datum is James M. Robinson and Helmut Koester, *Trajectories through Early Christianity* (Philadelphia: Fortress Press, 1971).

71. Robinson, "Introduction: The Dismantling and Reassembling of the Categories of New Testament Scholarship," in *Trajectories*, 16; and Koester, "GNOMAI DIAPHOROI," 114.

72. An introduction to, and an assessment of, the approach is given by Reginald H. Fuller, "New Testament Trajectories and Biblical Authority," in *Studia Evangelica* 7, ed. Elizabeth A. Livingstone, TU 126 (Berlin: Akademie Verlag, 1982), 189–99.

73. Robinson, "Introduction," 13.

74. Koester, "Conclusion: The Intention and Scope of Trajectories," in *Trajectories*, 272.

75. Robinson, "Introduction," 16.

76. Robinson, "Kerygma and History in the New Testament," in *Trajectories*, 63–69.

77. Major works here are those of Martin Dibelius, *From Tradition to Gospel*, 2d ed. (New York: Charles Scribner's Sons, 1934); and Rudolf Bultmann, *The History of the Synoptic Tradition*, 2d ed. (New York: Harper & Row, 1968).

78. Koester, "One Jesus and Four Primitive Gospels," in *Trajectories*, 166.

79. Robinson, "LOGOI SOPHON: On the Gattung of Q," in *Trajectories*, 71–74.

80. Ibid., 104.

81. Richard A. Edwards, *A Theology of Q: Eschatology, Prophecy, and Wisdom* (Philadelphia: Fortress Press, 1976), 151–52. The thesis has been elaborated in Burton Mack's *The Lost Gospel: The Book of Q and Christian Origins* (San Francisco: HarperSanFrancisco, 1993).

82. Koester, "Conclusion," 270.

83. Elaine H. Pagels, *The Gnostic Gospels* (New York: Random House, 1979), 148.

84. Koester, "The Structure and Criteria of Early Christian Beliefs," in *Trajectories*, 225; compare also pp. 229–31.

85. The History of Religions School is discussed (with examples of its work) in Werner G. Kümmel, *The New Testament: The History of the Investigation of Its Problems* (Nashville: Abingdon Press, 1972), 206–324. A brief account is by Kurt Rudolph, "Religionsgeschichtliche Schule," *EncRel* 12:293–96.

86. Koester, "One Jesus and Four Primitive Gospels," 186–87.

87. Robinson, "Kerygma and History in the New Testament," 43; and idem, "LOGOI SOPHON," 104–5, 113.

88. Actually Robinson seems to recognize this when he says that the genre under discussion "was open to a development" in the direction of Gnosticism "once a general drift toward Gnosticism set in," as he says in his essay, "LOGOI SOPHON," 104.

89. R. McL. Wilson, "Twenty Years After," in *Colloque international sur les textes de Nag Hammadi*, ed. Barc, 67. The same can be said about the use of such materials to elucidate "traditions" whose developments cannot be documented.

3. Confession and Community in Christian Tradition

1. See the chapter on "Religious Experience and Its Expression" in Joachim Wach, *Sociology of Religion* (Chicago: Univ. of Chicago Press, 1944), 17–27.

2. For what follows I am indebted largely to the essays of George Weckman, "Community," *EncRel* 3:566–71, and Joseph M. Kitagawa, "Religious Communities," *EncRel* 12:302–8.

3. Ferdinand Tönnies, *Community and Society* (New York: Harper & Row, 1957), 33–35. The first German edition appeared in 1887.

4. Ibid., 35.

5. Gerardus van der Leeuw, *Religion in Essence and Manifestation* (New York: Harper & Row, 1963; German original, 1933), 459–60.

6. Ibid., 650.

7. Wach, *Sociology of Religion*, 36.

8. A. R. Radcliff-Brown, "Religion and Society," in his *Structure and Function in Primitive Society: Essays and Addresses* (London: Cohen & West, 1952), 160–63, 177; and E. E. Evans-Pritchard, *Theories of Primitive Religion* (Oxford: Clarendon Press, 1965), 111–12.

9. Clifford Geertz, "Religion as a Cultural System," in his *The Interpretation of Cultures: Selected Essays* (New York: Basic Books, 1973), 90.

10. Clifford Geertz, "Ethos, World View, and the Analysis of Sacred Symbols," in his *Interpretation of Cultures*, 131.

11. Ibid., 126–27.

12. Clifford Geertz, "Religion: Anthropological Study," *EncRel* 13:406.

13. Ibid.

14. This is illustrated by Radcliff-Brown, "Religion and Society," 163–64, 171.

15. Cf. A. D. Nock, "The Historical Importance of Cult Associations," *CR* 38 (1924): 105–9; and Edwin A. Judge, *The Social Pattern of Christian Groups in the First Century* (London: Tyndale Press, 1960), 40–48.

16. Jacob Neusner, "A Religious System as a Theory of Society," in his *Understanding Seeking Faith: Essays on the Case of Judaism*, BJS 153, 3 vols. (Atlanta: Scholars Press, 1986–88), 3:10–11.

17. Jacob Neusner, *Jews and Christians: The Myth of a Common Tradition* (Philadelphia: Trinity Press International, 1991), 23–29.

18. Two of the best-known studies of the theologies of the New Testament, which respect the theological diversity within the New Testament, are those by Hans Conzelmann, *An Outline of the Theology of the New Testament* (New York: Harper & Row, 1969); and Leonhard Goppelt, *Theology of the New Testament*, 2 vols. (Grand Rapids, Mich.: Wm. B. Eerdmans, 1981–82).

19. Three contributions of note are those by Leander E. Keck, "On the Ethos of Early Christians," *JAAR* 42 (1974): 435–52; John H. Schütz, "Ethos of Early Christianity," *IDBSup* 289–93; and Birger Gerhardsson, *The Ethos of the Bible* (Philadelphia: Fortress Press, 1981). The last-named contains substantial studies of the communities of Matthew, Paul, and John. Attention to a single community is given by Holland Hendrix, "On the Form and Ethos of Ephesians," *USQR* 42 (1988): 3–15. Earlier work was done by Herbert Preisker, *Das Ethos des Urchristentums*, 2d ed. (Gütersloh: Verlagshaus Gerd Mohn, 1949).

20. The term *Jesus movement* has been popularized particularly in the writings of Gerd Theissen, *Sociology of Early Palestinian Christianity* (Philadelphia: Fortress Press, 1978); and idem, "Jesusbewegung als charismatische Wertrevolution," *NTS* 35 (1989): 343–60. According to Theissen, "the Jesus movement is the renewal movement within Judaism brought into being through Jesus and existing in the area of Syria and Palestine between about A.D. 30 and A.D. 70" (*Sociology*, p. 1).

21. A narrower definition that applies to "normative Christianity" is given by Petr Pokorný, *The Genesis of Christology: Foundations for a Theology of the New Testament* (Edinburgh: T. & T. Clark, 1987), 108. He says that the term *Christian* should be restricted only to those who affirm Jesus' resurrection, "which is the basis of the Christians' group identity."

22. Cf. Justin, *Apology* 1.26; Tertullian, *Adv. Marc.* 1.1; and Eusebius, *Hist. eccl.* 4.11.9.

4. The Beginnings of a
Normative Tradition

1. Helmut Koester, *Introduction to the New Testament*, 2 vols. (Philadelphia: Fortress Press, 1982), 2:92; and Dieter Georgi, *The Opponents of Paul in Second Corinthians* (Philadelphia: Fortress Press, 1986), 348.

2. Johannes Weiss, *Earliest Christianity: A History of the Period A.D. 30–150*, 2 vols. (New York: Harper & Row, 1959), 1:175–76; Henry J. Cadbury, "Names for Christians and Christianity in Acts," in *The Beginnings of Christianity*, ed. F. J. Foakes-Jackson and Kirsopp Lake, 5 vols. (New York: Macmillan, 1920–33), 5:282–86; Hans Conzelmann, *History of Primitive Christianity* (Nashville: Abingdon Press, 1973), 128, Martin Hengel, *Acts and the History of Earliest Christianity* (Philadelphia: Fortress Press, 1980), 103; Wayne A. Meeks and Robert L. Wilken, *Jews and Christians in Antioch in the First Four Centuries of the Common Era*, SBLSBS 13 (Missoula, Mont.: Scholars Press, 1978), 16; and John P. Meier, "Antioch," in *Antioch and Rome: New Testament Cradles of Catholic Christianity*, by Raymond E. Brown and John P. Meier (New York: Paulist Press, 1983), 35, 49.

3. According to Tacitus and Tertullian, Christians were commonly thought to bear the name of their founder, as in the case of Platonists, Epicureans, and Pythagoreans. So Tacitus, *Annals* 15.44; and Tertullian, *Apology* 3.6.

4. Ignatius, *Eph.* 11.2; *Magn.* 4.1; *Rom.* 3.2; *Pol.* 7.3.

5. It is interesting that the term *Christian* does not appear as a current self-designation of the church's members at Rome in *1 Clement* (ca. A.D. 96), even though Tacitus claims that it was applied by the masses of Rome already in the early 60s to identify those whom Nero punished for the great Roman fire (*Annals* 15.44).

6. Chronologies of Paul, which differ in detail but place the last of Paul's letters in the mid-50s, include those presented by Günther Bornkamm, *Paul* (New York: Harper & Row, 1971), 241–43; Werner G. Kümmel, *Introduction to the New Testament*, rev. ed. (Nashville: Abingdon Press, 1975), 252–55; Robert Jewett, *A Chronology of Paul's Life* (Philadelphia: Fortress Press, 1979); Gerd Luedemann, *Paul: Apostle to the Gentiles: Studies in Chronology* (Philadelphia: Fortress Press, 1984), which contains a chronological chart on pp. 262–63; and Jürgen Becker, *Paul: Apostle to the Gentiles* (Louisville: Westminster/John Knox Press, 1993), 17–32, with a chart on p. 31.

7. Kümmel, *Introduction to the NT*, 185–87; Gerhard A. Krodel, *Acts*, ACNT (Minneapolis: Augsburg, 1986); and Hans Conzelmann, *Acts of the Apostles*, Hermeneia (Philadelphia: Fortress Press, 1987), xxxiii. Earlier and later dates have been proposed. A date as early as A.D. 60–62 has been proposed by Colin J. Hemer, *The Book of Acts in the Setting of Hellenistic History*, WUNT 49 (Tübingen: J. C. B. Mohr [Paul Siebeck], 1989), 403. The 70s or 80s is maintained by F. F. Bruce, *The Acts of the Apostles*, 3d ed. (Grand Rapids, Mich.: Wm. B. Eerdmans, 1990), 9–18. A "decade later" than A.D. 125 (the date he proposes for the Gospel of Luke) is maintained by Koester, *Introduction to the NT*, 2:310.

8. Gerd Theissen, *Sociology of Early Palestinian Christianity* (Philadelphia: Fortress Press, 1978), 3. He writes: "In the case of the synoptic gospels we have to remove material which is of Hellenistic origin. We can make use of all the rest."

9. Such texts are in Eusebius, *Hist. eccl.* 2.1.3–5 and 2.23.3–18.

10. Josephus, *Ant.* 19.8.2.

11. A similar phrase appears at 1 Thess. 2:14. The authenticity of the passage, however, is contested. For the case that 1 Thess. 2:13-16 is an interpolation, see Birger A. Pearson, "1 Thessalonians 2:13-16: A Deutero-Pauline Interpolation," *HTR* 64 (1971): 79–94; Daryl Schmidt, "1 Thess. 2:13-16: Linguistic Evidence for an Interpolation," *JBL* 102 (1983): 269–79; and others surveyed by Schmidt. The authenticity of the passage is maintained by I. Howard Marshall, *1 and 2 Thessalonians*, NCB (Grand Rapids, Mich.: Wm. B. Eerdmans, 1983), 11–12; W. D. Davies, "Paul and the People of Israel," in his *Jewish and Pauline Studies* (Philadelphia: Fortress Press, 1984), 124–27; Karl P. Donfried, "Paul and Judaism: I Thessalonians 2:13–16 as a Test Case," *Int* 38 (1984): 244–45; and John W. Simpson, Jr., "The Problems Posed by 1 Thessalonians 2:15–16 and a Solution," *HorBT* 12 (1990): 42–72.

12. On the life of the community in general, cf. Eduard Schweizer, *Church Order in the New Testament*, SBT 32 (Naperville, Ill.: Alec R. Allenson, 1961), 34–50.

13. Martin Dibelius, "The Speeches in Acts and Ancient Historiography," in his *Studies in the Acts of the Apostles* (New York: Charles Scribner's Sons, 1956), 138–85

(esp. p. 165); Ulrich Wilckens, *Die Missionsreden der Apostlegeschichte*, 2d ed., WMANT 5.2 (Neukirchen-Vluyn: Neukirchener Verlag, 1963); and Eduard Schweizer, "Concerning the Speeches in Acts," in *Studies in Luke-Acts: Essays Presented in Honor of Paul Schubert*, ed. Leander E. Keck and J. Louis Martyn (Nashville: Abingdon Press, 1966), 208–16. It has been maintained that in the case of the speeches of Peter, there are significant differences within them at certain points, but that these can be accounted for on the basis of "varying functions of the individual speeches in their narrative settings." Such is the view of Robert C. Tannehill, "The Functions of Peter's Mission Speeches in the Narrative of Acts," *NTS* 37 (1991): 414.

14. Rudolf Pesch, *Die Apostelgeschichte*, 2 vols., EKKNT 5 (Neukirchen-Vluyn: Neukirchener Verlag, 1986), 1:42–45; Krodel, *Acts*, 36–37; and Bruce, *Acts*, 37–38.

15. The claim that Paul received this tradition from the Jerusalem church on his visit there in the early 30s is made by, among others, Rudolf Bultmann, *Theology of the New Testament*, 2 vols. (New York: Charles Scribner's Sons, 1951–55), 1:46; Oscar Cullmann, *The Christology of the New Testament*, rev. ed. (Philadelphia: Westminster Press, 1963), 76; Leonhard Goppelt, "The Easter Kerygma in the New Testament," in *The Easter Message Today: Three Essays*, by Leonhard Goppelt, Helmut Thielicke, and H. R. Müller-Schwefe (New York: Thomas Nelson, 1964), 36; Reginald H. Fuller, *The Foundations of New Testament Christology* (New York: Charles Scribner's Sons, 1965), 161; Werner G. Kümmel, *The Theology of the New Testament: According to Its Main Witnesses, Jesus-Paul-John* (Nashville: Abingdon Press, 1973), 115; and Helmut Koester, *Ancient Christian Gospels: Their History and Development* (Philadelphia: Trinity Press International, 1990), 51.

16. Johannes Behm, "*Klaō*," TDNT 3:729–30; Oscar Cullmann, *Early Christian Worship*, SBT 10 (Chicago: Henry Regnery, 1953), 14–15, 29; and Conzelmann, *Acts*, 23. The terminology of breaking bread is routinely used in eucharistic texts (1 Cor. 11:24; Mark 14:22//Matt. 26:26//Luke 22:19; cf. 24:38).

17. On the identity of the Hebrews and the Hellenists, see notes 41 and 42.

18. The singular is used in the earliest and best Greek witnesses (papyrus 74, Sinaiticus, Vaticanus, and others). Later witnesses have the plural ("churches").

19. The origins of the church at Lydda (Acts 9:32) are not indicated, but according to the perspective of Acts, it would have originated in the mission of the Hellenists who were driven out of Jerusalem and who evangelized Judea and Samaria (8:1). In any case, Peter visits "the saints" living there, heals Aeneas, and stays with him (9:32–35, 38).

20. Here we follow the chronologies of Bornkamm, *Paul*, 31; Kümmel, *Introduction to the NT*, 255; Conzelmann, *Acts*, 121; and Becker, *Paul*, 31. Luedemann, *Paul*, 262, sets the date at A.D. 47 (or perhaps 50). The date of A.D. 50 is maintained by Karl P. Donfried, "1 Thessalonians, Acts and the Early Paul," in *The Thessalonian Correspondence*, ed. Raymond F. Collins, BETL 87 (Louvain: Leuven Univ. Press, 1990), 8.

21. Eusebius, *Hist. eccl.* 2.1.2-3; 2.23.1. A survey of traditions about James and other brothers of Jesus is provided by A. Meyer and W. Bauer, "The Relatives of Jesus," in *New Testament Apocrypha*, ed. Edgar Hennecke and Wilhelm Schneemelcher,

2 vols. (Philadelphia: Westminster Press, 1963–65), 1:418–32; and Richard Bauckham, *Jude and the Relatives of Jesus in the Early Church* (Edinburgh: T. & T. Clark, 1990), 45–133. James is called "the chief of the bishops" and "the head bishop" in the Latin and Syriac texts, respectively, of the mid-second-century *Ascents of James* (1.68.1). Text, commentary, and evaluation of these designations of James as preeminent among bishops in the early church can be found in Robert E. Van Voorst, *The Ascents of James: History and Theology of a Jewish-Christian Community*, SBLDS 112 (Atlanta: Scholars Press, 1989), 150–51, 172–73. Van Voorst concludes that James is elevated in these texts to a position far above that which the historical James actually had. That the historical James ever was "bishop" (or patriarch) of Jerusalem is doubted by Hans von Campenhausen, "The Authority of Jesus' Relatives in the Early Church," in *Jerusalem and Rome: The Problem of Authority in the Early Church*, by Hans von Campenhausen and Henry Chadwick, FBHS 4 (Philadelphia: Fortress Press, 1966), 14–15.

22. Sources on the martyrdom of James are Josephus, *Ant.* 20.200, and Eusebius, *Hist. eccl.* 2.1.5; and 2.23.2–3.

23. Cf. E. P. Sanders, *Paul, the Law, and the Jewish People* (Philadelphia: Fortress Press, 1983), 19, 172.

24. Cf. Hans Dieter Betz, *Galatians*, Hermeneia (Philadelphia: Fortress Press, 1979), 81–83, 103–4; and Gerd Luedemann, *Opposition to Paul in Jewish Christianity* (Philadelphia: Fortress Press, 1989), 38–39.

25. Theissen, *Sociology of Early Palestinian Christianity*; idem, "Itinerant Radicalism: The Tradition of Jesus Sayings from the Perspective of the Sociology of Literature," *RadRel* 2 (1975): 84–93; and idem, "Jesusbewegung als charismatische Wertrevolution," *NTS* 35 (1989): 343–60.

26. Theissen, *Sociology of Early Palestinian Christianity*, 8.

27. Ibid., 1. In his essay "Itinerant Radicalism," 90, Theissen asserts that "its center was in Palestine."

28. Theissen, *Sociology of Early Palestinian Christianity*, 10.

29. Ibid., 8.

30. Ibid.

31. Ibid., 4.

32. Theissen, "Itinerant Radicalism," 85.

33. Theissen, *Sociology of Early Palestinian Christianity*, 3.

34. Ibid., 10–16.

35. Ibid., 9.

36. Cf. similar judgments by John E. Stambaugh and David L. Balch, *The New Testament in Its Social Environment* (Philadelphia: Westminster Press, 1986), 105; and Richard A. Horsley, *Sociology of the Jesus Movement* (New York: Crossroad Publishing Company, 1989), 43–46.

37. Horsley, *Sociology of the Jesus Movement*, 106. A review of major critiques of Theissen's work regarding the Jesus movement is presented by Bengt Holmberg, *Sociology and the New Testament: An Appraisal* (Minneapolis: Fortress Press, 1990), 50–54.

38. Horsley, *Sociology of the Jesus Movement*, 39.

39. Ibid., 117.

40. Ibid., 117–19.

41. The term *Hellenists* also appears at Acts 9:29. In this instance the term refers to Greek-speaking Jews who are not Christians. For discussion, cf. Krodel, *Acts*, 181; Bruce, *Acts*, 244; and Craig C. Hill, *Hellenists and Hebrews: Reappraising Division within the Earliest Church* (Minneapolis: Fortress Press, 1992), 23–24, who identifies the non-Christian Hellenists as "Greek-speaking Jews from the Diaspora" (p. 24).

42. Cf. Conzelmann, *Acts*, 45; Bruce, *Acts*, 181; Martin Hengel, "Between Jesus and Paul," in his *Between Jesus and Paul: Studies in the Earliest History of Christianity* (Philadelphia: Fortress Press, 1983), 7–10; and Hill, *Hellenists and Hebrews*, 19–24. Hill identifies the Hellenists as Jewish Christians who spoke Greek and the Hebrews as Jewish Christians who spoke Aramaic (p. 3, n. 7).

43. Hengel, *Acts*, 72–73; Bruce, *Acts*, 192. The antitemple stance could be historical, even if Stephen's speech cannot otherwise be taken as reliable information about the theology of the Hellenists. Cf. Hengel, "Between Jesus and Paul," 19–23; and Francis Watson, *Paul, Judaism and the Gentiles: A Sociological Approach*, SNTSMS 56 (Cambridge: Cambridge Univ. Press, 1986), 25–26. A lengthy discussion of tradition, redaction, and composition by Luke in the speech of Stephen is carried on by Hill, *Hellenists and Hebrews*, 50–101.

44. Meeks and Wilken, *Jews and Christians in Antioch*, 13–15.

45. The evidence is slim. Apollos of Alexandria, who arrived in Ephesus and Corinth in the early 50s (Acts 18:24; 19:1; 1 Cor. 1:12; 3:1-9, 21-23), may have become a Christian while still in Alexandria as a result of the mission of the Hellenists, if one can accept the reliability of the Western text of Acts 18:25 ("who was taught the word in his homeland"). The reliability of this tradition is maintained by, among others, C. Wilfred Griggs, *Early Egyptian Christianity: From Its Origins to 451 C.E.*, CS 2 (Leiden: E. J. Brill, 1990), 16–17. Further, the *Epistle of Barnabas*, conventionally thought to have been written in the era A.D. 70–135 at Alexandria, has some theological similarities to the speech of Stephen in Acts 7. Some similarities are illustrated by F. F. Bruce, *Peter, Stephen, James, and John: Studies in Early Non-Pauline Christianity* (Grand Rapids, Mich.: Wm. B. Eerdmans, 1980), 62–64. The Alexandrian origins A.D. 70–135 are held by Robert A. Kraft, *The Apostolic Fathers: 3, Barnabas and the Didache* (New York: Thomas Nelson, 1965), 45–56; Colin H. Roberts, *Manuscript, Society and Belief in Early Christian Egypt* (London: Oxford Univ. Press, 1979), 36; and Birger A. Pearson, "Early Christianity in Egypt: Some Observations," in *The Roots of Egyptian Christianity*, ed. Birger A. Pearson and James E. Goehring (Philadelphia: Fortress Press, 1986), 150–51.

46. Eusebius, *Hist. eccl.* 3.5.3; and Epiphanius, *Panarion* 29.7.7–8; idem, *Treatise on Weights and Measures* 15. For discussion of the historicity of this move, including a review of scholarship, cf. Craig Koester, "The Origin and the Significance of the Flight to Pella Tradition," *CBQ* 51 (1989): 90–106.

47. Walter Bauer, *Orthodoxy and Heresy in Earliest Christianity* (Philadelphia: Fortress Press, 1971), 86; Marie-Émile Boismard and Arnaud Lamouille, *L'Évangile de Jean* (Paris: Cerf, 1977), 1–62; and Stephen S. Smalley, *John: Evangelist and Interpreter* (Exeter: Paternoster Press, 1978), 119–21.

48. Eusebius, *Hist. eccl.* 3.19.1–3.20.7, quoting from the writings of Hegesippus; and 3.32.5–6. An assessment of this tradition, generally affirming its contents but questioning whether the rulership lasted until the time of Trajan, is made by Bauckham, *Jude and the Relatives of Jesus*, 94–106.

49. Epiphanius, *Panarion* 30.2.6; 30.23.1. The Ebionites are discussed by Weiss, *Earliest Christianity*, 2:730–39; Jean Daniélou, *The Theology of Jewish Christianity* (Chicago: Henry Regnery Company, 1964), 55–64; and Hans-Joachim Schoeps, *Jewish Christianity: Factional Disputes in the Early Church* (Philadelphia: Fortress Press, 1969).

50. The earliest use of the term *Ebionites* is late in the second century with Irenaeus, *Adv. Haer.* 1.26.3; and Hippolytus, *Ref.* 7.22. Schoeps, *Jewish Christianity*, 11, seems to want to trace their origins to the time of the flight of Jewish Christians from Jerusalem ca. A.D. 66–70. Daniélou, *Theology*, 56, claims, however, that the Ebionites cannot be identified with these persons. Weiss, *Earliest Christianity*, 2:731, grants that the Ebionites may have originated early, since their name seems to be "a relic of an earlier period" that perplexed later church leaders. Georg Strecker, "On the Problem of Jewish Christianity," an appendix to Bauer, *Orthodoxy and Heresy*, 273, suggests that the term *Ebionite* came into existence prior to the time of Irenaeus, but that it was still unknown to Justin, and then came to be applied to Jewish Christian groups in general.

51. On the tradition history of the Epistle of James, cf. Martin Dibelius, *James*, rev. Heinrich Greeven, Hermeneia (Philadelphia: Fortress Press, 1976), 11–26.

52. It appears that the first to use the designation Q was Johannes Weiss in an article published in 1890, according to Frans Neirynck, "Once More—The Symbol Q," *ETL* 55 (1979): 382–83; and Ivan Havener, *Q: The Sayings of Jesus* (Wilmington, Del.: Michael Glazier, 1987), 28–29. Both refer to the article of Johannes Weiss, "Die Verteidigung Jesu gegen den Vorwurf des Bündnisses mit Beelzebul," *TSK* 63 (1890): 555–69.

53. Examples include William R. Farmer, *The Synoptic Problem: A Critical Analysis* (New York: Macmillan, 1964), 199–232; David L. Dungan, "Mark—The Abridgment of Matthew and Luke," in *Jesus and Man's Hope*, ed. Donald G. Miller and Dikran Y. Hadidian, 2 vols. (Pittsburgh: Pittsburgh Theological Seminary, 1970–71), 1:50–97; and E. P. Sanders and Margaret Davies, *Studying the Synoptic Gospels* (Philadelphia: Trinity Press International, 1989), 51–119. The history of debate on Q up into the 1960s is in Kümmel, *Introduction to the NT*, 63–76.

54. Dieter Lührmann, "The Gospel of Mark and the Sayings Collection Q," *JBL* 108 (1989): 58–59. For a similar summary (listing seven basic assumptions, none contradicting those of Lührmann), cf. Koester, *Ancient Christian Gospels*, 133–34. Fewer points are made, but in far greater detail, by John S. Kloppenborg, *The Formation of Q: Trajectories in Ancient Wisdom Collections* (Philadelphia: Fortress Press, 1987), 41–88.

55. These include Athanasius Polag, *Fragmenta Q: Textheft zur Logienquelle*, 2d ed. (Neukirchen-Vluyn: Neukirchener Verlag, 1982); Howard C. Kee, *Jesus in History: An Approach to the Study of the Gospels*, 2d ed. (New York: Harcourt Brace Jovanovich, 1977), 76–120; and Richard A. Edwards, *A Theology of Q: Eschatology, Prophecy, and*

Wisdom (Philadelphia: Fortress Press, 1976), xi–xiii. An English translation of Polag's reconstruction is presented in Havener, *Q: The Sayings of Jesus*, 117–46.

56. Kümmel, *Introduction to the NT*, 70–71; Michael G. Steinhauser, "The Sayings Gospel Q: Introduction," in *Q-Thomas Reader* by John Kloppenborg et al. (Sonoma, Calif.: Polebridge Press, 1990), 6; Gerd Theissen, *The Gospels in Context: Social and Political History in the Synoptic Tradition* (Minneapolis: Fortress Press, 1991), 221–34 (and "in the 40s as most probable," p. 233); John S. Kloppenborg, "Literary Convention, Self-Evidence and the Social History of the Q People," in *Early Christianity, Q and Jesus: Semeia 55*, ed. John S. Kloppenborg and Leif E. Vaage (Atlanta: Scholars Press, 1992), 77–102; Arland D. Jacobson, *The First Gospel: An Introduction to Q* (Sonoma, Calif.: Polebridge Press, 1992), 259; and Burton L. Mack, *The Lost Gospel: The Book of Q and Christian Origins* (San Francisco: HarperSanFrancisco, 1993).

57. Dieter Lührmann, *Die Redaktion der Logienquelle*, WMANT 33 (Neukirchen-Vluyn: Neukirchener Verlag, 1969), 88. He maintains that the redaction of Q would have taken place in a Hellenistic community of the 50s or 60s, and that Syria is likely.

58. Edwards, *A Theology of Q*, 21, has written that there is not sufficient evidence to locate the community in a specific time or place, but then he concludes (p. 150) that northern Palestine or Syria during the 40s is a good possibility. Cf. also Havener, *Q: The Sayings of Jesus*, 42–45, "northern Galilee or western Syria"; and Koester, *Ancient Christian Gospels*, 165, "western Syria or Palestine," and (p. 170) "within the first three decades after the death of Jesus."

59. While not claiming a definite historical link, "intriguing and suggestive" correspondences between the Q community and the Hellenists of Acts 6 and 7 are noted by Ronald A. Piper, *Wisdom in the Q-Tradition: The Aphoristic Teaching of Jesus*, SNTSMS 61 (Cambridge: Cambridge Univ. Press, 1989), 187–92 (words quoted are from p. 192).

60. Cf. Luke 13:28-29//Matt. 8:11-12; also Luke 10:13-15//Matt. 11:21-23. The theme is developed by Paul D. Meyer, "The Gentile Mission in Q," *JBL* 89 (1970): 405–17. Cf. also Lührmann, *Redaktion der Logienquelle*, 86–88.

61. Lührmann, *Redaktion der Logienquelle*, 20–22; Arland D. Jacobson, "The History of the Composition of the Synoptic Sayings Source, Q," in *Society of Biblical Literature 1987 Seminar Papers*, ed. Kent H. Richards, SBLSPS 26 (Atlanta: Scholars Press, 1987), 285–94; idem, *The First Gospel*, 33–60; Dieter Zeller, "Redaktionsprozesse und weckselnder 'Sitz im Leben' beim Q-Material," in *Logia: Les Paroles de Jésus—The Sayings of Jesus: Mémorial Joseph Coppens*, ed. Joël Delobel, BETL 59 (Louvain: Leuven Univ. Press, 1982), 395–409; Kloppenborg, *Formation of Q*, 89–101; Migaku Sato, *Q und Prophetie: Studien zur Gattungs–und Traditionsgeschichte der Quelle Q*, WUNT 2/29 (Tübingen: J. C. B. Mohr [Paul Siebeck], 1988); Koester, *Ancient Christian Gospels*, 134; and Mack, *Lost Gospel*, 36–39, 44.

62. Kloppenborg, *Formation of Q*, 317.

63. Cf. here especially Jacobson, "The History of the Composition of the Synoptic Sayings Source," 285–94.

64. The strong eschatological emphasis of Q is widely affirmed; cf. Lührmann, *Die Redaktion der Logienquelle*, 69–83; Paul Hoffmann, *Studien zur Theologie der Logienquelle*,

NTAbh 8 (Münster: Aschendorff, 1972), 34–49; and Edwards, *Theology of Q*, 32–43. That Q shows signs of an awareness of the delay of the parousia, however, is maintained by Siegfried Schulz, *Q: Die Spruchquelle der Evangelisten* (Zurich: Theologischer Verlag, 1972), 268–322; and Havener, *Q: The Sayings of Jesus*, 57–62.

65. Walter Schmithals, *Jesus Christus in der Verkündigung der Kirche: Aktuelle Beiträge zum notwendigen Streit um Jesus* (Neukirchen-Vluyn: Neukirchener Verlag, 1972), 70–71.

66. The verse has some similarities to Mark 8:34. But there are differences, and it is regularly classified as a Q saying. Cf. T. W. Manson, *The Sayings of Jesus* (London: SCM Press, 1949; reprinted, Grand Rapids, Mich.: Wm. B. Eerdmans, 1979), 131–32; Polag, *Fragmenta Q*, 70; Piper, *Wisdom in the Q Tradition*, 197–202; Kloppenborg, *Formation of Q*, 231–32; Koester, *Ancient Christian Gospels*, 132; and Mack, *Lost Gospel*, 79.

67. Cf. Eduard Schweizer, *Lordship and Discipleship*, SBT 28 (Naperville, Ill.: Alec R. Allenson, 1960), 17; Joseph A. Fitzmyer, *The Gospel according to Luke*, 2 vols., AB 28–28A (Garden City, N.Y.: Doubleday, 1981–85), 1:784–85; 2:1061–62; and David Seeley, "Jesus' Death in Q," *NTS* 38 (1992): 226.

68. Quoted from the translation by Marvin W. Meyer in *Q-Thomas Reader* by Kloppenborg et al., 142; italics added.

69. Cf. M. Eugene Boring, *Sayings of the Risen Jesus: Christian Prophecy in the Synoptic Tradition*, SNTSMS 46 (Cambridge: Cambridge Univ. Press, 1982), 171–73; Fitzmyer, *Luke*, 2:1035; and Kloppenborg, *Formation of Q*, 227–29.

70. Cf. Boring, *Sayings of the Risen Jesus*, 172. In the midrash on Psalm 118:22–29 the verses are interpreted to signify final redemption. Cf. *The Midrash on Psalms*, trans. William G. Braude, 2 vols., YJS 13 (New Haven: Yale Univ. Press, 1959), 2:245.

71. Cf. Barnabas Lindars, *New Testament Apologetic: The Doctrinal Significance of the Old Testament Quotations* (Philadelphia: Westminster Press, 1961), 172; and Eduard Schweizer, *A Theological Introduction to the New Testament* (Nashville: Abingdon Press, 1991), 43.

72. Detailed reconstructions of the parable's origins and developments are presented by Fitzmyer, *Luke*, 2:1230–33; and Brendon B. Scott, *Hear Then the Parable: A Commentary on the Parables of Jesus* (Minneapolis: Fortress Press, 1989), 217–35.

73. Cf. Rudolf Bultmann, *History of the Synoptic Tradition*, 2d ed. (New York: Harper & Row, 1968), 176; C. H. Dodd, *The Parables of the Kingdom*, rev. ed. (New York: Charles Scribner's Sons, 1961), 114–15; Joachim Jeremias, *The Parables of Jesus*, rev. ed. (New York: Charles Scribner's Sons, 1963), 63; Schulz, *Q: Die Spruchquelle*, 293–98; Athanasius Polag, *Die Christologie der Logienquelle*, WMANT 45 (Neukirchen-Vluyn: Neukirchener Verlag, 1977), 165; Edward Schillebeeckx, *Jesus: An Experiment in Christology* (New York: Crossroad, 1981), 416; and Scott, *Hear Then the Parable*, 223–24.

74. Cf. Havener, *Q: The Sayings of Jesus*, 106–7; and Schweizer, *Theological Introduction to the NT*, 43.

75. Heinz E. Tödt, *The Son of Man in the Synoptic Tradition* (Philadelphia: Westminster Press, 1965), 250–53; Lührmann, *Redaktion der Logienquelle*, 94–97; Edwards, *Theology of Q*, 149; Havener, *Q: The Sayings of Jesus*, 32, 106; John Kloppenborg,

"'Easter Faith' and the Sayings Gospel Q," in *The Apocryphal Jesus and Christian Origins: Semeia 49*, ed. Ron Cameron (Atlanta: Scholars Press, 1990), 76–77, 84; Burton L. Mack, "Lord of the Logia: Savior or Sage?" in *Gospel Origins and Christian Beginnings: In Honor of James M. Robinson*, ed. James E. Goehring et al. (Sonoma, Calif.: Polebridge Press, 1990), 6, 19; Koester, *Ancient Christian Gospels*, 160; Jacobson, *The First Gospel*, 27–28, 260; and Mack, *Lost Gospel*, 139.

76. Kloppenborg, "'Easter Faith' and the Sayings Gospel Q," 84.

77. Ibid., 90.

78. Kloppenborg, *Formation of Q*, 2.

79. Ibid., 25.

80. Koester, *Ancient Christian Gospels*, 160. On the other hand, cf. Helmut Koester, "Jesus the Victim," *JBL* 111 (1992): 9: "While reflection about Jesus' death plays no central role in the more recent portraits of Jesus, all early Christian traditions are acutely aware of this fact. All sources—and this includes the tradition of the wisdom sayings and its theology—agree that the tradition about Jesus must be seen in this light: his rejection, suffering, and death."

81. On the presence and the future manifestation of the kingdom in Q, cf. Havener, *Q: The Sayings of Jesus*, 50–57.

82. Cf. Tödt, *Son of Man*, 264; and Edwards, *Theology of Q*, 149.

83. Koester, *Introduction to the NT*, 2:148.

84. Edwards, *Theology of Q*, 149.

85. Kloppenborg, "'Easter Faith' and the Sayings Gospel Q," 80. The deuteronomistic theme in Q had been discussed earlier by Odil H. Steck, *Israel und das gewaltsame Geschick der Propheten: Untersuchungen zur Überlieferung des deuteronomistischen Geschichtsbild im Alten Testament, Spätjudentum und Urchristentum*, WMANT 23 (Neukirchen-Vluyn: Neukirchener Verlag, 1967), 257–60 et passim; James M. Robinson, "Jesus as Sophos and Sophia: Wisdom Tradition and the Gospels," in *Aspects of Wisdom in Judaism and Early Christianity*, ed. Robert L. Wilken (Notre Dame: Univ. of Notre Dame Press, 1975), 13; and Arland D. Jacobson, "The Literary Unity of Q," *JBL* 101 (1982): 383–89.

86. Tödt, *Son of Man*, 252; Edwards, *Theology of Q*, 149–50; James M. Robinson, "Jesus from Easter to Valentinus (or to the Apostles' Creed)," *JBL* 101 (1982): 24; and Boring, *The Sayings of the Risen Jesus*, 182.

87. Kloppenborg, "'Easter Faith' and the Sayings Gospel Q," 90.

88. Ibid., 90–91.

89. This point has been made especially by Graham N. Stanton, "On the Christology of Q," in *Christ and Spirit in the New Testament: In Honour of Charles Francis Digby Moule*, ed. Barnabas Lindars and Stephen S. Smalley (Cambridge: Cambridge Univ. Press, 1973), 42; Martin Hengel, "Christology and New Testament Chronology: A Problem in the History of Earliest Christianity," in his *Between Jesus and Paul*, 37; Petr Pokorný, *The Genesis of Christology: Foundations for a Theology of the New Testament* (Edinburgh: T. & T. Clark, 1987), 90; Marinus de Jonge, *Christology in Context: The Earliest Christian Response to Jesus* (Philadelphia: Westminster Press, 1988), 83; and Athanasius Polag, "The Theological Center of the Sayings Source," in *The*

Gospel and the Gospels, ed. Peter Stuhlmacher (Grand Rapids, Mich.: Wm. B. Eerdmans, 1991), 101–2.

90. Cf. Edwards, *Theology of Q*, 18–21; Kloppenborg, "'Easter Faith' and the Sayings Gospel Q," 71; and Jacobson, *The First Gospel*, 33.

91. Tödt, *Son of Man*, 250. This had been maintained earlier by T. W. Manson, *Sayings of Jesus*, 16. Cf. also Leonhard Goppelt, *Theology of the New Testament*, 2 vols. (Grand Rapids, Mich.: Wm. B. Eerdmans, 1981–82), 1:5.

92. Tödt, *Son of Man*, 252.

93. Ernst Käsemann, "On the Subject of Primitive Christian Apocalyptic," in his *New Testament Questions of Today* (Philadelphia: Fortress Press, 1969), 119–20.

94. Kümmel, *Introduction to the NT*, 74.

95. De Jonge, *Christology in Context*, 83–84.

96. *A Testament of Hope: The Essential Writings of Martin Luther King, Jr.*, ed. James M. Washington (San Francisco: Harper & Row, 1986).

97. Polag, "The Theological Center of the Sayings Source," 102.

98. Cf. Pokorný, *Genesis of Christology*, 95, and also the remarks of Martin Hengel, "Aufgaben der neutestamentlichen Wissenschaft," forthcoming in *NTS* 40/3 (1994), who says that Q scholarship is "overgrown with hypotheses—not only one Q community (the existence of which I doubt), but several, with up to five different layers of redaction, in a text that can itself only be reconstructed in very fragmentary fashion. Why may it not simply be a collection of Jesus-sayings?" (quoted from an English translation by Philip E. Devenish).

99. Cf. Stanton, "On the Christology of Q," 42: "In view of the fact that both Matthew and Luke (and presumably their communities) had access to two very different and originally separate kinds of material about Jesus (Q and Mark), is it not at least possible that the Q community also had two different kinds of material?"

100. Kloppenborg, "Literary Convention, Self-Evidence and the Social History of the Q People," 79.

101. These ways are discussed in Arland J. Hultgren, *Christ and His Benefits: Christology and Redemption in the New Testament* (Philadelphia: Fortress Press, 1987), 76–89, 145–64. Cf. also Kenneth Grayston, *Dying, We Live: A New Enquiry into the Death of Christ in the New Testament* (New York: Oxford Univ. Press, 1990), 164–237, 282–323, 353–55, 356–58.

102. Cf. Eric Franklin, *Christ the Lord: A Study in the Purpose and Theology of Luke-Acts* (London: SPCK, 1975), 66; and Goppelt, *Theology of the NT*, 2:283.

103. W. R. G. Loader, "The Central Structure of Johannine Christology," *NTS* 30 (1984): 198.

104. Cf. note 85. The same can be said if one follows the claim that Q interprets the death of Jesus in light of Cynic-Stoic views on the nature of a teacher's death, as maintained by Seeley, "Jesus' Death in Q," 222–34.

105. The Holy Spirit in Q is discussed by Havener, *Q: The Sayings of Jesus*, 86–91.

106. Cf. Christopher M. Tuckett, "On the Stratification of Q: A Response," in *Early Christianity, Q and Jesus: Semeia 55*, ed. John S. Kloppenborg and Leif E. Vaage (Atlanta: Scholars Press, 1992), 216.

107. Major texts are Joel 2:28–29; 1 Macc. 4:46; *Sib. Or.* 3.781–82; *Pss. of Sol.* 17.37; 18.7; *T. Levi* 18.7; and *T. Judah* 24.2. Cf. the statement of David E. Aune, *Prophecy in Early Christianity and the Ancient Mediterranean World* (Grand Rapids, Mich.: Wm. B. Eerdmans, 1983), 193: "There was an apparently widespread view in early Judaism that at the end of the present age or in the age to come the Spirit of God would be poured out on all Israel and all Israelites would have the gift of prophesying."

108. Tödt, *Son of Man*, 252.

109. Cf. Pokorný, *Genesis of Christology*, 94–95, 105.

110. Edwards, *Theology of Q*, 148–49; and Kloppenborg, *Formation of Q*, 318–20. Additional aspects of the ethos of the Q community are discussed by John S. Kloppenborg, "Nomos and Ethos in Q," in *Gospel Origins and Christian Beginnings*, ed. J. Goehring, 35–48. Kloppenborg takes up the issue whether Q reflects a Torah-observant Jewish Christianity, concluding that Torah observance became an issue at one of the later stages of the composition of Q. Still more on the ethos of the Q community, and the function of the Q material in giving shape to it, can be found in the essay by Richard Horsley, "Logoi Prophētōn? Reflections on the Genre of Q," in *The Future of Early Christianity: Essays in Honor of Helmut Koester*, ed. Birger A. Pearson (Minneapolis: Fortress Press, 1991), 195–209 (esp. pp. 207–9).

111. Havener, *Q: The Sayings of Jesus*, 91–104. Cf. Theissen, *The Gospels in Context*, 233–34.

112. Boring, *Sayings of the Risen Jesus*, 182. Boring seems to go too far, however, in his statement: "What Jesus of Nazareth had said became dissolved in what the post-Easter Jesus said through his prophets."

113. Luke 6:47//Matt. 7:24; Luke 9:57-62//Matt. 8:19-22.

114. Luke 3:8//Matt. 3:8; Luke 15:7//Matt. 18:13.

115. Luke 17:6//Matt. 17:20.

116. Luke 12:8-9//Matt. 10:32-33.

117. Luke 12:22-34//Matt. 6:25-33; Luke 10:4//Matt. 10:9-11.

118. Luke 11:9-13//Matt. 7:7-11.

119. Luke 11:4//Matt. 6:12.

120. Luke 6:37//Matt. 7:1.

121. Luke 6:27-36//Matt. 5:39-47.

122. Luke 6:36//Matt. 5:48; Luke 11:4//Matt. 6:12.

123. Luke 6:20-21//Matt. 5:3, 6; Luke 7:22//Matt. 11:5; Luke 6:30//Matt. 5:42.

124. James M. Robinson, "Kerygma and History in the New Testament," and, "LOGOI SOPHON; On the Gattung of Q," in *Trajectories through Early Christianity* by James M. Robinson and Helmut Koester (Philadelphia: Fortress Press, 1971), 43, 104–5, 113.

125. Lührmann, *Die Redaktion der Logienquelle*, 91; and Kloppenborg, *Formation of Q*, 31. Cf. also the critique by Hans-Martin Schenke, "Die Tendenz der Weisheit zur Gnosis," in *Gnosis: Festschrift für Hans Jonas*, ed. Barbara Aland (Göttingen: Vandenhoeck & Ruprecht, 1978), 351–72 (esp. p. 361); and James D. G. Dunn, *Unity and Diversity in the New Testament: An Inquiry into the Character of Earliest Christianity*, 2d ed. (Philadelphia: Trinity Press International, 1990), 283–88. This point has now

been made also by James M. Robinson, "On Bridging the Gulf from Q to the Gospel of Thomas (or Vice Versa)," in *Nag Hammadi, Gnosticism, and Early Christianity*, ed. Charles W. Hedrick and Robert Hodgson, Jr. (Peabody, Mass.: Hendrickson Publishers, 1986), 136.

126. Helmut Koester, "One Jesus and Four Primitive Gospels," in *Trajectories*, 186; idem, *Ancient Christian Gospels*, 150. In another place Koester says that while it is not possible "to consider Q as the source of any of the sayings of the Gospel of Thomas," a "good portion of the Q parallels in the Gospel of Thomas are wisdom sayings and community instructions that appear in the formative stage of Q." Helmut Koester, "Q and Its Relatives," in *Gospel Origins and Christian Beginnings*, ed. Goehring et al., 56.

127. Koester, "One Jesus and Four Primitive Gospels," 186–87.

128. Kloppenborg, *Formation of Q*, 327–28. Kloppenborg calls the temptation story a "biographical-narrative preface" to Q (p. 327).

129. A list of "Q-Thomas Parallels" is given in Kloppenborg et al., *Q-Thomas Reader*, 159. Another listing of parallels between Q and the *Gospel of Thomas* is given by Koester, *Ancient Christian Gospels*, 87–89. In his list 88 verses of Q (as opposed to 78 in the list of Kloppenborg et al.) have parallels in the *Gospel of Thomas*. Working the other way, Koester says that 46 sayings in the latter have parallels in Q (pp. 87 and 107).

130. So Robinson, "On Bridging the Gulf from Q to the Gospel of Thomas," 136, has written: "It is, of course, the case that the genre of the sayings collection will not automatically end in gnosticism," and "the gnosticizing proclivity of the sayings collection does in fact need some catalyst to go into effect."

131. This principle has been enunciated clearly by, among others, John Knox, *Chapters in a Life of Paul*, rev. ed. (Macon, Ga.: Mercer Univ. Press, 1987), 3–28 (pp. 13–43 of the pioneering 1st ed., 1950); Jewett, *A Chronology of Paul's Life*, 22–24; Luedemann, *Paul*, 21–23; and Becker, *Paul*, 16.

132. Letters that are universally attributed to Paul as genuine are Romans, 1 and 2 Corinthians, Galatians, 1 Thessalonians, Philippians, and Philemon. For a brief but excellent discussion on authentic and deutero-Pauline letters, see Bornkamm, *Paul*, 241–43. For a more extended treatment of the issues, cf. Calvin J. Roetzel, *The Letters of Paul: Conversations in Context*, 3d ed. (Louisville: Westminster/John Knox Press, 1991), 131–55.

133. According to Colossians 1:6–7, for example, it was under Paul's supervision that Epaphras founded the church at Colossae.

134. The point has been made most forcefully and clearly by J. Christiaan Beker, *Paul the Apostle: The Triumph of God in Life and Thought* (Philadelphia: Fortress Press, 1980), 24.

135. This point is discussed in greater detail in Arland J. Hultgren, *Paul's Gospel and Mission: The Outlook from His Letter to the Romans* (Philadelphia: Fortress Press, 1985), 1–11.

136. The problems and possibilities are explored by Joseph Plevnik, "The Center of Pauline Theology," *CBQ* 51 (1989): 461–78; Ulrich Mauser, "Paul the Theologian," *HorBT* 11 (1989): 80–106; J. Christiaan Beker, *The Triumph of God: The Essence of Paul's*

Thought (Minneapolis: Fortress Press, 1990); and Victor Paul Furnish, "Paul the Theologian," in *The Conversation Continues: Studies in Paul and John in Honor of J. Louis Martyn*, ed. Robert T. Fortna and Beverly R. Gaventa (Nashville: Abingdon Press, 1990), 19–34.

137. This is the working principle of Judith M. Gundry Volf, *Paul and Perseverance: Staying in and Falling Away* (Louisville: Westminster/John Knox Press, 1991), 3.

138. But it is going too far to say that Paul's churches "were exclusively Gentile," as claimed by Lloyd Gaston, *Paul and the Torah* (Vancouver: Univ. of British Columbia Press, 1987), 8. Ephesus and Corinth had substantial Jewish populations in Paul's day, and we can expect that some became Christians, and the most probable explanation for Jewish persecution and flogging of Paul (2 Cor. 11:24, 26; 12:10) was due to his offending leaders of Jewish communities by having success among Jews and God-fearers. Cf. also 1 Cor. 7:18: persons circumcised at the time of call need not remove the marks. Finally, at 1 Cor. 9:20 Paul speaks of winning Jews to the faith.

139. Major studies include those of Oscar Cullmann, *The Earliest Christian Confessions* (London: Lutterworth Press, 1949); Vernon H. Neufeld, *The Earliest Christian Confessions*, NTTS 5 (Grand Rapids, Mich.: Wm. B. Eerdmans, 1963); and Jack T. Sanders, *The New Testament Christological Hymns: Their Historical Religious Background*, SNTSMS 15 (Cambridge: Cambridge Univ. Press, 1971).

140. Cf. BAGD, 838–39; Harald Riesenfeld, "*Hyper*," TDNT 8:508–09; and Goppelt, *Theology of the NT*, 2:92–98.

141. Closely related to these is the formula at Rom. 4:25 where Paul uses *dia* instead of *hyper*. Other instances of the *hyper* formula outside Paul's undisputed letters are at John 6:51; 11:51-52; Eph. 5:2, 25; 1 Tim. 2:16; Titus 2:14; Heb. 2:9; 1 Peter 2:21; 3:18; 1 John 3:16.

142. Other instances are found chiefly in the Johannine writings, e.g., John 3:17; 1 John 4:9. A similar pattern is found in Matt. 15:24 and Luke 4:18.

143. For more on this term and its applicability to redemptive Christology in the New Testament (and also a discussion of "christopractic" as another perspective), see Hultgren, *Christ and His Benefits*, 41–44. Cf. also a similar emphasis in the essay by C. A. Wanamaker, "Christ as Divine Agent in Paul," *SJT* 39 (1986): 517–28.

144. Cf. Charles B. Cousar, *A Theology of the Cross: The Death of Jesus in the Pauline Letters* (Minneapolis: Fortress Press, 1990), 61.

145. Paul mentions the cross at 1 Cor. 1:17, 18; Gal. 5:11; 6:12, 14; Phil. 2:8; 3:18; and he uses the verb (*crucify*) at 1 Cor. 1:23; 2:2, 8; 2 Cor. 13:4; Gal. 3:1. He uses the latter metaphorically at Gal. 5:24; 6:14 as well.

146. Ernst Lohmeyer, *Kyrios Jesus: Eine Untersuchung zu Phil. 2,5-11*, 2d ed. (Heidelberg: Carl Winter, Universitätsverlag, 1961), 45; Günther Bornkamm, "On Understanding the Christ Hymn: Philippians 2.6-11," in his *Early Christian Experience* (New York: Harper & Row, 1969), 113; and Ernst Käsemann, "The Saving Significance of the Death of Jesus in Paul," in his *Perspectives on Paul* (Philadelphia: Fortress Press, 1971), 36.

147. The phrase has been borrowed from Wolfhart Pannenberg, *Jesus, God and Man*, 2d ed. (Philadelphia: Westminster Press, 1977), 100.

148. The statement is confessional in context ("we believe that . . ."). It is probably pre-Pauline for three reasons: (1) Paul consistently uses the verb *egeirō* elsewhere on resurrection (*anistēmi* is used here); (2) the fact that it is active with "Jesus" as the subject (otherwise Paul uses a christological title alone or with "Jesus" as object, or as subject with a passive verb); and (3) the fact that it is introduced as a confessional formula. The view that it is a pre-Pauline formula is also maintained by Donfried, "1 Thessalonians, Acts and the Early Paul," 12.

149. Passages on God as the one who raised Jesus are at Rom. 4:24; 8:11; 10:9; 1 Cor. 6:14; 15:15; 2 Cor. 4:14; Gal. 1:1. Passages that use the divine passive are at Rom. 4:25; 6:4, 9; 7:4; 1 Cor. 15:4, 12, 20.

150. These themes, plus others, are discussed in a fine essay by Gerhard Friedrich, "Die Bedeutung der Auferweckung Jesu nach Aussagen des Neuen Testaments," in his *Auf das Wort kommt es an: Gesammelte Aufsätze zum 70. Geburtstag*, ed. J. H. Friedrich (Göttingen: Vandenhoeck & Ruprecht, 1978), 354–73; reprinted from *TZ* 27 (1971): 305–24.

151. This is demonstrated above all by the fact that Paul wrote letters to his churches, dealing with local problems in light of his gospel and confession. Galatians is perhaps the best example (see esp. 1:7; 5:10). Paul's visits to his churches and the use of emissaries to carry messages and correspondence to and from them show the same concern. Paul calls upon the Christians at Philippi to continue in what they have learned and received from him (Phil. 4:9), and he exhorts his churches to imitate him, i.e., his faith and life (1 Cor. 4:14-16; 11:1; Gal. 4:12; Phil. 3:17; 1 Thess. 1:6), as over against those who are enemies of the cross (Phil. 3:17-21). At the same time, Paul will not "lord it over" the faith of his churches (cf. 2 Cor. 1:24).

152. Wayne A. Meeks, *The First Urban Christians: The Social World of the Apostle Paul* (New Haven: Yale Univ. Press, 1983), 181; and Margaret Y. MacDonald, *The Pauline Churches: A Socio-Historical Study of Institutionalization in the Pauline and Deutero-Pauline Writings*, SNTSMS 60 (Cambridge: Cambridge Univ. Press, 1988), 72–83 (esp. pp. 76–77).

153. This point has been made particularly well in the writings of Käsemann, "On the Subject of Primitive Christian Apocalyptic," 132; and Cousar, *Theology of the Cross*, 102–3.

154. What is presented here is dealt with in greater detail in Arland J. Hultgren, "The Self-Definition of Paul and His Communities," *SEÅ* 56 (1991): 78–100.

155. The origins are discussed by Karl L. Schmidt, "*Ekklēsia*," TDNT 3:527–31; and Hans Conzelmann, *1 Corinthians*, Hermeneia (Philadelphia: Fortress Press, 1975), 21–23.

156. Cf. Schmidt, "*Ekklēsia*," 3:516; and Gerhard Lohfink, *Jesus and Community: The Social Dimensions of the Christian Faith* (Philadelphia: Fortress Press, 1984), 77.

157. Cf. Judg. 20:2; Neh. 13:1 for the former, and Deut. 23:2-4, 9; 1 Chr. 28:8; Mic. 2:5 for the latter. Schmidt, "*Ekklēsia*," 3:527–29, claims that, with four exceptions, *ekklēsia* always translates the Hebrew *qahal* (ca. a hundred times in the Old Testament). A more specific and intriguing proposal has been made by Harald Riesenfeld, "Sons of God and Ecclesia: An Intertestamental Analysis," in *Renewing the Judeo-Christian*

Wellsprings, ed. Val A. McInnes (New York: Crossroad Publishing Company, 1987), 89–104. Riesenfeld suggests that, from among the many passages in the LXX, the basis for the concept can be found at Psalm 86:6 (LXX, 88:6; RSV, 89:5). There the LXX has *ekklēsia hagiōn,* "assembly of the holy ones," for the Hebrew *qahal qedoshim* (pp. 102–3).

158. Philo, *Leg. All.* 3.8; 3.81; *Ebr.* 213. The term *qahal el* appears at 1QM 4.10; and *qahal* at 1QSa 1.20; 2.4; CD 7.17; 11.22; 12.6, signifying the community.

159. Examples are at Rom. 1:7; 12:13; 1 Cor. 1:2; 6:1; 2 Cor. 1:1; Phil. 4:21; 1 Thess. 3:13; Phlm. 5.

160. The plural participle *(hoi pisteuontes,* "believers") appears at Rom. 3:22; 4:11, 24; 1 Cor. 1:21; 14:22 (twice); Gal. 3:22; 1 Thess. 1:7; 2:10, 13. The singular form of the participle is used at Rom. 1:16; 4:5; 9:33; 10:4, 11. Cf. also the use of *pistos* as "believer" at 2 Cor. 6:15.

161. The word count does not include the two references to the (natural) brothers of Jesus (1 Cor. 9:5; Gal. 1:19). Paul uses the language of "father" for himself in relationship to his churches (1 Cor. 4:15; 2 Cor. 12:14; 1 Thess. 2:11; Phlm. 10). This imagery is dealt with by Bengt Holmberg, *Paul and Power: The Structure of Authority in the Primitive Church as Reflected in the Pauline Epistles,* ConBNT 11 (Lund: G. W. K. Gleerup, 1978), 79–81.

162. The wide range of sources is cited by Hans F. von Soden, "*Adelphos,*" TDNT 1:44–46.

163. Cf. Robert Banks, *Paul's Idea of Community: The Early House Churches in Their Historical Setting* (Grand Rapids, Mich.: Wm. B. Eerdmans, 1980), 59–60.

164. Charles H. Cooley, *Social Organization: A Study of the Larger Mind* (New York: Charles Scribner's Sons, 1909), 23–31; and Thomas J. Sullivan and Kendrick S. Thompson, *Sociology: Concepts, Issues, and Applications,* 2d ed. (New York: Macmillan, 1990), 109.

165. Cf. Robin Scroggs, "The Earliest Christian Communities as Sectarian Movement," in *Christianity, Judaism and Other Greco-Roman Cults: Studies for Morton Smith at Sixty,* ed. Jacob Neusner, 4 vols.; SJLA 12 (Leiden: E. J. Brill, 1975), 2:18.

166. Max Weber, "Zwischenbetrachtung: Theorie des Stufen und Richtungen religiöser Weltablehnung," in his *Gesammelte Aufsätze zur Religionssoziologie,* 3 vols. (Tübingen: J. C. B. Mohr [Paul Siebeck], 1920), 1:542–43; quotation from p. 543.

167. That some came from the lower strata of society is established by 1 Cor. 1:26. That some were of higher status has been argued by Edwin A. Judge, *Rank and Status in the World of the Caesars and St. Paul,* Univ. of Canterbury Publications 29 (Christchurch, New Zealand: Univ. of Canterbury, 1982), 9–13. Judge writes: "Of the 91 individuals named in the New Testament in connection with St. Paul, a third have Latin names" (p. 13), which he considers a higher proportion than one would expect, and he suggests that the use of Roman names by these persons was a mark of Roman citizenship.

168. Cf. Abraham Malherbe, *Social Aspects of Early Christianity,* 2d ed. (Philadelphia: Fortress Press, 1983), 86–87; and Gerd Theissen, "The Strong and the Weak in Corinth: A Sociological Analysis of a Theological Quarrel," in his *The Social Setting of Pauline Christianity: Essays on Corinth* (Philadelphia: Fortress Press, 1982), 121–43.

The range of social and economic urban life is described in the work of John E. Stambaugh, *The Ancient Roman City* (Baltimore: Johns Hopkins Univ. Press, 1988).

169. That tensions in the church at Corinth were caused by social stratification of its members has been argued by Gerd Theissen, "Social Stratification in the Corinthian Community: A Contribution to the Sociology of Early Hellenistic Christianity," in his *The Social Setting of Pauline Christianity*, 69–119. Cf. also Howard C. Kee, *Christian Origins in Sociological Perspective* (Philadelphia: Westminster Press, 1980), 93.

170. Edwin A. Judge, *The Social Pattern of Christian Groups in the First Century* (London: Tyndale Press, 1960), 60; and Malherbe, *Social Aspects of Early Christianity*, 87.

171. Cf. Ernst Käsemann, "The Pauline Doctrine of the Lord's Supper," in his *Essays on New Testament Themes*, SBT 41 (Naperville, Ill.: Alec R. Allenson, 1984), 109–10; idem, "The Theological Problem Presented by the Motif of the Body of Christ," in his *Perspectives on Paul*, 111; Conzelmann, *1 Corinthians*, 172; and Goppelt, *Theology of the NT*, 2:146–47.

172. Cullmann, *Early Christian Worship*, 26, 33–34; and Schweizer, *Church Order*, 92. The only use of "body of Christ" apart from worship is at Rom. 7:4.

173. Cf. E. Earle Ellis, "Christ Crucified," in *Reconciliation and Hope: New Testament Essays on Atonement and Eschatology Presented to L. L. Morris on His 60th Birthday*, ed. Robert Banks (Grand Rapids, Mich.: Wm. B. Eerdmans, 1974), 69–75; and Victor Paul Furnish, "Belonging to Christ: A Paradigm for Ethics in First Corinthians," *Int* 44 (1990): 145–57.

174. The "body of Christ" concept in Paul is dealt with in many works, including Eduard Schweizer, "*Sōma*," TDNT 7:1068–71; and Ernest Best, *One Body in Christ* (London: SPCK, 1955). A survey and commentary on contemporary studies is by Robert H. Gundry, *Sōma in Biblical Theology: With Emphasis on Pauline Anthropology*, SNTSMS 29 (Cambridge: Cambridge Univ. Press, 1976), 223–44. A more recent treatment of the theme, with critique of former views, is that of Gosnell L. O. R. Yorke, *The Church as the Body of Christ in the Pauline Corpus: A Re-examination* (Lanham, Md.: University Press of America, 1991).

175. Examples are in Seneca, *De Ira* 2.31.7–8; and Epictetus, *Dissertationes* 2.10.3. Many references are provided by Schweizer, "*Sōma*," 7:1036–41. Additional references and discussions of possible parallels are in the essays by T. W. Manson, "A Parallel to a N.T. Use of *Sōma*," *JTS* 37 (1936): 385; G. C. Richards, "Parallels to a N.T. Use of *Sōma*," *JTS* 38 (1937): 165; and W. L. Knox, "Parallels to the N.T. Use of *Sōma*," *JTS* 39 (1938): 243–46.

176. Cf. here especially Käsemann, "The Theological Problem Presented by the Motif of the Body of Christ," 118–20.

177. Rom. 12:9-10; 13:8-10; 14:15; 1 Cor. 13:1-13; 14:1; 16:14; 2 Cor. 5:14; Gal. 5:14, 22; Phil. 1:9; 1 Thess. 3:6, 12; 4:9-10; Phlm. 4, 7.

178. 1 Cor. 10:21; 12:7; Gal. 6:2, 9-10; Phil. 2:4; 1 Thess. 5:15.

179. Rom. 12:16, 18; 14:17-18; 15:5; 2 Cor. 13:11; 1 Thess. 5:13.

180. Bauer, *Orthodoxy and Heresy*, 70–75, 101–02, 86–89.

181. Perhaps ca. A.D. 54/55. Cf. Bornkamm, *Paul*, 241–42; and Becker, *Paul*, 31.

182. Cf. a similar judgment by Luedemann, *Opposition to Paul*, 106.

183. Bauer, *Orthodoxy and Heresy*, 72–73.

184. Cf. 1 John 4:2-3; 2 John 7; Ignatius, *Trall.* 9.1–2; 10.1; *Smyrn.* 2.1.

185. Hans F. von Campenhausen, *Polykarp von Smyrna und die Pastoralbriefe*, SHA (Heidelberg: C. Winter, 1951), 40–41.

186. There is debate whether one can speak of one letter or two (chapters 1–12; 13–14) that have been combined. The treatment above assumes a single letter, but the results would not be different if there were two. The two-letter hypothesis was championed by P. N. Harrison, *Polycarp's Two Epistles to the Philippians* (Cambridge: Cambridge Univ. Press, 1936). The theory is critiqued and rejected by William R. Schoedel, *The Apostolic Fathers: 5, Polycarp, Martyrdom of Polycarp, Fragments of Papias* (New York: Thomas Nelson, 1967), 4, 29, 37.

187. Cf. Kümmel, *Introduction to the NT*, 257–60; Ernest Best, *A Commentary on the First and Second Epistles to the Thessalonians*, HNTC (New York: Harper & Row, 1972), 7–13; Koester, *Introduction to the NT*, 2:112; Robert Jewett, *The Thessalonian Correspondence: Pauline Rhetoric and Millenarian Piety* (Philadelphia: Fortress Press, 1986), 59–60; and Becker, *Paul*, 31.

188. Jewett, *The Thessalonian Correspondence*, 102–4.

189. This is discussed by Abraham J. Malherbe, *Paul and the Thessalonians: The Philosophic Tradition of Pastoral Care* (Philadelphia: Fortress Press, 1987), 68–78. See also John M. G. Barclay, "Thessalonica and Corinth: Social Contrasts in Pauline Christianity," *JSNT* 47 (1992): 50–52.

190. Pauline authorship and dating of ca. A.D. 50 is held by Kümmel, *Introduction to the NT*, 264–69; Best, *First and Second Epistles to the Thessalonians*, 58–59; and Jewett, *The Thessalonian Correspondence*, 60. Deutero-Pauline authorship is maintained by Bornkamm, *Paul*, 243; Willi Marxsen, *Introduction to the New Testament* (Philadelphia: Fortress Press, 1968), 42–44; Koester, *Introduction to the NT*, 2:242–46; and Becker, *Paul*, 11.

191. The term is borrowed from Reginald H. Fuller, *A Critical Introduction to the New Testament* (London: Gerald Duckworth, 1966), 59.

192. Walter Schmithals, *Paul and the Gnostics* (Nashville: Abingdon Press, 1972), 123–218.

193. See critique by Jewett, *The Thessalonian Correspondence*, 147–49; cf. Koester, *Introduction to the NT*, 2:244–45.

194. Bauer, *Orthodoxy and Heresy*, 74–75.

195. Bishop Melito is quoted by Eusebius, *Hist. eccl.* 4.26.10.

196. Joseph B. Tyson, "Paul's Opponents in Galatia," *NovT* 10 (1968): 241–54; Robert Jewett, "The Agitators and the Galatian Congregation," *NTS* 17 (1971): 198–212; Betz, *Galatians*, 5–9; Luedemann, *Paul*, 44–45; idem, *Opposition to Paul*, 97–103; J. Louis Martyn, "A Law-Observant Mission to Gentiles: The Background of Galatians," *SJT* 38 (1985): 307–24; and George Howard, *Paul: Crisis in Galatia: A Study in Early Christian Theology*, 2d ed., SNTSMS 35 (Cambridge: Cambridge Univ. Press, 1990), 1–19.

197. Aspects of "Paulinism" in 1 Peter are discussed in various commentaries, e.g., Francis W. Beare, *The First Epistle of Peter* (Oxford: Basil Blackwell, 1961), 9–10, 25–26; J. N. D. Kelly, *A Commentary on the Epistles of Peter and Jude*, HNTC (New York: Harper & Row, 1969), 11–15; Ernest Best, *1 Peter*, NCB (London: Marshall,

Morgan & Scott, 1971), 32–36; J. Ramsey Michaels, *1 Peter*, WBC (Waco, Tex.: Word Books, 1988), xliii–xlv; and Peter H. Davids, *The First Epistle of Peter*, NICNT (Grand Rapids, Mich.: Wm. B. Eerdmans, 1990), 4–7.

198. Cf. Bornkamm, *Paul*, xi; and Kümmel, *Introduction to the NT*, 252–55.

199. On Paul's sources of information about Corinth, cf. John C. Hurd, Jr., *The Origin of I Corinthians*, 2d ed. (Macon, Ga.: Mercer Univ. Press, 1983), 47–50.

200. So Conzelmann, *1 Corinthians*, 33–34; Fuller, *Introduction to the NT*, 43–45, 50; and Koester, *Introduction to the NT*, 2:121. Luedemann, *Opposition to Paul*, 79–80, contends that the opposition to Paul at Corinth was from Jewish Christian missionaries that made up the "Cephas party." Against this view, it has been maintained that, in the letter itself, the solidarity of both Cephas and Apollos with Paul speaks against such. Cf. Nils A. Dahl, "Paul and the Church at Corinth according to 1 Corinthians 1:10—4:21," in *Christian History and Interpretation: Studies Presented to John Knox*, ed. William R. Farmer et al. (Cambridge: Cambridge Univ. Press, 1967), 323.

201. The major work is by Walter Schmithals, *Gnosticism in Corinth: An Investigation of the Letters to the Corinthians* (Nashville: Abingdon Press, 1971).

202. Robert McL. Wilson, "How Gnostic Were the Corinthians?" *NTS* 19 (1972): 65–74; idem, "Gnosis at Corinth," in *Paul and Paulinism: Essays in Honour of C. K. Barrett*, ed. Morna D. Hooker and S. G. Wilson (London: SPCK, 1982), 102–14; Conzelmann, *1 Corinthians*, 15 (who uses the term *proto-Gnostics*); Kurt Rudolph, " 'Gnosis' and 'Gnosticism'—The Problems of Their Definition and Their Relation to the Writings of the New Testament," in *The New Testament and Gnosis: Essays in Honour of Robert McL. Wilson*, ed. A. H. B. Logan and A. J. M. Wedderburn (Edinburgh: T. & T. Clark, 1983), 31–32; and Dunn, *Unity and Diversity*, 275–79. An essay that shows that major features of Gnosticism were not present at Corinth or elsewhere in the Pauline churches is that of Frederik Wisse, "The 'Opponents' in the New Testament in Light of the Nag Hammadi Writings," in *Colloque international sur les textes de Nag Hammadi*, ed. Bernard Barc (Quebec: Les Presses de l'Université Laval, 1981), 99–120. That the background of tendencies at Corinth is to be found in Hellenistic Judaism's wisdom speculation is maintained by Birger A. Pearson, "Hellenistic-Jewish Wisdom Speculation and Paul," in *Aspects of Wisdom in Judaism and Early Christianity*, ed. Wilken, 43–66; and Richard A. Horsley, "Gnosis at Corinth: I Corinthians 8.1-6," *NTS* 27 (1979): 32–51.

203. Advocates for the hypothesis (with slight variations) include, among others, Bornkamm, *Paul*, 74–77, 244–46; Georgi, *The Opponents of Paul in Second Corinthians*, 9–18, 335; Marxsen, *Introduction to the NT*, 77–82; Fuller, *Introduction to the NT*, 46–49; and Koester, *Introduction to the NT*, 2:53–54, 126–30. For critique and rejection of the hypothesis, cf. Kümmel, *Introduction to the NT*, 287–93.

204. That the opponents of Paul in 2 Corinthians are different from those in 1 Corinthians has been maintained by various interpreters, e.g., C. K. Barrett, "Christianity at Corinth," *BJRL* 46 (1964): 269–97; Fuller, *Introduction to the NT*, 49–50; and Georgi, *The Opponents of Paul in Second Corinthians*, 317–19.

205. Bauer, *Orthodoxy and Heresy*, 101–2.

206. William R. Schoedel, "The Apostolic Fathers," in *The New Testament and Its Modern Interpreters*, ed. Eldon J. Epp and George W. MacRae (Philadelphia: Fortress

Press, 1989), 461, with references. The theology of this letter and its concerns have been treated in depth by Barbara E. Bowe, *Church in Crisis: Ecclesiology and Paraenesis in Clement of Rome*, HDR 23 (Minneapolis: Fortress Press, 1989), who interprets the letter primarily as an appeal to restore harmony and to seek the common good of the community in place of an individualism inspired by competing claims of spiritual gifts.

207. Quoted by Eusebius, *Hist. eccl.* 4.22.2.

208. Ibid., 4.23.1-7.

209. Ibid., 4.23.11.

210. Cf. Bornkamm, *Paul*, xii; and Becker, *Paul*, 31.

211. Cf. Betz, *Galatians*, 12.

212. Philippians and Philemon are assigned to an Ephesian imprisonment by Bornkamm, *Paul*, 241–42; and Koester, *Introduction to the NT*, 2:130–31. For a survey of other views, cf. Kümmel, *Introduction to the NT*, 324–32, 348–49.

213. Major interpreters who have adopted this view include T. W. Manson, "St. Paul's Letter to the Romans—And Others," *BJRL* 31 (1948): 224–40; reprinted in *The Romans Debate*, ed. Karl P. Donfried, rev. ed. (Peabody, Mass.: Hendrickson Publishers, 1991), 3–15; Bornkamm, *Paul*, 247; and Koester, *Introduction to the NT*, 2:138–39.

214. Cf. the remarks by Karl P. Donfried, "Introduction 1991: The Romans Debate since 1977," in *The Romans Debate*, ed. Donfried, lxx, and the discussion by Becker, *Paul*, 340–43.

215. Bornkamm, *Paul*, 86; Kümmel, *Introduction to the NT*, 480–81; Eduard Lohse, *Colossians and Philemon*, Hermeneia (Philadelphia: Fortress Press, 1971), 177–83; and Nils A. Dahl, "Ephesians," *IDBSup*, 268. Various theories concerning the collection of the Pauline letters into a corpus are surveyed by Harry Y. Gamble, *The New Testament Canon: Its Making and Meaning* (Philadelphia: Fortress Press, 1985), 36–46; and Bruce M. Metzger, *The Canon of the New Testament: Its Origin, Development, and Significance* (Oxford: Clarendon Press, 1987), 257–66.

5. The Shaping of
Normative Christianity

1. An important exception is the work of John A. T. Robinson, *Redating the New Testament* (Philadelphia: Westminster Press, 1976), who tries to place all of the books of the New Testament prior to A.D. 70. Among the various reviews that take Robinson's work to task is that of Robert M. Grant in *JBL* 97 (1978): 294–96.

2. For a survey of scholarly opinion, cf. Werner G. Kümmel, *Introduction to the New Testament*, rev. ed. (Nashville: Abingdon Press, 1975), 97–98.

3. Cf. Wayne A. Meeks and Robert L. Wilken, *Jews and Christians in Antioch in the First Four Centuries of the Christian Era*, SBLSBS 13 (Missoula, Mont.: Scholars Press, 1978), 13–15.

4. The viewpoint held here is that Acts 15 and Galatians 2 refer to the same course of events, seen from two perspectives, following Hans Dieter Betz, *Galatians*, Hermeneia (Philadelphia: Fortress Press, 1979), 81–83; John P. Meier, "Antioch,"

in *Antioch and Rome: New Testament Cradles of Catholic Christianity*, by Raymond E. Brown and John P. Meier (New York: Paulist Press, 1983), 36–37 (n. 86); Gerhard Krodel, *Acts*, ACNT (Minneapolis: Augsburg, 1986), 265–66; Hans Conzelmann, *Acts of the Apostles*, Hermeneia (Philadelphia: Fortress Press, 1987), 121; James D. G. Dunn, *Jesus, Paul, and the Law: Studies in Mark and Galatians* (Louisville: Westminster/John Knox Press, 1990), 159–60; and Dieter Lührmann, *Galatians: A Continental Commentary* (Minneapolis: Fortress Press, 1992), 24–25. That Galatians 2 narrates events prior to those in Acts 15 is maintained by F. F. Bruce, *The Acts of the Apostles*, 3d ed. (Grand Rapids, Mich.: Wm. B. Eerdmans, 1990), 331. That it narrates events after those in Acts 15 is the view of Paul J. Achtemeier, *The Quest for Unity in the New Testament Church: A Study in Paul and Acts* (Philadelphia: Fortress Press, 1987), 48, 58–61.

5. These are discussed in greater detail in three works from which the abbreviated summary here has been drawn: Meeks and Wilken, *Jews and Christians in Antioch*, 16–18; Meier, "Antioch," 36–44; and Krodel, *Acts*, 267–70.

6. Detailed analyses of events and the nature of the controversy can be found in studies by Dunn, *Jesus, Paul, and the Law*, 129–82; E. P. Sanders, "Jewish Association with Gentiles and Galatians 2:11-14," in *The Conversation Continues: Studies in Paul and John in Honor of J. Louis Martyn*, ed. Robert T. Fortna and Beverly R. Gaventa (Nashville: Abingdon Press, 1990), 170–88; and Paula Fredriksen, "Judaism, the Circumcision of Gentiles, and Apocalyptic Hope: Another Look at Galatians 1 and 2," *JTS* 42 (1991): 532–64.

7. Alan F. Segal, *Paul the Convert: The Apostolate and Apostasy of Saul the Pharisee* (New Haven: Yale Univ. Press, 1990), 231.

8. *Jub.* 22.16; *Joseph and Aseneth* 7.1; 3 Macc. 3:4; Jdt. 12:1-2; Tob. 1:10-12; and *Aristeas* 142. Cf. also Acts 10:28. These matters have been discussed by, among others, George F. Moore, *Judaism in the First Centuries of the Christian Era: The Age of the Tannaim*, 3 vols. (Cambridge: Harvard Univ. Press, 1927–30), 2:75; Dunn, *Jesus, Paul, and the Law*, 137–48; and Bengt Holmberg, "Sociologiska perspektiv på Gal 2:11-14 (21)," *SEÅ* 55 (1990): 71–92 (esp. 75–80).

9. Paul C. Böttger, "Paulus und Petrus in Antiochien: Zum Verständnis von Galater 2.11-21," *NTS* 37 (1991): 78–79.

10. D. J. Verseput, "Paul's Gentile Mission and the Jewish Christian Community: A Study of the Narrative in Galatians 1 and 2," *NTS* 39 (1993): 51–57.

11. Cf. James D. G. Dunn, *Unity and Diversity in the New Testament: An Inquiry into the Character of Earliest Christianity*, 2d ed. (Philadelphia: Trinity Press International, 1990), 254; Helmut Koester, *Introduction to the New Testament*, 2 vols. (Philadelphia: Fortress Press, 1982), 2:107; and Achtemeier, *Quest for Unity*, 59.

12. Meier, "Antioch," 40.

13. The depth of the distinction between church and synagogue is exemplified particularly in Matthean opposition to Pharisaic interpretations of the law (15:1-14; 23:23-24) and in the designations "their synagogues" (4:23; 9:35; 10:17; 12:9; 13:54; cf. 23:34) and "their scribes" (7:29), referring to the opposition of the evangelist's day, retrojected into the ministry of Jesus. On Matthew and the scribes and Pharisees, cf. Reinhart Hummel, *Die Auseinandersetzung zwischen Kirche und Judentum im Matthäusevangelium*, BEvT 33 (Munich: Kaiser Verlag, 1963), 12–18; Douglas R.

A. Hare, *The Theme of Jewish Persecution in the Gospel according to Matthew*, SNTSMS 6 (Cambridge: Cambridge Univ. Press, 1967), 85–96; Graham Stanton, "The Gospel of Matthew and Judaism," *BJRL* 66 (1984): 264–84; and J. Andrew Overman, *Matthew's Gospel and Formative Judaism: The Social World of the Matthean Community* (Minneapolis: Fortress Press, 1990), 115–17.

14. This view is widely held in critical scholarship, such as in the following works: Kümmel, *Introduction to the NT*, 119–20; Eduard Schweizer, *The Good News according to Matthew* (Atlanta: John Knox Press, 1975), 15–17; idem, "Matthew's Church," in *The Interpretation of Matthew*, ed. Graham Stanton, IRT 3 (Philadelphia: Fortress Press, 1983), 129; idem, *A Theological Introduction to the New Testament* (Nashville: Abingdon Press, 1991), 128–29; Koester, *Introduction to the NT*, 2:172; Meier, "Antioch," 15–27; Jack D. Kingsbury, *Matthew*, 2d ed., PC (Philadelphia: Fortress Press, 1986), 106; W. D. Davies and Dale C. Allison, *A Critical and Exegetical Commentary on the Gospel according to Saint Matthew*, 3 vols., ICC (Edinburgh: T. & T. Clark, 1988—), 1:127–47; Ulrich Luz, *Matthew 1–7: A Commentary* (Minneapolis: Fortress Press, 1989), 90–93; and Graham N. Stanton, *A Gospel for a New People: Studies in Matthew* (Edinburgh: T. & T. Clark, 1992), 378. Overman, *Matthew's Gospel*, 159, posits "a Galilean city, either Tiberias or Sepphoris, as the most plausible location for the Matthean community."

15. On Peter in the Gospel of Matthew, cf. Jack D. Kingsbury, "The Figure of Peter in Matthew's Gospel as a Theological Problem," *JBL* 98 (1979): 67–87; Overman, *Matthew's Gospel*, 136–40; and Reinhard Feldmeier, "The Portrayal of Peter in the Synoptic Gospels," in *The Gospel and the Gospels*, ed. Peter Stuhlmacher (Grand Rapids, Mich.: Wm. B. Eerdmans, 1991), 254. The postapostolic origin of Matt. 16:18 in Syria is maintained by Ulrich Luz, "The Primacy Text (Mt. 16:18)," *PSB* 12 (1991): 41–55. Thorough discussion of the arguments for and against authenticity, leaving the question open, is provided in Davies and Allison, *Saint Matthew*, 2:602–15.

16. Quoted from *The Nag Hammadi Library in English*, ed. James M. Robinson, 3d ed. (San Francisco: Harper & Row, 1988), 127–28.

17. Cf. R. McL. Wilson, *Studies in the Gospel of Thomas* (London: A. R. Mowbray, 1960), 111–12; and Michael Fieger, *Das Thomasevangelium: Einleitung, Kommentar, und Systematik*, NTAbh 22 (Münster: Aschendorff Verlag, 1991), 9, 66–71.

18. Quoted from *New Testament Apocrypha*, ed. Edgar Hennecke and Wilhelm Schneemelcher, 2 vols. (Philadelphia: Westminster Press, 1963–65), 2:464. Traditions of Thomas in Syrian sources are discussed by Richard Bauckham, *Jude and the Relatives of Jesus in the Early Church* (Edinburgh: T. & T. Clark, 1990), 32–36.

19. On matters of date for the *Gospel of Thomas*, see note 33 of chapter 2. Logion 13 of this Gospel actually presupposes the association of Peter and Matthew in the Matthean community, since it elevates Thomas above them. The claim for the primacy of Thomas over these other two apostles can hardly be explained otherwise. Cf. Fieger, *Thomasevangelium*, 66–71.

20. A list of "Q-Thomas Parallels" (utilizing some 78 verses in Q) is given in John Kloppenborg et al., *Q-Thomas Reader* (Sonoma, Calif.: Polebridge Press, 1990), 159.

21. These parallels are at Luke 5:39; 12:13-15; 12:16b-20; 12:49; 23:29 and, respectively, *Gos. Thom.* 47, 72, 63, 10, 79. In addition, the parable of the great banquet in *Gos. Thom.* 64 is more like that in Luke 14:15-24 than Matt. 22:1-10. It has been emphasized that when the *Gos. Thom.* has parallels to Q or to the triple tradition, generally the wording is closest to that of Luke. Cf. Wilson, *Studies in the Gospel of Thomas*, 45–88; and Bertil Gärtner, *The Theology of the Gospel of Thomas* (London: Collins, 1961), 66–68.

22. Although the *Gospel of Thomas* is often considered gnostic, it has been contended that even more it is "tinged with Encratism." So Henri-Charles Puech, "Gnostic Gospels and Related Documents," in *NT Apocrypha*, ed. Hennecke and Schneemelcher, 1:306. An Encratite character of this Gospel is also affirmed by Gilles Quispel, "The *Gospel of Thomas* Revisited," in *Colloque international sur les textes de Nag Hammadi*, ed. Bernard Barc (Quebec: Les Presses de l'Université Laval, 1981), 219, 234–36, 254–59.

23. Ignatius, *Eph.* 17.1; *Smyrn.* 1.1; 6.1; *Pol.* 1.3; 2.2. That Ignatius knew and used the Gospel of Matthew is the view of Édouard Massaux, *The Influence of the Gospel of Saint Matthew on Christian Literature before Saint Irenaeus: The First Ecclesiastical Writers*, NGS 5/1 (Macon, Ga.: Mercer Univ. Press, 1990), 85–96; and John P. Meier, "Matthew and Ignatius: A Response to William R. Schoedel," in *Social History of the Matthean Community: Cross-Disciplinary Approaches*, ed. David L. Balch (Minneapolis: Fortress Press, 1991), 178–86.

24. Cf. Helmut Koester, *Synoptische Überlieferung bei den apostolischen Vätern*, TU 65 (Berlin: Akademie Verlag, 1957), 24–61; and William R. Schoedel, *Ignatius of Antioch*, Hermeneia (Philadelphia: Fortress Press, 1985), 9; idem, "Ignatius and the Reception of the Gospel of Matthew in Antioch," in *Social History of the Matthean Community*, ed. Balch, 129–77; and Arthur J. Bellinzoni, "The Gospel of Matthew in the Second Century," *SC* 9 (1992): 206–7.

25. For the conventional dating of the Gospel of Matthew, see the works listed previously in note 14.

26. That the Matthean church was composed of both Jews and Gentiles has been contended by many interpreters, including Schweizer, *Matthew*, 237–38; Meier, "Antioch," 46–57; Luz, *Matthew 1-7*, 84–87; and Stanton, *Gospel for a New People*, 161, 379. Overman, *Matthew's Gospel*, 158, contends that the Matthean community was "mostly, if not thoroughly, Jewish but in the process of turning to the wider Gentile world."

27. Cf. further the essay, Arland J. Hultgren, "Things New and Old at Matthew 13:52," in *All Things New: Essays in Honor of Roy A. Harrisville*, ed. Arland J. Hultgren, Donald H. Juel, and Jack D. Kingsbury (*Word & World* Supplement Series 1, 1992), 109–17. Cf. also O. Lamar Cope, *Matthew: A Scribe Trained for the Kingdom of Heaven*, CBQMS 5 (Washington, D.C.: Catholic Biblical Association, 1976), 10 et passim; and David E. Orton, *The Understanding Scribe: Matthew and the Apocalyptic Ideal*, JSNTSup 25 (Sheffield: JSOT Press, 1989). The range of possible meanings of "old" and "new" other than that given here is presented in Davies and Allison, *Saint Matthew*, 2:447.

28. These are attested as follows: Christ 14 times, Lord 30 times, Son of God 17 times, Son of Man 31 times, and Son of David 8 times.

29. Jack D. Kingsbury, *Matthew: Structure, Christology, Kingdom* (Philadelphia: Fortress Press, 1975), 40–83; and James D. G. Dunn, *Christology in the Making: A New Testament Inquiry into the Origins of the Doctrine of the Incarnation* (Philadelphia: Westminster Press, 1980), 48; and Daniel J. Harrington, *The Gospel of Matthew*, SPS 1 (Collegeville, Minn.: Liturgical Press, 1991), 18.

30. Edward P. Blair, *Jesus in the Gospel of Matthew* (Nashville: Abingdon Press, 1960), 83.

31. Willoughby C. Allen, *A Critical and Exegetical Commentary on the Gospel according to S. Matthew*, ICC, 3d ed. (Edinburgh: T. & T. Clark, 1912), lxvi–lxvii; and Floyd V. Filson, *A Commentary on the Gospel according to St. Matthew*, HNTC, 2d ed. (New York: Harper & Row, 1971), 27–28.

32. Wolfgang Trilling, *Das wahre Israel: Studien zur Theologie des Matthäusevangeliums*, SANT 10, 3d ed. (Munich: Kösel Verlag, 1964), 21–51.

33. Gerhard Barth, "Matthew's Understanding of the Law," in *Tradition and Interpretation in Matthew*, by Günther Bornkamm, Gerhard Barth, and Heinz J. Held (Philadelphia: Westminster Press, 1963), 77. Cf. also Klyne R. Snodgrass, "Matthew's Understanding of the Law," *Int* 46 (1992): 368–78.

34. Birger Gerhardsson, *The Ethos of the Bible* (Philadelphia: Fortress Press, 1981), 44–45. Cf. also W. D. Davies, *The Setting of the Sermon on the Mount* (Cambridge: Cambridge Univ. Press, 1964), 428–31.

35. M. Jack Suggs, *Wisdom, Christology, and Law in Matthew's Gospel* (Cambridge: Harvard Univ. Press, 1970). According to Suggs, the Matthean Jesus is the "incarnation of Wisdom" (p. 130). Since, however, incarnation implies preexistence (a concept lacking in Matthew), it is better to say that for Matthew "Jesus 'incarnated,' or 'embodied,' God's wisdom," as does Reginald H. Fuller, "Christology in Matthew and Luke," in *Who Is This Christ? Gospel Christology and Contemporary Faith*, by Reginald H. Fuller and Pheme Perkins (Philadelphia: Fortress Press, 1983), 85.

36. The redemptive Christology of Matthew (and its distinctiveness) is discussed in Arland J. Hultgren, *Christ and His Benefits: Christology and Redemption in the New Testament* (Philadelphia: Fortress Press, 1987), 69–76.

37. Cf. Hans von Campenhausen, *Ecclesiastical Authority and Spiritual Power in the Church of the First Three Centuries* (Stanford: Stanford Univ. Press, 1969), 126; and Herbert Braun, *Jesus: Der Mann aus Nazareth und seine Zeit*, Themen der Theologie 1; 2d ed. (Stuttgart: Kreuz Verlag, 1969), 145.

38. Günther Bornkamm, "The Authority to 'Bind' and 'Loose' in the Church in Matthew's Gospel," in *The Interpretation of Matthew*, ed. Stanton, 85–97; Schweizer, *Matthew*, 371–72; and Richard H. Hiers, "'Binding' and 'Loosing': The Matthean Authorization," *JBL* 104 (1985): 233–50. Hiers writes that "Matthew may have intended his authorization to encompass not only matters of doctrine but also excommunication, and even determination of the ultimate destiny of church members" (p. 249).

39. The term is borrowed from Eduard Schweizer, *Church Order in the New Testament*, SBT 32 (Naperville, Ill.: Alec R. Allenson, 1961), 56; cf. Kingsbury, *Matthew*, 94.

40. The meaning of the passage is disputed. Do those to whom acts of kindness are to be done include any in need, or are they simply emissaries of Christ? For

discussion (with review of alternatives), see Hultgren, *Christ and His Benefits*, 231–32 (n. 44). Cf. also Schweizer, "Matthew's Church," 138–39; Gerhardsson, *The Ethos of the Bible*, 51–52; Stanton, *Gospel for a New People*, 207–31; and Douglas R. A. Hare, *Matthew* (Louisville: Westminster/John Knox Press, 1993), 288–91. A history of the interpretation of this passage has been written by Sherman W. Gray, *The Least of My Brothers: Matthew 25:31-46: A History of Interpretation*, SBLDS 114 (Atlanta: Scholars Press, 1989).

41. Ernst von Dobschütz, "Matthew as Rabbi and Catechist," in *The Interpretation of Matthew*, ed. Stanton, 25–26 (German ed. of essay, 1928); G. D. Kilpatrick, *The Origins of the Gospel according to St. Matthew* (Oxford: Clarendon Press, 1946), 135–37; Krister Stendahl, *The School of St. Matthew and Its Use of the Old Testament*, 2d ed. (Philadelphia: Fortress Press, 1968), 24–27, 29, 35.

42. Raymond E. Brown, *The Churches the Apostles Left Behind* (New York: Paulist Press, 1984), 134–35.

43. Kingsbury, *Matthew*, 105.

44. Cf. Schweizer, "Matthew's Church," 139; and Overman, *Matthew's Gospel*, 123. The Greek term translated here as "master" is *kathēgētēs* and is otherwise not found in the New Testament. It seems to have had the connotation of "school-teacher" in the New Testament era and is equivalent to "professor" in modern Greek. Cf. James H. Moulton and George Milligan, *The Vocabulary of the Greek Testament Illustrated from the Papyri and Other Non-Literary Sources* (Grand Rapids, Mich.: Wm. B. Eerdmans, 1949), 312.

45. Schweizer, "Matthew's Church," 140.

46. Ibid., 130–35; Overman, *Matthew's Church*, 113–24; and Graham N. Stanton, "The Communities of Matthew," *Int* 46 (1992): 384.

47. Cf. Cope, *Matthew: A Scribe Trained for the Kingdom of Heaven*, 10 et passim; and Davies and Allison, *Saint Matthew*, 2:445–46.

48. These matters are discussed in detail in Arland J. Hultgren, *1 and 2 Timothy, Titus*, ACNT (Minneapolis: Augsburg, 1984), 12–19.

49. The details are in ibid., 21–25.

50. On the basis of internal evidence within 2 Timothy alone (1:16–17; 4:6), and dispensing with other considerations, that letter would be assigned to Rome.

51. That the Pastorals were produced in Ephesus or Asia Minor is held by C. K. Barrett, *The Pastoral Epistles* (Oxford: Clarendon Press, 1963), 18–19; Kümmel, *Introduction to the NT*, 384–87; Koester, *Introduction to the NT*, 2:305; A. T. Hanson, *The Pastoral Epistles*, NCBC (Grand Rapids, Mich.: Wm. B. Eerdmans, 1982), 14; Jürgen Roloff, *Der erste Brief an Timotheus*, EKKNT 15 (Zurich: Benziger Verlag, 1988), 42–43; and J. Christiaan Beker, *Heirs of Paul: Paul's Legacy in the New Testament and in the Church Today* (Minneapolis: Fortress Press, 1991), 36–38. That the Pastorals were written from Rome, and were addressed to churches at Ephesus and Crete, as they claim to be, is the view of Jerome D. Quinn, *The Letter to Titus*, AB 35 (New York: Doubleday, 1990), 20–21. He posits A.D. 80–85 as their date of composition (p. 19). The traditional claim for Pauline authorship in Rome (ca. A.D. 61–64) is maintained by, among others, George W. Knight, *The Pastoral Epistles: A Commentary on the Greek Text*, NIGTC (Grand Rapids, Mich.: Wm. B. Eerdmans, 1992), 3–54.

Walter Bauer, *Orthodoxy and Heresy in Earliest Christianity* (Philadelphia: Fortress Press, 1971), 84, considers the Pastoral Epistles to exhibit Christianity at Ephesus at a stage later than the letters of Ignatius.

52. Cf. 1 Tim. 1:4-5; 2:10; 3:7; 4:12; 5:10, 23; 6:3, 6, 18; 2 Tim. 1:13; 2:22; 3:12, 16; Titus 1:18; 2:2-7, 12, 14; 3:2, 8.

53. Texts are cited in Str-B 4:467-70.

54. Hans Windisch, "Zur Christologie der Pastoralbriefe," *ZNW* 34 (1935): 213–21; and Hanson, *The Pastoral Epistles*, 40. Those who affirm that the Pastorals teach (or at least assume) preexistence include Barrett, *The Pastoral Epistles*, 25; and Reginald H. Fuller, *A Critical Introduction to the New Testament* (London: Gerald Duckworth, 1966), 134. That the author of the Pastorals expressed a Christology in terms of an "epiphany" that is functionally equivalent to preexistence and incarnation in the writings of Paul and John is maintained by I. Howard Marshall, "The Christology of the Pastoral Epistles," *SNTU* 13 (1988): 157–77.

55. "Lord" is used as a christological title at 1 Tim. 1:2, 12; 6:3, 14; 2 Tim. 1:2, 18a; 4:8.

56. For discussion of this contested verse, cf. Hultgren, *Christ and His Benefits*, 244–45 (n. 74).

57. Such distinctions are evident at 1 Tim. 1:1; 2:5-6; 5:21; 2 Tim. 4:1; Titus 1:4; 3:4-6.

58. For a survey and critique of various views, see Hultgren, *Christ and His Benefits*, 110–11.

59. Rudolf Bultmann, *Theology of the New Testament*, 2 vols. (New York: Charles Scribner's Sons, 1951–55), 2:183 (cf. 2:186).

60. Kümmel, *Introduction to the NT*, 384.

61. Cf. the discussion of Martin Dibelius and Hans Conzelmann, *The Pastoral Epistles*, Hermeneia (Philadelphia: Fortress Press, 1972), 50–51.

62. Ignatius, *Magn.* 6.1; *Trall.* 2.3; Hippolytus, *Apostolic Tradition* 9.

63. Schweizer, *Church Order in the New Testament*, 85; and apparently Quinn, *Titus*, 16. More recently Schweizer has suggested that "presbyter" might have been the actual title of an office, and that "bishop" might have been the presbyter's "functional designation"; *Theological Introduction to the NT*, 102.

64. *1 Clem.* 44.4–5; and Irenaeus, *Adv. Haer.* 3.3.4; 4.26.2.

65. Dibelius and Conzelmann, *The Pastoral Epistles*, 54–57; Barrett, *The Pastoral Epistles*, 32; Hanson, *The Pastoral Epistles*, 32–33; and Roloff, *Timotheus*, 176. The picture has been altered in the work of Kevin Giles, *Patterns of Ministry among the First Christians* (San Francisco: HarperCollins, 1991), 38–40, 85–89. He suggests that a bishop was the leader of a house church, and that the council of elders (presbyters), made up of bishops and other elders, was the overseeing unit of a city.

66. The views are summarized, with references, in Hultgren, *1 and 2 Timothy, Titus*, 74–75 (and notes 15–18, p. 184). In addition to those listed there, Susanne Heine, *Women and Early Christianity: A Reappraisal* (Minneapolis: Augsburg, 1988), 136, maintains also that the passage refers to female deacons.

67. The important role of widows in offering intercessory prayer is referred to by Polycarp, *Phil.* 4.3.

68. The term *office* is used by Heine, *Women and Early Christianity*, 136–37, and *order* by Bonnie Bowman Thurston, *The Widows: A Woman's Ministry in the Early Church* (Philadelphia: Fortress Press, 1989), 36–55, who also summarizes other scholarship.

69. Ignatius, *Smyrn.* 13.1; *Pol.* 4.1; Polycarp, *Phil.* 4.3. Thurston, *Widows*, 92–105, presents material on widows from the third century.

70. Cf. 1 Tim. 1:4-6; 4:1-2, 7; 6:4, 15, 20; 2 Tim. 2:14-17, 23; 3:2-6, 13; 4:3-4; Titus 1:11, 14-16; 3:9.

71. The heretical teachings are discussed by, among others, Barrett, *The Pastoral Epistles*, 12–18; Robert J. Karris, "The Background and Significance of the Polemic of the Pastoral Epistles," *JBL* 92 (1973): 549–64; and Roloff, *Timotheus*, 228–39.

72. R. McL. Wilson, *Gnosis and the New Testament* (Philadelphia: Fortress Press, 1968), 41–44; Frederik Wisse, "Prolegomena to the Study of the New Testament and Gnosis," in *The New Testament and Gnosis: Essays in Honour of Robert McL. Wilson*, ed. A. H. B. Logan and A. J. M. Wedderburn (Edinburgh: T. & T. Clark, 1983), 142–43; Kurt Rudolph, *Gnosis: The Nature and History of Gnosticism* (San Francisco: Harper & Row, 1983), 302–3; Roloff, *Timotheus*, 234; and idem, "Der Kampf gegen die Irrlehrer: Wie geht man miteinander um?" *BK* 46 (1991): 114–20.

73. Quoted from *NHLE*, 56. In the introduction to this text, Malcolm M. Peel considers the document to have been composed by a Valentinian Gnostic late in the second century (pp. 52–53).

74. A similar approach has been taken by Margaret Y. MacDonald, *The Pauline Churches: A Socio-historical Study of Institutionalization in the Pauline and Deutero-Pauline Writings*, SNTSMS 60 (Cambridge: Cambridge Univ. Press, 1988), 229–34.

75. Of course the gnostic interpretation of Paul was still only in its infancy and would flourish later, especially in the works of Valentinians, as demonstrated by Elaine H. Pagels, *The Gnostic Paul: Gnostic Exegesis of the Pauline Letters* (Philadelphia: Fortress Press, 1975).

76. On the opposition at Ephesus, cf. Schoedel, *Ignatius of Antioch*, 58–60, 65.

77. Kümmel, *Introduction to the NT*, 246; Oscar Cullmann, *The Johannine Circle* (Philadelphia: Westminster Press, 1976), 95–99; Raymond E. Brown, *The Community of the Beloved Disciple* (New York: Paulist Press, 1979), 23; Koester, *Introduction to the NT*, 2:185; idem, *Ancient Christian Gospels: Their History and Development* (Philadelphia: Trinity Press International, 1990), 267; D. Moody Smith, *John*, 2d ed., PC (Philadelphia: Fortress Press, 1986), 76; Martin Hengel, *The Johannine Question* (Philadelphia: Trinity Press International, 1989), 80–81; Schweizer, *Theological Introduction to the NT*, 152; and John Painter, *The Quest for the Messiah: The History, Literature and Theology of the Johannine Community* (Edinburgh: T. & T. Clark, 1991), 45–55. A slightly earlier date (ca. A.D. 80) is suggested by Robert Kysar, *John*, ACNT (Minneapolis: Augsburg, 1986), 15–16.

78. Kümmel, *Introduction to the NT*, 445, 452; Brown, *Community*, 23, 97; and Stephen S. Smalley, *1, 2, 3 John*, WBC (Waco, Tex.: Word Books, 1984), xxxii.

79. Major proposals include those of J. Louis Martyn, "Glimpses into the History of the Johannine Community," in his *The Gospel of John in Christian History: Essays for Interpreters* (New York: Paulist Press, 1979), 90–121; Brown, *Community*, 22–24, 166–

67; and Kysar, *John*, 14–15. Other proposals are surveyed by Brown, *Community*, 171–82.

80. This important insight into the background of the Gospel of John has been pioneered by J. Louis Martyn, *History and Theology in the Fourth Gospel*, rev. ed. (Nashville: Abingdon Press, 1979), 50–62. The first edition was published in 1968 (New York: Harper & Row). The texts of the Babylonian and Palestinian recensions of the *Shemonah Esreh* are printed (along with discussion) in Emil Schürer, *The History of the Jewish People in the Age of Jesus Christ (175 B.C.–A.D. 135)*, rev. Geza Vermes, Fergus Millar, and Martin Goodman, 3 vols. (Edinburgh: T. & T. Clark, 1973–87), 2:454–63. For discussion of this text, cf. William Horbury, "The Benediction of the *Minim* and Early Jewish-Christian Controversy," *JTS* 33 (1982): 19–61.

81. Brown, *Community*, 95–96; idem, *The Epistles of John*, AB 30 (Garden City, N.Y.: Doubleday, 1982), 19–30; and Smalley, *1, 2, 3 John*, xxii. Cf. also the earlier works of Willi Marxsen, *Introduction to the New Testament* (Philadelphia: Fortress Press, 1968), 264, 269; and Rudolf Bultmann, *The Johannine Epistles*, Hermeneia (Philadelphia: Fortress Press, 1973), 1. That 2 and 3 John were written by someone other than the author of 1 John is maintained by Judith Lieu, *The Second and Third Epistles of John: History and Background* (Edinburgh: T. & T. Clark, 1986). Common authorship of the Gospel and Epistles of John is maintained, however, by Kümmel, *Introduction to the NT*, 442–45, 449–51.

82. C. H. Dodd, *The Interpretation of the Fourth Gospel* (Cambridge: Cambridge Univ. Press, 1953), 3–9, 444–53; Rudolf Schnackenburg, *The Gospel according to St. John*, 3 vols. (New York: Herder & Herder, Seabury, Crossroad, 1968–82), 1:149–52; Raymond E. Brown, *The Gospel according to John*, AB 29–29A (Garden City, N.Y.: Doubleday, 1966–70), 1:lxxx–lxxxvi, ciii–civ; C. K. Barrett, *The Gospel according to St. John*, 2d ed. (Philadelphia: Westminster Press, 1978), 123–34; Smalley, *1, 2, 3 John*, xxxii; and Hengel, *The Johannine Question*, 80–81.

83. Kümmel, *Introduction to the NT*, 246–47; and Koester, *Introduction to the NT*, 2:185.

84. Martyn, "Glimpses into the History of the Johannine Community," 115–21; Brown, *Community*, 90; and Kysar, *John*, 163.

85. Floyd V. Filson, "The Significance of the Early House Churches," *JBL* 58 (1939): 110. The possibility of an overlap of Pauline and Johannine forms of Christianity at Ephesus is discussed by Rudolf Schnackenburg, "Ephesus: Entwicklung einer Gemeinde von Paulus zu Johannes," *BZ* 35 (1991): 41–64.

86. Although Jesus is accused of making himself equal to God in the Gospel of John (5:18; cf. 10:33), the Son is subordinate to the Father (14:28). This is explored in detail by C. K. Barrett, " 'The Father Is Greater than I': John 14:28, Subordinationist Christology in the New Testament," in his *Essays on John* (Philadelphia: Westminster Press, 1982), 19–36.

87. Data on these titles is presented in Hultgren, *Christ and His Benefits*, 146, 156 (and notes).

88. Ibid., 147 (references in notes 15 and 16, p. 255).

89. Ernst Haenchen, *John*, Hermeneia, 2 vols. (Philadelphia: Fortress Press, 1984), 1:96.

90. The term is borrowed from C. K. Barrett, "Christocentric or Theocentric? Observations on the Theological Method of the Fourth Gospel," in his *Essays on John*, 8; idem, *St. John*, 72–73. Cf. also Schnackenburg, *St. John*, 2:185.

91. Bultmann, *Theology of the NT*, 2:10–14. Bultmann describes the so-called Gnostic Redeemer Myth at 1:66–67; and idem, *Primitive Christianity in Its Contemporary Setting* (Cleveland: World Publishing Company, 1956), 163–64.

92. This point has been emphasized by Carsten Colpe, *Die religionsgeschichtliche Schule: Darstellung und Kritik ihres Bildes vom gnostischen Erlösermythos*, FRLANT 78 (Göttingen: Vandenhoeck & Ruprecht, 1961); and Rudolph, *Gnosis*, 121–31.

93. Cf. the guarded estimation of Wilson, *Gnosis and the NT*, 45–58.

94. Cf. Brown, *John*, 1:lii–lvi.

95. The scholarship on this point is impressive and cannot be reviewed in detail here. Much of it is summarized and furthered by the work of Rodney A. Whitacre, *Johannine Polemic: The Role of Tradition and Theology*, SBLDS 67 (Chico, Calif.: Scholars Press, 1982).

96. Brown, *Community*, 67.

97. Martyn, *History and Theology*, 72, 78–81; idem, "Glimpses into the History of the Johannine Community," 104–5.

98. The background of John 5:18 and related passages is discussed by Wayne A. Meeks, "Equal to God," in *The Conversation Continues*, ed. Fortna and Gaventa, 309–21.

99. Gerhardsson, *The Ethos of the Bible*, 98, 110.

100. Schweizer, *Church Order in the New Testament*, 124; and Brown, *The Churches the Apostles Left Behind*, 90–94.

101. Ernst Käsemann, *The Testament of Jesus: A Study of the Gospel of John in Light of Chapter 17* (Philadelphia: Fortress Press, 1968), 73.

102. Cf. Marinus de Jonge, "Variety and Development in Johannine Christology," in his *Jesus: Stranger from Heaven and Son of God: Jesus Christ and the Christians in Johannine Perspective*, SBLSBS 11 (Missoula, Mont.: Scholars Press, 1977), 200–206; and Brown, *Community*, 109–35.

103. Harald Riesenfeld, "*Peri*," TDNT 6:55.

104. Present and future aspects of eschatology in the letters are discussed further by Brown, *The Epistles of John*, 99–100; and idem, *Community*, 135–38.

105. That perfectionist self-understanding was a major contributor to the sectarianism of the Johannine community is the thesis of John Bogart, *Orthodox and Heretical Perfectionism in the Johannine Community as Evident in the First Epistle of John*, SBLDS 33 (Missoula, Mont.: Scholars Press, 1977).

106. Karl P. Donfried, "Ecclesiastical Authority in 2–3 John," in *L'Évangile de Jean: Sources, rédaction, théologie*, ed. Marinus de Jonge, BETL 44 (Gembloux: Duculot, 1977), 325–33; Brown, *The Epistles of John*, 650–51; and Smalley, *1, 2, 3 John*, 317.

107. Brown, *Community*, 151–55, 167; and Smalley, *1, 2, 3 John*, xxx–xxxi.

108. Gnostic interpretations of the Fourth Gospel are explored by J. N. Sanders, *The Fourth Gospel in the Early Church* (Cambridge: Cambridge Univ. Press, 1943), 47–66; Maurice F. Wiles, *The Spiritual Gospel: The Interpretation of the Fourth Gospel in the Early Church* (Cambridge: Cambridge Univ. Press, 1960), 96–111; and Elaine H.

Pagels, *The Johannine Gospel in Gnostic Exegesis: Heracleon's Commentary on John*, SBLMS 17 (Nashville: Abingdon Press, 1973).

109. Brown, *Community*, 155–62, 167; and Smalley, *1, 2, 3 John*, xxxi–xxxii.

110. The parallels are demonstrated by Bruce M. Metzger, *The Canon of the New Testament: Its Origins, Development, and Significance* (Oxford: Clarendon Press, 1987), 46–48.

111. Christian Maurer, *Ignatius von Antioch und das Johannesevangelium* (Zurich: Zwingli Verlag, 1949); and Robert M. Grant, *After the New Testament* (Philadelphia: Fortress Press, 1967), 41.

112. Cf. Schoedel, *Ignatius of Antioch*, 9.

113. Irenaeus, *Adv. Haer.* 3.11.8; cf. also 3.1.1–2.

114. A date of ca. A.D. 200 (and discussions concerning alternatives) is posited for this document by Harry Y. Gamble, *The New Testament Canon: Its Making and Meaning* (Philadelphia: Fortress Press, 1985), 32; and Metzger, *Canon of the NT*, 194.

115. The popularity of the *Diatessaron* is demonstrated by Bruce M. Metzger, *The Early Versions of the New Testament: Their Origin, Transmission, and Limitations* (Oxford: Clarendon Press, 1977), 10–25.

116. Cf. Irenaeus, *Adv. Haer.* 3.2.2—3.5.1.

117. The evidence for the use of apostles and other disciples of Jesus as authorities in various gnostic Christian documents is surveyed by Pheme Perkins, *The Gnostic Dialogue: The Early Church and the Crisis of Gnosticism* (New York: Paulist Press, 1980), 113–56; and Douglas M. Parrott, "Gnostic and Orthodox Disciples in the Second and Third Centuries," in *Nag Hammadi, Gnosticism, and Early Christianity*, ed. Charles W. Hedrick and Robert Hodgson, Jr. (Peabody, Mass: Hendrickson Publishers, 1986), 193–219. Ways in which various writers (Papias, Gnostics, and others) appealed to ancient and apostolic authorities is surveyed by Hans von Campenhausen, *The Formation of the Christian Bible* (Philadelphia: Fortress Press, 1972), 129–42.

6. The Limits to Diversity

1. Such is the view of major interpreters of Acts: Johannes Munck, *The Acts of the Apostles*, AB 31 (Garden City, N.Y.: Doubleday, 1967), 56; Ernst Haenchen, *The Acts of the Apostles: A Commentary* (Philadelphia: Westminster Press, 1971), 264; and F. F. Bruce, *The Acts of the Apostles*, 3d ed. (Grand Rapids, Mich.: Wm. B. Eerdmans, 1990), 185. Cf. also Eduard Schweizer, *Church Order in the New Testament*, SBT 32 (Naperville, Ill.: Alec R. Allenson, 1961), 47.

2. Ceslas Spicq, "L'épître aux Hébreux: Apollos, Jean-Baptiste, les Hellénistes et Qumrân," *RevQ* 1 (1958–59): 365–90.

3. Cf. Hans Conzelmann, *Acts of the Apostles*, Hermeneia (Philadelphia: Fortress Press, 1987), 46.

4. Justin, *Apology* 1.26; 1.56; 2.15; Irenaeus, *Adv. Haer.* 1.23.1-4; Hippolytus, *Ref.* 6.2–15; 10.8; Origen, *Contra Celsum* 1.57; *Ps. Clem. H.* 2.22-25; and Epiphanius, *Panarion* 21.

5. Irenaeus, *Adv. Haer.* 1.23.2. Epiphanius, *Panarion* 26.1.1, however, claims that the Gnostics "sprout from Nicolaus like fruit from a dunghill," referring to the Nicolaus of Acts 6:5, who is then (perhaps wrongly) considered the originator of the Nicolaitans of Rev. 2:6, 14-15. The issues are discussed by Adolf von Harnack, "The Sect of the Nicolaitans and Nicolaus, the Deacon in Jerusalem," *JR* 3 (1923): 413–22. Doubt about the origin of the Nicolaitans from Nicolaus of Acts is expressed by Robert M. Grant, *Gnosticism: A Source Book of Heretical Writings from the Early Christian Period* (New York: Harper & Brothers, 1961), 43.

6. Oscar Cullmann, *The Johannine Circle* (Philadelphia: Westminster Press, 1976), 46–49, 57; and Raymond E. Brown, *The Community of the Beloved Disciple* (New York: Paulist Press, 1979), 35–40, 48, 56, 77.

7. Cf. C. K. Barrett, *A Commentary on the First Epistle to the Corinthians*, HNTC (New York: Harper & Row, 1968), 43; Birger A. Pearson, "Hellenistic-Jewish Wisdom Speculation and Paul," in *Aspects of Wisdom in Judaism and Early Christianity*, ed. Robert L. Wilken (Notre Dame: Univ. of Notre Dame Press, 1975), 59; and C. Wilfred Griggs, *Early Egyptian Christianity: From Its Origins to 451 C.E.*, CS 2 (Leiden: E. J. Brill, 1990), 16–17.

8. On the "God-fearers," see the extensive data and treatment in Emil Schürer, *The History of the Jewish People in the Age of Jesus Christ (175 B.C.–A.D. 135)*, rev. Geza Vermes, Fergus Millar, and Martin Goodman, 3 vols. (Edinburgh: T. & T. Clark, 1973–87), 3/1:150–76 (especially pp. 160–72); and John G. Gager, "Jews, Gentiles and Synagogues in the Book of Acts," *HTR* 79 (1986): 91–99.

9. References to inscriptions are made in essays by K. G. Kuhn and H. Stegemann, "Proselyten," *PWSup* 9:1248–83; M. J. Mellink, "Archaeology in Asia Minor," *AJA* 81/3 (1977): 305–6; and Gager, "Jews," 97–98. Gager and (revised) Schürer, *History of the Jewish People*, 3/1:25–26, cite the important evidence of synagogue inscriptions from ancient Aphrodisias, which has been published subsequently in the book by Joyce M. Reynolds and Robert Tannenbaum, *Jews and God-Fearers at Aphrodisias: Greek Inscriptions with Commentary*, CPSSV 12 (Cambridge: Cambridge Philological Society, 1987). Cf. also Robert F. Tannenbaum, "Jews and God-Fearers in the Holy City of Aphrodite," *BAR* 12/5 (1986): 54–57; and the comprehensive treatment by Paul R. Trebilco, *Jewish Communities in Asia Minor*, SNTSMS 69 (Cambridge: Cambridge Univ. Press, 1991), 145–66; he concludes from both inscriptions and literary references that God-fearers existed in at least some synagogues of Asia Minor in the first five centuries A.D. For critique of earlier views, cf. A. Thomas Kraabel, "The Disappearance of the 'God-Fearers,'" *Numen* 28 (1981): 113–26, and a response to his essay by J. Andrew Overman, "The God-Fearers: Some Neglected Features," *JSNT* 32 (1988): 17–26. For support of the view that Paul evangelized among God-fearers, cf. Arland J. Hultgren, *Paul's Gospel and Mission: The Outlook from His Letter to the Romans* (Philadelphia: Fortress Press, 1985), 137–45; Etienne Trocmé, "The Jews as Seen by Paul and Luke," in *To See Ourselves as Others See Us*, ed. Jacob Neusner and Ernest S. Frerichs (Chico, Calif.: Scholars Press, 1985), 159; and Karl P. Donfried, "1 Thessalonians, Acts and the Early Paul," in *The Thessalonian Correspondence*, ed. Raymond F. Collins, BETL 87 (Louvain: Leuven Univ. Press, 1990), 22.

10. Jacob Jervell, "The Church of Jews and Godfearers," in *Luke-Acts and the Jewish People: Eight Critical Perspectives,* ed. Joseph B. Tyson (Minneapolis: Augsburg, 1988), 11–20.

11. Still useful on the gentile backgrounds of early Christianity is the work of Arthur Darby Nock, *Early Gentile Christianity and Its Hellenistic Background* (New York: Harper & Row, 1964).

12. A major study in this area is by Gerd Lüdemann, *Untersuchungen zur simonianischen Gnosis,* GTA 1 (Göttingen: Vandenhoeck & Ruprecht, 1975).

13. Gerd Lüdemann, "The Acts of the Apostles and the Beginnings of Simonian Gnosticism," *NTS* 33 (1987): 420–26; and Jarl Fossum, "Sects and Movements," in *The Samaritans,* ed. Alan D. Crown (Tübingen: J. C. B. Mohr [Paul Siebeck], 1989), 360–61.

14. Eusebius, *Hist. eccl.* 4.7.1–15; Epiphanius, *Panarion* 26.

15. These include Adolf von Harnack, *History of Dogma,* 7 vols. (Boston: Little, Brown, & Company, 1898–1902), 1:226–28; Nock, *Early Gentile Christianity,* xiii–xvii; idem, "Gnosticism," *HTR* 57 (1964): 275; Edwin M. Yamauchi, *Pre-Christian Gnosticism: A Survey of the Proposed Evidences,* 2d ed. (Grand Rapids, Mich.: Baker Book House, 1983); Simone Pétrement, *A Separate God: The Christian Origins of Gnosticism* (San Francisco: Harper & Row, 1990), 4 et passim; and Giovanni Filoramo, *A History of Gnosticism* (Cambridge, Mass.: Basil Blackwell, 1990), 2, 147–52, 157–59. The history of modern scholarship is surveyed by Kurt Rudolph, *Gnosis: The Nature and History of Gnosticism* (San Francisco: Harper & Row, 1983), 30–34.

16. Robert M. Grant, *Gnosticism and Early Christianity,* rev. ed. (New York: Harper & Row, 1966), 39; Rudolph, *Gnosis,* 277–82; Petr Pokorný, "Der sociale Hintergrund der Gnosis," in *Gnosis und Neues Testament: Studien aus Religionswissenschaft und Theologie,* ed. Karl-Wolfgang Tröger (Gütersloh: Gerd Mohn, 1973), 78; George W. MacRae, "Nag Hammadi and the New Testament," in *Gnosis: Festschrift für Hans Jonas,* ed. Barbara Aland (Göttingen: Vandenhoeck & Ruprecht, 1978), 150; Birger A. Pearson, "Early Christianity and Gnosticism: A Review Essay," *RSR* 13 (1987): 6; idem, "Jewish Elements in Gnosticism and the Development of Gnostic Self-Definition," in *Jewish and Christian Self-Definition,* ed. E. P. Sanders et al., 3 vols. (Philadelphia: Fortress Press, 1980–82), 1:151–52; Gilles Quispel, "Gnosticism from Its Origins to the Middle Ages," *EncRel* 5:567; and Henry A. Green, *The Economic and Social Origins of Gnosticism,* SBLDS 77 (Atlanta: Scholars Press, 1985), 174–210. For a survey of scholarship into the early 1970s, cf. Robert McL. Wilson, " 'Jewish Gnosis' and Gnostic Origins: A Survey," *HUCA* 45 (1974): 177–89.

17. Grant, *Gnosticism and Early Christianity,* 39; and Rudolph, *Gnosis,* 277.

18. Pokorný, "Der sociale Hintergrund der Gnosis," 78; MacRae, "Nag Hammadi and the New Testament," 150; and Quispel, "Gnosticism from Its Origins," 567.

19. Willem C. van Unnik, "Gnosis und Judentum," in *Gnosis,* ed. Aland, 65–86.

20. The view that the origins of Gnosticism can be found in influences from oriental philosophical and religious traditions (Persian and Babylonian) which developed in Hellenism is expressed by Wilhelm Bousset, *Kyrios Christos* (Nashville: Abingdon Press, 1970; 1st German ed., 1913), 245; Richard Reitzenstein, *Hellenistic Mystery-Religions: Their Basic Ideas and Significance,* PTMS 15 (Pittsburgh: Pickwick

Press, 1978; 1st German ed., 1910), 66–67; Rudolf Bultmann, *Primitive Christianity in Its Contemporary Setting* (Cleveland: World Publishing Company, 1956), 162; and Geo Widengren, *The Gnostic Attitude* (Santa Barbara, Calif.: Institute of Religious Studies, Univ. of California, 1973).

21. Hans Jonas, *The Gnostic Religion: The Message of the Alien God and the Beginnings of Christianity*, 2d ed. (Boston: Beacon Press, 1963), 34.

22. Hans Jonas, "Delimitation of the Gnostic Phenomenon—Typological and Historical," in *Le Origini dello Gnosticismo*, ed. Ugo Bianchi, SHR 12 (Leiden: E. J. Brill, 1967), 103.

23. The stages suggested here are based on those of Pheme Perkins, "Gnosticism as a Christian Heresy," *EncRel* 5:578–80.

24. The term *incipient Gnosticism* is used by, among others, Robert McL. Wilson, *Gnosis and the New Testament* (Philadelphia: Fortress Press, 1968), 30–32.

25. Eusebius, *Hist. eccl.* 4.22.5. A shorter list from earlier times is given by Justin, *Dialogue with Trypho*, 35.

26. A major English translation of Book I (Sects 1–46) of three books is *The Panarion of Epiphanius of Salamis*, trans. Frank Williams, NHS 35 (Leiden: E. J. Brill, 1987). Epiphanius dealt with eighty sects altogether in his three books, but not all are Christian heresies.

27. This figure is given by Quispel, "Gnosticism from Its Origins," 5:570.

28. Major works in which the search takes place are Friedrich Schleiermacher, *On Religion: Speeches to Its Cultured Despisers* (New York: Harper & Brothers, 1958; 1st German ed., 1799); Ludwig Feuerbach, *The Essence of Christianity* (New York: Harper & Brothers, 1957; 1st German ed., 1841); Ernst Troeltsch, *The Absoluteness of Christianity and the History of Religions* (Richmond: John Knox Press, 1971; 1st German ed., 1902); and Adolf von Harnack, *What Is Christianity?* (New York: G. P. Putnam's Sons, 1901; reprinted, Philadelphia: Fortress Press, 1986; 1st German ed., 1900). A more recent attempt along these lines, and including review and critique of the above and other writers, is that of Stephen Sykes, *The Identity of Christianity: Theologians and the Essence of Christianity from Schleiermacher to Barth* (Philadelphia: Fortress Press, 1984).

29. Harnack, *What Is Christianity?* 10–18, 51, 56, 63–74.

30. This theme has been developed in particular by Gerhard Ebeling, "Jesus and Faith," in his *Word and Faith* (Philadelphia: Fortress Press, 1963), 201–46 (esp. pp. 235–36); and Willi Marxsen, *The Beginnings of Christology: A Study in Its Problems*, FBBS 22 (Philadelphia: Fortress Press, 1969), 20, 44–57.

31. Cf. Matt. 19:19; Rom. 8:28; 1 Cor. 2:9; 8:3; James 1:12; 2:5; and 1 John 4:20-21; 5:2.

32. Among the many references that can be given are the following: Mark 11:22; Rom. 1:17; 4:12-20; 1 Cor. 13:13; Gal. 2:16-20; 1 Thess. 1:8; Eph. 1:15; 2:8; Col. 1:4; Heb. 6:1; 11:1-39; and 1 Peter 1:29.

33. Love for others appears as the central moral teaching across the New Testament canon. To the references already given can be added, among others, John 13:34; 15:12, 17; Rom. 13:8-10; 1 Cor. 13:13; Gal. 5:14; 1 Thess. 4:9; Heb. 10:24; James 2:8; 1 Peter 1:22; 2:17; 1 John 3:11, 23; 4:7, 19-21; Jude 2; and Rev.

2:19. On the subject, cf. Birger Gerhardsson, *The Ethos of the Bible* (Philadelphia: Fortress Press, 1981), 122–24.

34. Passages on trustworthiness include Matt. 25:21-23 par.; 1 Cor. 4:2, 17; Eph. 1:1; 1 Tim. 1:12; and 1 Peter 5:12.

35. Robert L. Wilken, "Diversity and Unity in Early Christianity," *SC* 1 (1981): 106–7.

36. Ibid., 107.

37. Ibid., 108.

38. Ibid., 110.

39. Tertullian, *Adv. Marc.* 1.21; quoted from *Tertullian Adversus Marcionem*, ed. and trans. Ernest Evans, 2 vols. (Oxford: Clarendon Press, 1972), 1:55. Subsequent quotations from Tertullian's work against Marcion will be from this version. According to Evans, this work by Tertullian was completed in its first edition in A.D. 198, the second between 207 and 208. Tertullian makes a similar statement in his *De Praesc. Haer.* 34.

40. Irenaeus, *Adv. Haer.* 1.26.2; Hippolytus, *Ref.* 7.22.

41. Hippolytus, *Ref.* 8.13.

42. Ibid., 8.12.

43. Adolf von Harnack, *Marcion: The Gospel of the Alien God* (Durham, N.C.: Labyrinth Press, 1990), 2–3, 10–12, 19, 147–48 (n. 5); E. C. Blackman, *Marcion and His Influence* (London: SPCK, 1948), 1, 86–87; W. H. C. Frend, "Marcion," *ExpTim* 80 (1969): 328–32; and Robert L. Wilken, "Marcion," *EncRel* 9:195.

44. Gnostic allegorical interpretation is discussed by Robert M. Grant, *The Letter and the Spirit* (New York: Macmillan, 1957), 25, 66–73.

45. This latter point of view has been suggested by David S. Williams, "Reconsidering Marcion's Gospel," *JBL* 108 (1989): 477–96.

46. Illustrations of the work of Marcion are provided by Robert M. Grant, *Heresy and Criticism: The Search for Authenticity in Early Christian Literature* (Louisville: Westminster/John Knox Press, 1993), 33–47.

47. Irenaeus, *Adv. Haer.* 1.23.2; cf. also *Ps. Clem. H.* 22.2.

48. Irenaeus, *Adv. Haer.* 1.23.5; Epiphanius, *Panarion* 22; Eusebius, *Hist. eccl.* 3.26.1.

49. Justin, *Apology* 1.26; 1.56.

50. Eusebius, *Hist. eccl.* 3.26.3.

51. Acts 8:10 portrays Simon as having a following, prior to his baptism, who hail him as the "Great Power of God," an honorific title for a "divine man" figure or even an emanation from the highest God. The likelihood of his being a Gnostic prior to his contact with Christianity is affirmed also by Jonas, *The Gnostic Religion*, 103; Wilson, *Gnosis and the New Testament*, 2; Johannes Quasten, *Patrology*, 4 vols. (Westminster, Md.: Christian Classics, 1983–86), 1:254–55; Lüdemann, "The Acts of the Apostles and the Beginnings of Simonian Gnosticism," 420–26; and Fossum, "Sects and Movements," 357–89.

52. Irenaeus, *Adv. Haer.* 1.23.5; Epiphanius, *Panarion* 22.1.2.

53. Quasten, *Patrology*, 1:256.

54. For this figure, known by both names, "Saturninus" is adopted, which is the preference in *The Oxford Dictionary of the Christian Church*, 2d ed., ed. F. L. Cross and E. A. Livingstone (London: Oxford Univ. Press, 1974), 1238.

55. Irenaeus, *Adv. Haer.* 1.24.1–2.

56. Ibid., 1.24.1; cf. Hippolytus, *Ref.* 7.16; and Epiphanius, *Panarion* 23.

57. Irenaeus, *Adv. Haer.* 1.25.1.

58. Ibid., 1.26.1; Hippolytus, *Ref.* 7.21; 10.17.

59. Hippolytus, *Ref.* 7.26; 10.16; Epiphanius, *Panarion* 44.

60. On Basilides, cf. Irenaeus, *Adv. Haer.* 1.24.3; Epiphanius, *Panarion* 24; on Valentinus and his followers, cf. Irenaeus, *Adv. Haer.* 1.1.1–8. Their systems are discussed by Rudolph, *Gnosis*, 309–13, 317–25.

61. On Basilides, cf. Irenaeus, *Adv. Haer.* 1.24.4; Epiphanius, *Panarion* 24; on Valentinus and his followers, cf. Irenaeus, *Adv. Haer.* 1.1.5.

62. Irenaeus, *Adv. Haer.* 1.1.5; Hippolytus, *Ref.* 6.28.

63. Irenaeus, *Adv. Haer.* 1.27.2; Hippolytus, *Ref.* 7.17; Tertullian, *Adv. Marc.* 1.11 and 1.19. Marcion's theology is discussed by Rudolph, *Gnosis*, 313–16.

64. Tertullian, *Adv. Marc.* 1.6.

65. Hippolytus, *Ref.* 7.17; Tertullian, *Adv. Marc.* 1.2.

66. Tertullian, *Adv. Marc.* 1.6.

67. Ibid., 1.19.

68. Eusebius, *Hist. eccl.* 4.11.9; 5.16.21; Epiphanius, *Panarion* 42.3.1–2.

69. *Tri. Trac.* 112.20–35, *NHLE* 91; *Gos. Eg.* 63.4–25, *NHLE* 216.

70. Major studies here are those of Alan F. Segal, *Two Powers in Heaven: Early Rabbinic Reports about Christianity and Gnosticism*, SJLA 25 (Leiden: E. J. Brill, 1977); and Jarl E. Fossum, *The Name of God and the Angel of the Lord: Samaritan and Jewish Concepts of Intermediation and the Origin of Gnosticism*, WUNT 36 (Tübingen: J. C. B. Mohr [Paul Siebeck], 1985). Cf. also Quispel, "Gnosticism from Its Origins," 5:569.

71. Philo, *Quaest. Gen.* 2.62.

72. A carefully nuanced discussion on this matter is that of Larry W. Hurtado, *One God, One Lord: Early Christian Devotion and Ancient Jewish Monotheism* (Philadelphia: Fortress Press, 1988), 44–48.

73. This is discussed by Jonas, *The Gnostic Religion*, 51–54; and idem, "Delimitation of the Gnostic Phenomenon," 100. Cf. also Grant, *Gnosticism: A Source Book*, 15.

74. Cf. Nils A. Dahl, "The Arrogant Archon and the Lewd Sophia: Jewish Traditions in Gnostic Revolt," in *The Rediscovery of Gnosticism*, ed. Bentley Layton, 2 vols., SHR 41 (Leiden: E. J. Brill, 1980–81), 2:689–90.

75. Tertullian, *Adv. Marc.* 1.2.

76. *Gos. Phil.* 75.2–3, *NHLE* 154.

77. Cf. George W. MacRae, "Why the Church Rejected Gnosticism," in *Jewish and Christian Self-Definition*, ed. Sanders et al., 1:130–31.

78. Harnack, *Marcion*, 101. The text is not provided in the English version. It is published within an appendix in Adolf von Harnack, *Marcion: Das Evangelium vom fremden Gott*, 2d ed. (Leipzig: J. C. Hinrichs Verlag, 1924; reprinted, Darmstadt: Wissenschaftliche Buchgesellschaft, 1960), 353.

79. The terminology is developed in more detail with illustrations in Arland J. Hultgren, *Christ and His Benefits: Christology and Redemption in the New Testament* (Philadelphia: Fortress Press, 1987), 41–44 et passim.

80. Ibid., 167–74.

81. Eusebius, *Hist. eccl.* 3.27.2; cf. also 6.17.1. Irenaeus, *Adv. Haer.* 1.26.1, and Hippolytus, *Ref.* 7.22, claim that the Ebionites' Christology was like that of the gnostic teachers Cerinthus and Carpocrates. The point of similarity was not in their total Christologies but in that together they claimed that Jesus was conceived and born naturally. These gnostic teachers could say so, since for them the Christ descended upon the human Jesus at his baptism. Cf. Georg Strecker, "On the Problem of Jewish Christianity," an appendix in Walter Bauer, *Orthodoxy and Heresy in Earliest Christianity* (Philadelphia: Fortress Press, 1971), 276–77.

82. Irenaeus, *Adv. Haer.* 1.23.2; Hippolytus, *Ref.* 6.14.

83. Ignatius, *Trall.* 10.1; *Smyrn.* 5.2.

84. Irenaeus, *Adv. Haer.* 1.27.2; Hippolytus, *Ref.* 10.15; Tertullian, *Adv. Marc.* 1.24; 3.8; 3.10.

85. Irenaeus, *Adv. Haer.* 1.21.1; cf. Hippolytus, *Ref.* 7.21.

86. Irenaeus, *Adv. Haer.* 1.26.1.

87. The Christology of Saturninus is summarized by Irenaeus, *Adv. Haer.* 1.24.1, and Hippolytus, *Ref.* 7.16; that of Basilides by Irenaeus, *Adv. Haer.* 1.24.4.

88. Irenaeus, *Adv. Haer.* 1.24.4.

89. Hippolytus, *Ref.* 6.30; Irenaeus, *Adv. Haer.* 1.7.2.

90. The issues are discussed by Robert McL. Wilson, "Valentinianism and the *Gospel of Truth*," in *The Rediscovery of Gnosticism*, ed. Layton, 1:133–41.

91. *Gos. Truth* 31.5–6, *NHLE* 46.

92. *Gos. Phil.* 57.28—58.10; *Treat. Seth* 56.4–19; *Apoc. Peter* 81.3–24, *NHLE* 144–45, 365, 377.

93. Cf. Pheme Perkins, "Gnostic Christologies and the New Testament," *CBQ* 43 (1981): 590–606; and idem, "John's Gospel and Gnostic Christologies: The Nag Hammadi Evidence," in *Christ and His Communities: Essays in Honor of Reginald H. Fuller*, ed. Arland J. Hultgren and Barbara Hall (Cincinnati: Forward Movement Publications, 1990), 68–76. The phrase quoted is from p. 76 of the latter essay.

94. The major study in this area is that of Ernst Käsemann, *The Testament of Jesus: A Study of the Gospel of John in the Light of Chapter 17* (Philadelphia: Fortress Press, 1968). See esp. pp. 8–9, 20, 27, 75. The place and consequences of Johannine Christology are discussed by P. Maurice Casey, *From Jewish Prophet to Gentile God: The Origins and Development of New Testament Christology* (Louisville: Westminster/John Knox Press, 1991), 23–40, 156–59.

95. Cf. Elaine H. Pagels, *The Johannine Gospel in Gnostic Exegesis: Heracleon's Commentary on John*, SBLMS 17 (Nashville: Abingdon Press, 1973).

96. These assertions are explored by Marianne Meye Thompson, *The Humanity of Jesus in the Fourth Gospel* (Philadelphia: Fortress Press, 1988).

97. On gnostic exposition of this verse, and orthodox reaction to it, see Pagels, *The Johannine Gospel in Gnostic Exegesis*, 37–43; on Marcion's inability to speak of the incarnation, see Harnack, *Marcion*, 83.

98. Ignatius, *Trall.* 9.1; quoted from *The Apostolic Fathers*, trans. Kirsopp Lake, 2 vols., LCL (New York: G. P. Putnam's Sons, 1912–13), 1.221.

99. Hippolytus, *Against the Heresy of One Noetus* 18; quoted from the translation by S. D. F. Salmond in *The Ante-Nicene Fathers*, ed. Alexander Roberts and James Donaldson, 10 vols. (Buffalo: Christian Literature Company, 1885–96), 5:230.

100. Tertullian, *Adv. Marc.* 3.8.

101. Cf. Matt. 5:16; 7:17; Luke 3:8; 8:15; John 15:2-16; 2 Cor. 9:6-15; Eph. 2:10; Col. 1:10; and Heb. 10:24.

102. Irenaeus, *Adv. Haer.* 1.23.2; 1.23.5; cf. Epiphanius, *Panarion* 21 and 22.

103. Irenaeus, *Adv. Haer.* 1.24.1–2; Epiphanius, *Panarion* 22.

104. Irenaeus, *Adv. Haer.* 1.26.1; Hippolytus, *Ref.* 7.21.

105. Irenaeus, *Adv. Haer.* 1.25.6; Hippolytus, *Ref.* 7.20.

106. Irenaeus, *Adv. Haer.* 1.25.6; Eusebius, *Hist. eccl.* 4.7.9.

107. Irenaeus, *Adv. Haer.* 1.25.5; quoted from *Gnosis: A Selection of Gnostic Texts*, ed. Werner Foerster, 2 vols. (Oxford: Clarendon Press, 1972-74), 1:38.

108. Quoted from "Proposal for a Terminological and Conceptual Agreement with Regard to the Theme of the Colloquium," in *Le Origini dello Gnosticismo*, ed. Bianchi, xxvi.

109. On the elitism of the Gnostics, cf. Rudolph, *Gnosis*, 209–10; and Green, *Origins of Gnosticism*, 210–16.

110. Irenaeus, *Adv. Haer.* 1.24.4.

111. Ibid., 1.24.6; cf. Epiphanius, *Panarion* 24.5. A similar saying appears in *Gos. Thom.* 38.1–2 (logion 23), *NHLE* 129.

112. Irenaeus, *Adv. Haer.* 1.6.1-2; 1.7.5; 1.8.3; Hippolytus, *Ref.* 5.6.7; and Epiphanius, *Panarion* 31.7.8-11.

113. Irenaeus, *Adv. Haer.* 1.6.2.

114. Ibid., 1.3.1.

115. Theodotus, *Excerpta* 78. The text is provided in *The Excerpta ex Theodoto of Clement of Alexandria*, ed. Robert P. Casey (London: Christophers, 1934), 89.

116. Cf. the assessment of Rudolph, *Gnosis*, 319, and note 90 above.

117. *Gos. Truth* 37.37-38; *Gos. Phil.* 77.15-30, *NHLE* 49, 155.

118. *Tri. Trac.* 118.14-34, *NHLE* 94-95.

119. *Ap. Jas.* 8.26-27, *NHLE* 33.

120. *Ap. John* 31.30-31, *NHLE* 123.

121. *Soph. Jes. Chr.* 93.18-19, *NHLE* 223.

122. *Apoc. Peter* 73.17-18, *NHLE* 374.

123. *Testim. Truth* 31.22-25 and 45.1-4, *NHLE* 450 and 454.

124. Irenaeus, *Adv. Haer.* 1.25.5.

125. *Ap. Jas.* 8.11-15; 11.1-2, *NHLE* 33, 34.

126. *Ap. Jas.* 12.10-15, *NHLE* 35.

127. Irenaeus, *Adv. Haer.* 1.24.4.

128. These are, respectively, at *Treat. Res.* 46.5-21; *Tri. Trac.* 128.2-17; and *Gos. Phil.* 52.17-18, *NHLE* 55, 99, 142.

129. Irenaeus, *Adv. Haer.* 1.27.3. The scope of redemption in Marcion's teaching is discussed by Harnack, *Marcion*, 88–89.

130. On Hellenistic Judaism, cf. Wis. 2:13; Philo, *Deus Imm.* 143; for Qumran texts, cf. 1QS 4.6; 1QH 4.11. Many more references are given by Rudolf Bultmann, "*Ginōskō, Gnōsis,*" *TDNT* 1:696–703.

131. *Gos. Thom.* 39; *Oxy. Pap.* 655; *Ps. Clem. H.* 18.16.

132. Cf. Arland J. Hultgren, "Jesus and Gnosis: The Saying on Hindering Others in Luke 11:52 and Its Parallels," *FFF* 7/3–4 (1991): 165–82.

133. Cf. Joseph A. Fitzmyer, *The Gospel according to Luke*, AB 28–28A, 2 vols. (Garden City, N.Y.: Doubleday, 1981–85), 2:946: "The key of knowledge was given to [the lawyers], the key to unlock the knowledge of God and his will in the Torah and its traditions; it was the key to the house that wisdom built (Prov. 9:1)."

134. The relationship of faith and knowledge in the Pauline corpus is discussed by Robert J. Banks, *Paul's Idea of Community* (Grand Rapids, Mich.: Wm. B. Eerdmans, 1980), 74–79.

135. Cf. Gerd Theissen, "The Strong and the Weak in Corinth: A Sociological Analysis of a Theological Quarrel," in his *The Social Setting of Pauline Christianity: Essays on Corinth* (Philadelphia: Fortress Press, 1982), 130–37.

136. Rudolph, *Gnosis*, 301.

137. Eduard Lohse, *Colossians and Philemon*, Hermeneia (Philadelphia: Fortress Press, 1971), 82–83; and Eduard Schweizer, *The Letter to the Colossians* (Minneapolis: Augsburg, 1982), 117–18.

138. Major studies in New Testament ethics include those of J. L. Houlden, *Ethics and the New Testament* (Baltimore: Penguin Books, 1973); Wolfgang Schrage, *The Ethics of the New Testament* (Philadelphia: Fortress Press, 1988); and Eduard Lohse, *Theological Ethics of the New Testament* (Minneapolis: Fortress Press, 1991).

139. Texts are cited by E. R. Dodds, *Pagan and Christian in an Age of Anxiety* (Cambridge: Cambridge Univ. Press, 1965), 136.

140. Ibid., 136–38.

141. Cf. the reservations of Henry Chadwick, "The Domestication of Gnosis," in *The Rediscovery of Gnosticism*, ed. Layton, 1:7–8; and Robert McL. Wilson, "Ethics and the Gnostics," in *Studien zum Text und zur Ethik des Neuen Testaments: Festschrift zum 80. Geburtstag von Heinrich Greeven*, ed. Wolfgang Schrage (Berlin: Walter de Gruyter, 1986), 440–49. A survey of charges of immorality against various groups (Jews, orthodox Christians, gnostic Christians, and others) by their critics has been made by Robert M. Grant, "Charges of 'Immorality' against Various Religious Groups in Antiquity," in *Studies in Gnosticism and Hellenistic Religions: Presented to Gilles Quispel on the Occasion of His 65th Birthday*, ed. R. van den Broek and M. J. Vermaseren (Leiden: E. J. Brill, 1981), 161–70.

142. Justin, *Apology* 1.26 and 1.56; Irenaeus, *Adv. Haer.* 1.23.2 and 1.23.5; cf. Epiphanius, *Panarion* 21 and 22.

143. Irenaeus, *Adv. Haer.* 1.23.2; Hippolytus, *Ref.* 6.14.

144. Justin, *Apology* 1.26.

145. Irenaeus, *Adv. Haer.* 1.26.3; Hippolytus, *Ref.* 7.24. Eusebius, *Hist. eccl.* 3.29.3, quotes Clement of Alexandria, who says that Nicolaus himself was faithful to his wife, but that his followers were promiscuous. Epiphanius, *Panarion* 25.1.5, attributes

to Nicolaus the saying, "Unless one copulates every day, he cannot have eternal life."

146. On the Carpocratians, cf. Irenaeus, *Adv. Haer.* 1.25.3; and Clement of Alexandria, *Stromateis* 3.2; on Basilides and his followers, cf. Irenaeus, *Adv. Haer.* 1.24; and Epiphanius, *Panarion* 24.3.7.

147. On Saturninus, cf. Irenaeus, *Adv. Haer.* 1.24.2; on Marcion, cf. Hippolytus, *Ref.* 10.15; Epiphanius, *Panarion* 42.3.3.; and Tertullian, *Adv. Marc.* 1.29.

148. Irenaeus, *Adv. Haer.* 1.6.3–4; cf. also 1.13.6.

149. Cf. Foerster, *Gnosis*, 1:313, who cites materials lacking hints of libertinism in the *Excerpto ex Theodoto* and Heracleon's commentary on John; and Green, *Origins of Gnosticism*, 216 (n. 242), 223.

150. *Gos. Phil.* 64.31—65.1; 81.34—82.10, *NHLE* 148, 157–58. On the possible Valentinian origin of this document, cf. Rudolph, *Gnosis*, 319.

151. Cf. MacRae, "Why the Church Rejected Gnosticism," 1:129.

152. *Gos. Phil.* 66.10–13, *NHLE* 149.

153. Irenaeus, *Adv. Haer.* 1.25.4.

154. Tertullian, *Adv. Marc.* 4.16; 4.35; 4.38. Cf. Harnack, *Marcion*, 85.

155. Cf. Rudolph, *Gnosis*, 319; and the introduction to these tractates by, respectively, Harold W. Attridge and George W. MacRae (*Gos. Truth*) and Harold W. Attridge and Elaine H. Pagels (*Tri. Trac.*), *NHLE* 38–39, 58–60.

156. *Gos. Truth* 33.1–9, *NHLE* 47.

157. *Tri. Trac.* 121.22–38, *NHLE* 96.

158. Cf. the introduction to the tractate, *NHLE*, 503, by Frederik Wisse.

159. The libertine and ascetic tendencies are surveyed by Green, *Origins of Gnosticism*, 216–38. He concludes that Valentinus himself "adhered to conventional codes of moral conduct" (p. 216, n. 242); but see also his citation of Valentinian libertinism (p. 223).

160. Cf. Gerhard Lohfink, *Jesus and Community: The Social Dimension of Christian Faith* (Philadelphia: Fortress Press, 1984), 9–12, 31–73; and the statement of Eduard Schweizer, *A Theological Introduction to the New Testament* (Nashville: Abingdon Press, 1991), 18: "It is important to the whole tradition that Jesus gathered around himself both the circle of the twelve and a larger group of followers, including women (Mark 15:41; Luke 8:1-3). Since after Easter the twelve had no clear function, this group was certainly not formed at that time. It made sense as the core of a re-establishing of the twelve tribes, which is typical certainly of Jesus, but in only a limited way or not at all for the post-Easter community."

161. The case for this view has been argued well by Robert L. Wilken, "The Durability of Orthodoxy," *WW* 8 (1988): 124–32. Concerning subsequent centuries, Andrew Greeley has written: "Catholicism . . . is a rich, complex, pluralistic heritage. Anyone who has read Catholic history is well aware that its tradition has always been pluralistic and that it has defined its boundaries out as far as possible, to include everyone it can." Quoted from his article "For Centuries, Catholics Have Gone Their Own Way," Minneapolis *Star Tribune* (25 Aug. 1993), 15A.

162. The definition of a sect along these lines is given by Bryan R. Wilson, *Sects and Society* (Berkeley: Univ. of California Press, 1961), 1; further in idem, "The

Sociology of Sects," in his *Religion in a Sociological Perspective* (Oxford: Oxford Univ. Press, 1982), 89–120. Wilson builds upon, and also departs from, the earlier work of Ernst Troeltsch, *The Social Teaching of the Christian Churches*, 2 vols. (New York: Macmillan, 1931), 1:331–43.

163. Origen, *Contra Celsum* 1.57.

164. Justin, *Apology* 1.26.4.

165. Epiphanius, *Panarion* 22.2.1.

166. Justin, *Apology* 1.26; Irenaeus, *Adv. Haer.* 1.23.1.

167. Irenaeus, *Adv. Haer.* 1.23.5.

168. Cf. a similar judgment by Foerster, *Gnosis*, 1:32.

169. Irenaeus, *Adv. Haer.* 1.26.3; Hippolytus, *Ref.* 7.36.3; Eusebius, *Hist. eccl.* 3.29.1; and Epiphanius, *Panarion* 25.1.1.

170. Eusebius, *Hist. eccl.* 3.29.1.

171. Justin, *Apology* 1.26.5–6; Eusebius, *Hist. eccl.* 4.11.9.

172. Tertullian, *Adv. Marc.* 4.5.

173. Evidence is cited by Blackman, *Marcion*, 4; and H. E. W. Turner, *The Pattern of Christian Truth: A Study in Relations between Orthodoxy and Heresy in the Early Church* (London: A. R. Mowbray, 1954), 158, who cites Origen.

174. On bishops, cf. Tertullian, *Adv. Marc.* 4.5; on presbyters, Eusebius, *Hist. eccl.* 4.15.46. Additional evidence for these offices and for deacons is provided by Harnack, *Marcion*, 100, 165 (n. 3); Turner, *The Pattern of Christian Truth*, 159–60; and Blackman, *Marcion*, 5. The view that Marcionism rejected church structures typical of the orthodox movement is put forth by R. Joseph Hoffmann, "How Then Know This Troublous Teacher? Further Reflections on Marcion and His Church," *SC* 6 (1987–88): 185–86.

175. Eusebius, *Hist. eccl.* 5.16.21.

176. References to baptism are in Tertullian, *Adv. Marc.* 1.29; and Epiphanius, *Panarion* 42.3.6; to the Lord's Supper in Epiphanius, *Panarion* 42.3.3.

177. Epiphanius, *Panarion* 42.3.6.

178. Tertullian, *Adv. Marc.* 1.29.

179. Hippolytus, *Ref.* 10.15; Tertullian, *Adv. Marc.* 1.29; and Epiphanius, *Panarion* 42.3.3.

180. Epiphanius, *Panarion* 42.3.3.

181. For example, Irenaeus, *Adv. Haer.* 1.27.3; Hippolytus, *Ref.* 10.15; and Epiphanius, *Panarion* 42.4.6.

182. Irenaeus, *Adv. Haer.* 1.27.3.

183. Harnack, *Marcion*, 100–103.

184. Ibid., 99: "The Marcionites constantly sought to exact a missionary influence upon [the great church] and to absorb the whole Christian tradition." That the Marcionites drew members from catholic churches is a complaint of Tertullian, *De Praesc. Haer.* 42. Cf. also Blackman, *Marcion*, 13; and Thomas A. Robinson, *The Bauer Thesis Examined: The Geography of Heresy in the Early Christian Church*, SBEC 11 (Lewistown, N.Y.: Edwin Mellen Press, 1988), 48–51.

185. Eusebius, *Hist. eccl.* 4.7.12.

186. Epiphanius, *Panarion* 24.1.4.

187. Irenaeus, *Adv. Haer.* 1.24.6.

188. Ibid.

189. Ibid., 1.6.4.

190. Ibid.

191. Ibid. 1.3.1; Epiphanius, *Panarion* 31.7.5.

192. Important studies on Valentinian churches and social structures are those of Klaus Koschorke, "Gnostic Instructions on the Organization of the Congregation: The Tractate Interpretation of Knowledge from CG XI," in *The Rediscovery of Gnosticism,* ed. Layton, 2:757–69; and Green, *Origins of Gnosticism,* 242–58.

193. Cf. the introduction to *Val. Exp.* by Elaine H. Pagels, *NHLE* 481.

194. *Tri. Trac.* 127.26–34; *Gos. Phil.* 67.19–21; 67.27–30, *NHLE* 99, 150.

195. *Gos. Phil.* 67.27–30, *NHLE* 150.

196. Cf. the introduction to *Interp. Know.* by Elaine H. Pagels, *NHLE* 472–73.

197. *Gos. Truth* 43.20–24, *NHLE* 51.

198. *Tri. Trac.* 132.20–28, *NHLE* 101.

199. *Tri. Trac.* 118.14—119.34, *NHLE* 94–95.

200. *Soph. Jes. Chr.* 93.18–19, *NHLE* 223.

201. *Gos. Thom.* 41.27–30 (logion 49), *NHLE* 132.

202. The text is given in *NHLE* 473–80.

203. Koschorke, "Gnostic Instructions on the Organization of the Congregation," 2:759–60; and Elaine H. Pagels, "Introduction: NHC XI,1: The Interpretation of Knowledge," in *Nag Hammadi Codices XI, XII, XIII,* ed. Charles W. Hedrick, NHS 28 (Leiden: E. J. Brill, 1990), 22–24. Hereafter abbreviated *NHC XI–XIII.*

204. *Interp. Know.* 15.35–38; 16.31–35, *NHLE* 478.

205. *Interp. Know.* 17.25–28, *NHLE* 478.

206. *Interp. Know.* 18.28–34, *NHLE* 479. The term *sōma* is in the text at *NHC XI–XIII,* 69.

207. *Interp. Know.* 17.14–21; 18.17–38, *NHLE* 479.

208. *Interp. Know.* 16.20–27; 17.31–34, *NHLE* 478.

209. *Interp. Know.* 15.26–36, *NHLE* 478.

210. Pagels, "Introduction," *NHC XI–XIII,* 28.

211. *Interp. Know.* 19.20–37, *NHLE* 479. On the meaning, see Pagels, "Introduction," *NHC XI–XIII,* 28–29.

212. Koschorke, "Gnostic Instructions on the Organization of the Congregation," 2:757.

213. Ibid., 2:758; and Pagels, "Introduction," *NHC XI–XIII,* 22.

214. Pearson, "Jewish Elements in Gnosticism and the Development of Gnostic Self-Definition," 1:159.

215. Frederik Wisse, "Prolegomena to the Study of the New Testament and Gnosis," in *The New Testament and Gnosis: Essays in Honour of Robert McL. Wilson,* ed. A. H. B. Logan and A. J. M. Wedderburn (Edinburgh: T. & T. Clark, 1983), 141–42.

216. Pearson, "Jewish Elements in Gnosticism and the Development of Gnostic Self-Definition," 1:159; and Green, *Origins of Gnosticism,* 259.

217. Rudolph, *Gnosis,* 367.

218. On itinerant missionaries and the Q community, cf. Ivan Havener, *Q: The Sayings of Jesus* (Wilmington, Del.: Michael Glazier, 1987), 91–104; and Gerd Theissen, *The Gospels in Context: Social and Political History in the Synoptic Tradition* (Minneapolis: Fortress Press, 1991), 233.

219. All of this had its origins in the time of Paul. Cf. E. Earle Ellis, "Paul and His Co-Workers," *NTS* 17 (1971): 439–52; and Banks, *Paul's Idea of Community*, 48, who cites such passages as Rom. 16:1; 2 Cor. 8:11-13; 8:14. Particularly important and well done is the discussion of "The Infrastructure of the Pauline Mission Field" by Jürgen Becker, in *Paul: Apostle to the Gentiles* (Louisville: Westminster/John Knox Press, 1993), 178–85.

220. John Koenig, *New Testament Hospitality: Partnership with Strangers as Promise and Mission* (Philadelphia: Fortress Press, 1985), 2.

221. Cf. Rowen Williams, "Does It Make Sense to Speak of Pre-Nicene Orthodoxy?" in *The Making of Orthodoxy: Essays in Honour of Henry Chadwick*, ed. Rowen Williams (Cambridge: Cambridge Univ. Press, 1989), 12; and Petr Pokorný, *The Genesis of Christology: Foundations for a Theology of the New Testament* (Edinburgh: T. & T. Clark, 1987), 158–60, 205–06.

222. On this matter, cf. S. C. Barton and G. H. R. Horsley, "A Hellenistic Cult Group and the New Testament Churches," *JAC* 24 (1981): 28–29.

223. Justin, *Apology* 1.26.

224. Tertullian, *Adv. Marc.* 4.5.

225. Ibid., 5.19.

226. Epiphanius, *Panarion* 42.1.2.

227. Eusebius, *Hist. eccl.* 5.13.1–4.

228. Harnack, *Marcion*, 104.

229. Rudolph, *Gnosis*, 217–18.

230. Cf. Williams, "Does It Make Sense to Speak of Pre-Nicene Orthodoxy?" 11. Cf. also Rudolph, *Gnosis*, 216–17, who does, however, suggest that some cohesiveness among communities existed.

231. Irenaeus, *Adv. Haer.* 1.22.1; Hippolytus, *Ref.* 5.1; Tertullian, *Against the Valentinians* 4; idem, *De Praesc. Haer.* 41 and 42; Clement of Alexandria, *Stromateis* 7.17; Eusebius, *Hist. eccl.* 4.7.12–14; and 5.13.1–4. The claim that heretics cannot get along with each other is attested earlier at 1 Tim. 6:3-5 and in *Barn.* 20.1-2.

232. Cf. the introductions to these works by Birger A. Pearson and Elaine H. Pagels, respectively, in *NHLE* 448–49 and 481–82.

233. *Treat. Res.* 50.15, *NHLE* 57.

234. Green, *Origins of Gnosticism*, 245.

235. Justin, *Dialogue with Trypho* 47.

236. Irenaeus, *Adv. Haer.* 1.26.3; Hippolytus, *Ref.* 7.22. Cf. Strecker, "On the Problem of Jewish Christianity," 273, 276, and 278. Strecker suggests that the term *Ebionite* came into existence prior to the time of Irenaeus, but that it was still unknown to Justin, and then came to be applied to Jewish Christian groups in general.

237. Eusebius, *Hist. eccl.* 3.27.1–6.

238. Ibid., 6.17.1.

239. Hans-Joachim Schoeps, *Jewish Christianity: Factional Disputes in the Early Church* (Philadelphia: Fortress Press, 1969), 36–37; and F. F. Bruce, *Peter, Stephen, James, and John: Studies in Early Non-Pauline Christianity* (Grand Rapids, Mich.: Wm. B. Eerdmans, 1980), 118–19.

240. Hippolytus, *Ref.* 7.22.

241. The point has been made well by Chadwick, "The Domestication of Gnosis," 14–15, and illustrated by Bentley Layton, "General Introduction," in his *The Gnostic Scriptures* (Garden City, N.Y.: Doubleday, 1987), xx–xxi.

242. Layton, "General Introduction," *Gnostic Scriptures*, xviii.

243. Cf. Hans Dieter Betz, "Orthodoxy and Heresy in Primitive Christianity," *Int* 29 (1965): 308–9; Reginald H. Fuller, "New Testament Trajectories and Biblical Authority," in *Studia Evangelica* 7, ed. Elizabeth A. Livingstone, TU 126 (Berlin: Akademie Verlag, 1982), 198–99; and Martin Hengel, "Aufgaben der neutestamentlichen Wissenschaft," forthcoming in *NTS* 40/3 (1994). Among other things, Hengel rejects "the widespread opinion today" that in the early church there was "only a multitude of contradictory messages" and affirms that there was indeed "an original *unity* of the church given through the Christ-event" (quoted from an English translation by Philip E. Devenish).

7. Normative Christianity and the Legacy of Jesus

1. For discussion of this theme in the message of Jesus, cf. Günther Bornkamm, *Jesus of Nazareth* (New York: Harper & Brothers, 1960), 109–17.

2. Its impact on and through New Testament writings can be seen in the work of Victor P. Furnish, *The Love Command in the New Testament* (Nashville: Abingdon Press, 1972).

3. Both aspects have multiple attestation in the synoptic tradition. The kingdom as a present (or imminent) reality is declared in Matt. 6:33//Luke 12:31 (Q); Mark 10:15; and Luke 17:21 (L). The kingdom as future expectation is declared in Matt. 8:11//Luke 7:29 (Q); Mark 9:47; 14:25; and Luke 14:15 (L).

4. Texts and scholarship are surveyed on this by Ben Witherington, *The Christology of Jesus* (Minneapolis: Fortress Press, 1990), 216–21.

5. Cf. Bornkamm, *Jesus of Nazareth*, 57–58.

6. Ibid., 169–78.

7. Marinus de Jonge, *Christology in Context: The Earliest Christian Response to Jesus* (Philadelphia: Westminster Press, 1988), 208–11; and Witherington, *The Christology of Jesus*, 268.

8. The question has been raised specifically concerning Jesus' understanding of his death by Daniel J. Antwi, "Did Jesus Consider His Death to Be an Atoning Sacrifice?" *Int* 45 (1991): 17–28.

9. Cf. Bornkamm, *Jesus of Nazareth*, 82–84; Herbert Braun, *Jesus of Nazareth: The Man and His Time* (Philadelphia: Fortress Press, 1979), 105–15; John Riches, *Jesus and the Transformation of Judaism* (New York: Seabury Press, 1981), 98–111; and

Leonhard Goppelt, *Theology of the New Testament*, 2 vols. (Grand Rapids, Mich.: Wm. B. Eerdmans, 1981–82), 1:127–34.

10. Cf. de Jonge, *Christology in Context*, 208–11. A discussion that takes seriously the deeds of Jesus in regard to his apparent self-understanding is that of E. P. Sanders, *Jesus and Judaism* (Philadelphia: Fortress Press, 1985), 294–318, 334–35.

11. This is elaborated in Arland J. Hultgren, *Christ and His Benefits: Christology and Redemption in the New Testament* (Philadelphia: Fortress Press, 1987), 31–39.

12. Charles W. Hedrick, "Introduction: The Tyranny of the Synoptic Jesus," *Semeia* 44 (1988): 2.

13. Among the various assessments on issues here are the following: Bernard B. Scott, *Hear Then the Parable: A Commentary on the Parables of Jesus* (Minneapolis: Fortress Press, 1989), 30–35 et passim; and Stephen J. Patterson, *The Gospel of Thomas and Jesus* (Sonoma, Calif.: Polebridge Press, 1992).

14. Cf. too the remark made by Helmut Koester, "Jesus the Victim," *JBL* 111 (1992): 9: "All early Christian traditions are acutely aware of [Jesus' death]. All sources—and this includes the tradition of the wisdom sayings and its theology— agree that the tradition about Jesus must be seen in this light: his rejection, suffering, and death."

15. Cf. Rudolf Bultmann, *Theology of the New Testament*, 2 vols. (New York: Charles Scribner's Sons, 1951–55), 1:46; Oscar Cullmann, *The Christology of the New Testament*, rev. ed. (Philadelphia: Westminster Press, 1963), 76; Reginald H. Fuller, *The Foundations of New Testament Christology* (New York: Charles Scribner's Sons, 1965), 161; Leonhard Goppelt, *Theology of the New Testament*, 2 vols. (Grand Rapids, Mich.: Wm. B. Eerdmans, 1981–82), 1:232–34; and Helmut Koester, *Ancient Christian Gospels: Their History and Development* (Philadelphia: Trinity Press International, 1990), 51. On the early Palestinian origins of the formula, cf. Ferdinand Hahn, *The Titles of Jesus in Christology: Their History in Early Christianity* (Cleveland: World Publishing Company, 1969), 175–89; and Peter Stuhlmacher, "The Pauline Gospel," in *The Gospel and the Gospels*, ed. Peter Stuhlmacher (Grand Rapids, Mich.: Wm. B. Eerdmans, 1991), 157–58. It has been argued that "Cephas" in this and other passages is not Simon Peter, by Bart D. Ehrman, "Cephas and Peter," *JBL* 109 (1990): 463–74. Against that view, the two names are certainly applied to the same person in Gal. 1:18; 2:9, 11, 14 (Cephas) and 2:7 (Peter), as well as in John 1:42. Cf. Hans Dieter Betz, *Galatians*, Hermeneia (Philadelphia: Fortress Press, 1979), 76–77; Hans Conzelmann, *1 Corinthians*, Hermeneia (Philadelphia: Fortress Press, 1975), 32–33, 256–57; Raymond E. Brown, *The Gospel according to John*, AB 29–29A, 2 vols. (Garden City, N.Y.: Doubleday, 1966–70), 1:76; and Dale C. Allison, "Peter and Cephas: One and the Same," *JBL* 111 (1992): 489–95.

16. John A. T. Robinson, "The Most Primitive Christology of All?" in his *Twelve New Testament Studies*, SBT 34 (Naperville, Ill.: Alec R. Allenson, 1962), 139–53.

17. Ibid., 144.

18. Hahn, *Titles of Jesus*, 93–103.

19. Helmut Koester, *Introduction to the New Testament*, 2 vols. (Philadelphia: Fortress Press, 1982), 2:148. Cf. also Richard A. Edwards, *A Theology of Q: Eschatology, Prophecy,*

and Wisdom (Philadelphia: Fortress Press, 1976), 149–50; and Ivan Havener, Q: *The Sayings of Jesus* (Wilmington, Del.: Michael Glazier, 1987), 106–07.

20. The passage contains terminology and theological emphases characteristic of Luke-Acts in several respects. These are surveyed in Hultgren, *Christ and His Benefits,* 17–19.

21. Helmut Koester, "The Structure and Criteria of Early Christian Beliefs," in *Trajectories through Early Christianity,* by James M. Robinson and Helmut Koester (Philadelphia: Fortress Press, 1971), 225.

22. It also led to the rise of orthodoxy. Cf. Petr Pokorný, *The Genesis of Christology: Foundations for a Theology of the New Testament* (Edinburgh: T. & T. Clark, 1987), 219: "Because faith is lived, orthodoxy consists not in a closed correct doctrinal system but in the capacity to make the individual groups aware of their common basis in the Easter event and to co-ordinate their witness within an eschatological perspective."

Bibliography

Achtemeier, Paul J. *The Quest for Unity in the New Testament Church: A Study in Paul and Acts.* Philadelphia: Fortress Press, 1987.

Aland, Barbara, ed. *Gnosis: Festschrift für Hans Jonas.* Göttingen: Vandenhoeck & Ruprecht, 1978.

Allen, Willoughby C. *A Critical and Exegetical Commentary on the Gospel according to S. Matthew.* ICC. 3d ed. Edinburgh: T. & T. Clark, 1912.

Allison, Dale C. "Peter and Cephas: One and the Same." *JBL* 111 (1992): 489–95.

Aune, David E. *Prophecy in Early Christianity and the Ancient Mediterranean World.* Grand Rapids: Wm. B. Eerdmans, 1983.

Balch, David L. *Social History of the Matthean Community: Cross-Disciplinary Approaches.* Minneapolis: Fortress Press, 1991.

Banks, Robert. *Paul's Idea of Community: The Early House Churches in Their Historical Setting.* Grand Rapids: Wm. B. Eerdmans, 1980.

———, ed. *Reconciliation and Hope: New Testament Essays on Atonement and Eschatology Presented to L. L. Morris on His 60th Birthday.* Grand Rapids: Wm. B. Eerdmans, 1974.

Barc, Bernard, ed. *Colloque international sur les textes de Nag Hammadi.* Quebec: Les Presses de l'Université Laval, 1981.

Barclay, John M. G. "Thessalonica and Corinth: Social Contrasts in Pauline Christianity." *JSNT* 47 (1992): 49–74.

Barnard, L. W. "The Origins and Emergence of the Church in Edessa during the First Two Centuries A.D." *VC* 22 (1968): 161–75.

Barrett, C. K. *A Commentary on the First Epistle to the Corinthians.* HNTC. New York: Harper & Row, 1968.

———. *Essays on John.* Philadelphia: Westminster Press, 1982.

———. *The Gospel according to St. John.* 2d ed. Philadelphia: Westminster Press, 1978.

———. "Christianity at Corinth." *BJRL* 46 (1964): 269–97.

———. *The Pastoral Epistles.* Oxford: Clarendon Press, 1963.

Barton, S. C., and G. H. R. Horsley. "A Hellenistic Cult Group and the New Testament Churches." *JAC* 24 (1981): 7–41.

Bauckham, Richard. *Jude and the Relatives of Jesus in the Early Church.* Edinburgh: T. & T. Clark, 1990.

Bauer, Walter. *Orthodoxy and Heresy in Earliest Christianity.* Philadelphia: Fortress Press, 1971.

Beare, Francis W. *The First Epistle of Peter.* Oxford: Basil Blackwell, 1961.

Becker, Jürgen. *Paul: Apostle to the Gentiles.* Louisville: Westminster/John Knox Press, 1993.

Beker, J. Christiaan. *Heirs of Paul: Paul's Legacy in the New Testament and in the Church Today.* Minneapolis: Fortress Press, 1991.

———. *Paul the Apostle: The Triumph of God in Life and Thought.* Philadelphia: Fortress Press, 1980.

———. *The Triumph of God: The Essence of Paul's Thought.* Minneapolis: Fortress Press, 1990.

Best, Ernest. *A Commentary on the First and Second Epistles to the Thessalonians.* HNTC. New York: Harper & Row, 1972.

———. *1 Peter.* NCB. London: Marshall, Morgan & Scott, 1971.

———. *One Body in Christ.* London: SPCK, 1955.

Betz, Hans Dieter. *Galatians.* Hermeneia. Philadelphia: Fortress Press, 1979.

———. "Orthodoxy and Heresy in Primitive Christianity." *Int* 29 (1965): 299–311.

Bianchi, Ugo, ed. *Le Origini dello Gnosticismo.* SHR 12. Leiden: E. J. Brill, 1967.

Blackman, E. C. *Marcion and His Influence.* London: SPCK, 1948.

Blair, Edward P. *Jesus in the Gospel of Matthew.* Nashville: Abingdon Press, 1960.

Böttger, Paul C. "Paulus und Petrus in Antiochien: Zum Verständnis von Galater 2.11–21." *NTS* 37 (1991): 77–100.

Bogart, John. *Orthodox and Heretical Perfectionism in the Johannine Community as Evident in the First Epistle of John.* SBLDS 33. Missoula, Mont.: Scholars Press, 1977.

Boring, M. Eugene. *Sayings of the Risen Jesus: Christian Prophecy in the Synoptic Tradition.* SNTSMS 46. Cambridge: Cambridge Univ. Press, 1982.

Bornkamm, Günther. *Early Christian Experience.* New York: Harper & Row, 1969.

———. *Jesus of Nazareth.* New York: Harper & Brothers, 1960.

———. *Paul.* New York: Harper & Row, 1971.

————, Gerhard Barth, and Heinz J. Held. *Tradition and Interpretation in Matthew*. Philadelphia: Westminster Press, 1963.

Bousset, Wilhelm. *Kyrios Christos: A History of Belief in Christ from the Beginnings of Christianity to Irenaeus*. Nashville: Abingdon Press, 1970.

Bowe, Barbara E. *Church in Crisis: Ecclesiology and Paraenesis in Clement of Rome*. HDR 23. Minneapolis: Fortress Press, 1989.

Braude, William G., trans. *The Midrash on Psalms*. 2 vols. YJS 13. New Haven: Yale Univ. Press, 1959.

Braun, Herbert. *Jesus of Nazareth: The Man and His Time*. Philadelphia: Fortress Press, 1979.

Broek, R. van, and M. J. Vermaseren, eds. *Studies in Gnosticism and Hellenistic Religions: Presented to Gilles Quispel on the Occasion of His 65th Birthday*. Leiden: E. J. Brill, 1981.

Brown, Raymond E., and John P. Meier. *Antioch and Rome: New Testament Cradles of Catholic Christianity*. New York: Paulist Press, 1983.

————. *The Churches the Apostles Left Behind*. New York: Paulist Press, 1984.

————. *The Community of the Beloved Disciple*. New York: Paulist Press, 1979.

————. *The Epistles of John*. AB 30. Garden City, N.Y.: Doubleday, 1982.

————. *The Gospel according to John*. AB 29–29A. Garden City, N.Y.: Doubleday, 1966–70.

————, et al., eds. *Peter in the New Testament*. Minneapolis: Augsburg, 1973.

Bruce, F. F. *The Acts of the Apostles*. 3d ed. Grand Rapids: Wm. B. Eerdmans, 1990.

————. *Peter, Stephen, James, and John: Studies in Early Non-Pauline Christianity*. Grand Rapids: Wm. B. Eerdmans, 1980.

Bultmann, Rudolf. *The History of the Synoptic Tradition*. 2d ed. New York: Harper & Row, 1968.

————. *The Johannine Epistles*. Hermeneia. Philadelphia: Fortress Press, 1973.

————. *Primitive Christianity in Its Contemporary Setting*. Cleveland: World Publishing Company, 1956.

————. *Theology of the New Testament*. 2 vols. New York: Charles Scribner's Sons, 1951–55.

Cameron, Ron, ed. *The Apocryphal Jesus and Christian Origins*. Semeia 49. Atlanta: Scholars Press, 1990.

————. *The Other Gospels: Non-Canonical Gospel Texts*. Philadelphia: Westminster Press, 1982.

Campenhausen, Hans von. *Ecclesiastical Authority and Spiritual Power in the Church of the First Three Centuries*. Stanford: Stanford Univ. Press, 1969.

————. *The Formation of the Christian Bible*. Philadelphia: Fortress Press, 1972.

————. *Jerusalem and Rome: The Problem of Authority in the Early Church*. FBHS 4. Philadelphia: Fortress Press, 1966.

————. *Polykarp von Smyrna und die Pastoralbriefe.* SHA. Heidelberg: C. Winter, 1951.

Casey, P. Maurice. *From Jewish Prophet to Gentile God: The Origins and Development of New Testament Christology.* Louisville: Westminster/John Knox Press, 1991.

Casey, Robert P., ed. *The Excerpta ex Theodoto of Clement of Alexandria.* London: Christophers, 1934.

Charlesworth, James H., ed. *The Old Testament Pseudepigrapha.* 2 vols. Garden City, N.Y.: Doubleday, 1983–85.

Christie-Murray, David. *A History of Heresy.* New York: Oxford Univ. Press, 1989.

Collins, Raymond F., ed. *The Thessalonian Correspondence.* BETL 87. Louvain: Leuven Univ. Press, 1990.

Colpe, Carsten. *Die religionsgeschichtliche Schule: Darstellung und Kritik ihres Bildes vom gnostischen Erlösermythos.* FRLANT 78. Göttingen: Vandenhoeck & Ruprecht, 1961.

Conzelmann, Hans. *Acts of the Apostles.* Hermeneia. Philadelphia: Fortress Press, 1987.

————. *1 Corinthians.* Hermeneia. Philadelphia: Fortress Press, 1975.

————. *History of Primitive Christianity.* Nashville: Abingdon Press, 1973.

————. *An Outline of the Theology of the New Testament.* New York: Harper & Row, 1969.

Cooley, Charles H. *Social Organization: A Study of the Larger Mind.* New York: Charles Scribner's Sons, 1909.

Cope, O. Lamar. *Matthew: A Scribe Trained for the Kingdom of Heaven.* CBQMS 5. Washington, D.C.: Catholic Biblical Association, 1976.

Court, John, and Kathleen Court. *The New Testament World.* Cambridge: Cambridge Univ. Press, 1990.

Cousar, Charles B. *A Theology of the Cross: The Death of Jesus in the Pauline Letters.* Minneapolis: Fortress Press, 1990.

Crown, Alan D., ed. *The Samaritans.* Tübingen: J. C. B. Mohr (Paul Siebeck), 1989.

Cullmann, Oscar. *The Christology of the New Testament.* Rev. ed. Philadelphia: Westminster Press, 1963.

————. *The Earliest Christian Confessions.* London: Lutterworth Press, 1949.

————. *Early Christian Worship.* SBT 10. Chicago: Henry Regnery, 1953.

————. "The Gospel of Thomas and the Problem of the Age of the Tradition Contained Therein." *Int* 16 (1962): 418–38.

————. *The Johannine Circle.* Philadelphia: Westminster Press, 1976.

Danielou, Jean. *The Theology of Jewish Christianity.* Chicago: Henry Regnery Company, 1964.

Dart, John. *The Jesus of Heresy and History: The Discovery and Meaning of the Nag Hammadi Gnostic Library.* San Francisco: Harper & Row, 1986.

Davids, Peter H. *The First Epistle of Peter*. NICNT. Grand Rapids: Wm. B. Eerdmans, 1990.

Davies, Stevan. *The Gospel of Thomas and Christian Wisdom*. New York: Seabury Press, 1983.

Davies, W. D. *Jewish and Pauline Studies*. Philadelphia: Fortress Press, 1984.

———. *The Setting of the Sermon on the Mount*. Cambridge: Cambridge Univ. Press, 1964.

Davies, W. D., and Dale Allison. *A Critical and Exegetical Commentary on the Gospel according to Saint Matthew*. 3 vols. ICC. Edinburgh: T. & T. Clark, 1988–.

Delobel, Joël, ed. *Logia: Les Paroles de Jésus—The Sayings of Jesus: Mémorial Joseph Coppens*. BETL 59. Louvain: Leuven Univ. Press, 1982.

Desjardins, Michael. "Bauer and Beyond: On Recent Scholarly Discussions of *Hairesis* in the Early Christian Era." *SC* 8 (1991): 65–82.

———. "Where Was the Gospel of Thomas Written?" *TJT* 8 (1992): 121–33.

Dibelius, Martin. *From Tradition to Gospel*. 2d ed. New York: Charles Scribner's Sons, 1934.

———. *James*. Rev. Heinrich Greeven. Hermeneia. Philadelphia: Fortress Press, 1976.

———, and Hans Conzelmann. *The Pastoral Epistles*. Hermeneia. Philadelphia: Fortress Press, 1972.

———. *Studies in the Acts of the Apostles*. New York: Charles Scribner's Sons, 1956.

Dodd, C. H. *The Interpretation of the Fourth Gospel*. Cambridge: Cambridge Univ. Press, 1953.

———. *The Parables of the Kingdom*. Rev. ed. New York: Charles Scribner's Sons, 1961.

Dodds, E. R. *Pagan and Christian in an Age of Anxiety*. Cambridge: Cambridge Univ. Press, 1965.

Donfried, Karl P. "Paul and Judaism: I Thessalonians 2:13-16 as a Test Case." *Int* 38 (1984): 242–53.

———. ed. *The Romans Debate*. Rev. ed. Peabody, Mass.: Hendrickson Publishers, 1991.

Drijvers, H. J. W. "Edessa und das jüdische Christentum." *VC* 24 (1970): 4–33.

Dunn, James D. G. *Christology in the Making: A New Testament Inquiry into the Origins of the Doctrine of the Incarnation*. Philadelphia: Westminster Press, 1980.

———. *Jesus, Paul, and the Law: Studies in Mark and Galatians*. Louisville: Westminster/John Knox Press, 1990.

————. *Unity and Diversity in the New Testament: An Inquiry into the Character of Earliest Christianity.* 2d ed. Philadelphia: Trinity Press International, 1990.

Ebeling, Gerhard. *Word and Faith.* Philadelphia: Fortress Press, 1963.

Edwards, Richard A. *A Theology of Q: Eschatology, Prophecy, and Wisdom.* Philadelphia: Fortress Press, 1976.

Ehrman, Bart D. "Cephas and Peter." *JBL* 109 (1990): 463–74.

Eliade, Mircea, ed. *The Encyclopedia of Religion.* 16 vols. New York: Macmillan, 1987.

Epp, Eldon J., and George W. MacRae, eds. *The New Testament and Its Modern Interpreters.* Philadelphia: Fortress Press, 1989.

Eusebius. *The History of the Church from Christ to Constantine.* Trans. G. A. Williamson. Minneapolis: Augsburg, 1975.

Evans, Ernest, ed. and trans. *Tertullian Adversus Marcionem.* 2 vols. Oxford: Clarendon Press, 1972.

Evans-Pritchard, E. E. *Theories of Primitive Religion.* Oxford: Clarendon Press, 1965.

Farmer, William R., et al., eds. *Christian History and Interpretation: Studies Presented to John Knox.* Cambridge: Cambridge Univ. Press, 1967.

————. *The Synoptic Problem: A Critical Analysis.* New York: Macmillan, 1964.

Feuerbach, Ludwig. *The Essence of Christianity.* New York: Harper & Brothers, 1957.

Fieger, Michael. *Das Thomasevangelium: Einleitung, Kommentar, und Systematik.* NTAbh 22. Münster: Aschendorff Verlag, 1991.

Filoramo, Giovanni. *A History of Gnosticism.* Cambridge, Mass.: Basil Blackwell, 1990.

Filson, Floyd V. *A Commentary on the Gospel according to St. Matthew.* HNTC. 2d ed. New York: Harper & Row, 1971.

————. "The Significance of the Early House Churches." *JBL* 58 (1939): 105–12.

Fitzmyer, Joseph A. *The Gospel according to Luke.* 2 vols. AB 28–28A. Garden City, N.Y.: Doubleday, 1981–85.

Foakes-Jackson, F. J., and Kirsopp Lake, eds. *The Beginnings of Christianity.* 5 vols. New York: Macmillan, 1920–33.

Foerster, Werner, ed. *Gnosis: A Selection of Gnostic Texts.* 2 vols. Oxford: Clarendon Press, 1972–74.

Fornberg, Tord. *An Early Church in a Pluralistic Society: A Study of 2 Peter.* ConBNT 9. Lund: Carl Bloms Boktryckeri, 1977.

Fortna, Robert T., and Beverly R. Gaventa, eds. *The Conversation Continues: Studies in Paul and John in Honor of J. Louis Martyn.* Nashville: Abingdon Press, 1990.

Fossum, Jarl E. *The Name of God and the Angel of the Lord: Samaritan and Jewish Concepts of Intermediation and the Origin of Gnosticism.* WUNT 36. Tübingen: J. C. B. Mohr (Paul Siebeck), 1985.

Franklin, Eric. *Christ the Lord: A Study in the Purpose and Theology of Luke-Acts.* London: SPCK, 1975.

Fredriksen, Paula. "Judaism, the Circumcision of Gentiles, and Apocalyptic Hope: Another Look at Galatians 1 and 2." *JTS* 42 (1992): 532–64.

Freedman, David N., ed. *The Anchor Bible Dictionary.* 6 vols. New York: Doubleday, 1992.

Frend, W. H. C. "The Gospel of Thomas: Is Rehabilitation Possible?" *JTS* 18 (1967): 13–26.

———. "Marcion." *ExpTim* 80 (1969): 328–32.

———. *The Rise of Christianity.* Philadelphia: Fortress Press, 1984.

Friedrich, Gerhard. *Auf das Wort kommt es an: Gesammelte Aufsätze zum 70. Geburtstag.* Göttingen: Vandenhoeck & Ruprecht, 1978.

Fuller, Reginald H. *A Critical Introduction to the New Testament.* London: Gerald Duckworth, 1966.

———. *The Foundations of New Testament Christology.* New York: Charles Scribner's Sons, 1965.

———, and Pheme Perkins. *Who Is This Christ? Gospel Christology and Contemporary Faith.* Philadelphia: Fortress Press, 1983.

Furnish, Victor Paul. "Belonging to Christ: A Paradigm for Ethics in First Corinthians." *Int* 44 (1990): 145–57.

———. *The Love Command in the New Testament.* Nashville: Abingdon Press, 1972.

Gager, John. "Jews, Gentiles and Synagogues in the Book of Acts." *HTR* 79 (1986): 91–99.

Gamble, Harry Y. *The New Testament Canon: Its Making and Meaning.* Philadelphia: Fortress Press, 1985.

Gärtner, Bertil. *The Theology of the Gospel according to Thomas.* New York: Harper & Bros., 1961.

Gaston, Lloyd. *Paul and the Torah.* Vancouver: Univ. of British Columbia Press, 1987.

Geertz, Clifford. *The Interpretation of Cultures: Selected Essays.* New York: Basic Books, 1973.

Georgi, Dieter. *The Opponents of Paul in Second Corinthians.* Philadelphia: Fortress Press, 1986.

Gerhardsson, Birger. *The Ethos of the Bible.* Philadelphia: Fortress Press, 1981.

Giles, Kevin. *Patterns of Ministry among the First Christians.* San Francisco: HarperCollins, 1991.

Goehring, James E., et al., eds. *Gospel Origins and Christian Beginnings: In Honor of James M. Robinson.* Sonoma, Calif.: Polebridge Press, 1990.

Goppelt, Leonhard. *Theology of the New Testament.* 2 vols. Grand Rapids: Wm. B. Eerdmans, 1981–82.

———, et al. *The Easter Message Today: Three Essays.* New York: Thomas Nelson, 1964.

Grant, Robert M. *After the New Testament.* Philadelphia: Fortress Press, 1967.

———. *Gnosticism: A Source Book of Heretical Writings from the Early Christian Period.* New York: Harper & Brothers, 1961.

———. *Gnosticism and Early Christianity.* Rev. ed. New York: Harper & Row, 1966.

———. *Heresy and Criticism: The Search for Authenticity in Early Christian Literature.* Louisville: Westminster/John Knox Press, 1993.

———. *The Letter and the Spirit.* New York: Macmillan, 1957.

Gray, Sherman W. *The Least of My Brothers: Matthew 25:31-46: A History of Interpretation.* SBLDS 114. Atlanta: Scholars Press, 1989.

Grayston, Kenneth. *Dying, We Live: A New Enquiry into the Death of Christ in the New Testament.* New York: Oxford Univ. Press, 1990.

Green, Henry A. *The Economic and Social Origins of Gnosticism.* SBLDS 77. Atlanta: Scholars Press, 1985.

Griggs, C. Wilfred. *Early Egyptian Christianity: From Its Origins to 451 C.E.* CS 2. Leiden: E. J. Brill, 1990.

Guillaumont, A., trans. *The Gospel according to Thomas.* New York: Harper & Bros., 1959.

Gundry, Robert H. *Sōma in Biblical Theology: With Emphasis on Pauline Anthropology.* SNTSMS 29. Cambridge: Cambridge Univ. Press, 1976.

Haenchen, Ernst. *The Acts of the Apostles: A Commentary.* Philadelphia: Westminster Press, 1971.

———. *John.* Hermeneia. 2 vols. Philadelphia: Fortress Press, 1984.

Hahn, Ferdinand. *The Titles of Jesus in Christology: Their History in Early Christianity.* Cleveland: World Publishing Company, 1969.

Hanson, A. T. *The Pastoral Epistles.* NCBC. Grand Rapids: Wm. B. Eerdmans, 1982.

Hare, Douglas R. A. *Matthew.* Louisville: Westminster/John Knox Press, 1993.

———. *The Theme of Jewish Persecution in the Gospel according to Matthew.* SNTSMS 6. Cambridge: Cambridge Univ. Press, 1967.

Harnack, Adolf von. *History of Dogma.* 7 vols. Boston: Little, Brown, and Company, 1898–1902.

———. *Marcion: The Gospel of the Alien God.* Durham, N.C.: Labyrinth Press, 1990.

———. "The Sect of the Nicolaitans and Nicolaus, the Deacon in Jerusalem." *JR* 3 (1923): 413–22.

———. *What Is Christianity?* New York: G. P. Putnam's Sons, 1901.

Harrington, Daniel J. *The Gospel of Matthew.* SPS 1. Collegeville, Minn.: Liturgical Press, 1991.

————. "The Reception of Walter Bauer's *Orthodoxy and Heresy in Earliest Christiantiy* during the Last Decade." *HTR* 73 (1980): 289–98.

Harrison, P. N. *Polycarp's Two Epistles to the Philippians.* Cambridge: Cambridge Univ. Press, 1936.

Havener, Ivan. *Q: The Sayings of Jesus.* Wilmington, Del.: Michael Glazier, 1987.

Hedrick, Charles W., ed. *The Historical Jesus and the Rejected Gospels.* Semeia 44. Atlanta: Scholars Press, 1988.

————, ed. *Nag Hammadi Codices XI, XII, XIII.* NHS 28. Leiden: E. J. Brill, 1990.

Hedrick, Charles W., and Robert Hodgson, Jr., eds. *Nag Hammadi, Gnosticism, and Early Christianity.* Peabody, Mass.: Hendrickson Publishers, 1986.

Heine, Susanne. *Women and Early Christianity: A Reappraisal.* Minneapolis: Augsburg, 1988.

Hemer, Colin J. *The Book of Acts in the Setting of Hellenistic History.* WUNT 49. Tübingen: J. C. B. Mohr (Paul Siebeck), 1989.

Hendrix, Holland. "On the Form and Ethos of Ephesians." *USQR* 42 (1988): 3–15.

Hengel, Martin. *Acts and the History of Earliest Christianity.* Philadelphia: Fortress Press, 1980.

————. *Between Jesus and Paul: Studies in the Earliest History of Christianity.* Philadelphia: Fortress Press, 1983.

————. *The Johannine Question.* Philadelphia: Trinity Press International, 1989.

Hennecke, Edgar, and Wilhelm Schneemelcher, eds. *New Testament Apocrypha.* 2 vols. Philadelphia: Westminster Press, 1963–65.

Hiers, Richard H. " 'Binding' and 'Loosing': The Matthean Authorization." *JBL* 104 (1985): 233–50.

Hill, Craig C. *Hellenists and Hebrews: Reappraising Division within the Earliest Church.* Minneapolis: Fortress Press, 1992.

Hills, Julian V. *Tradition and Composition in the* Epistula Apostolorum. HDR 24. Minneapolis: Fortress Press, 1990.

Hoffmann, R. Joseph. "How Then Know This Troublous Teacher? Further Reflections on Marcion and His Church." *SC* 6 (1987–88): 173–91.

Hoffmann, Paul. *Studien zur theologie der Logienquelle.* NTAbh 8. Münster: Aschendorff, 1972.

Holmberg, Bengt. *Paul and Power: The Structure of Authority in the Primitive Church as Reflected in the Pauline Epistles.* ConBNT 11. Lund: G. W. K. Gleerup, 1978.

————. "Sociologiska perspektiv på Gal 2:11-14 (21)." *SEÅ* 55 (1990): 71–92.

————. *Sociology and the New Testament: An Appraisal.* Minneapolis: Fortress Press, 1990.

Hooker, Morna D., and S. G. Wilson, eds. *Paul and Paulinism: Essays in Honour of C. K. Barrett.* London: SPCK, 1982.

Horbury, William. "The Benediction of the *Minim* and Early Jewish-Christian Controversy." *JTS* 33 (1982): 19–61.

Hornschuh, Manfred. *Studien zur Epistula Apostolorum.* PTS 5. Berlin: Walter de Gruyter, 1965.

Horsley, Richard A. "Gnosis at Corinth: I Corinthians 8.1-6." *NTS* 27 (1970): 32–51.

————. *Sociology of the Jesus Movement.* New York: Crossroad Publishing Company, 1989.

Houlden, J. L. *Ethics and the New Testament.* Baltimore: Penguin Books, 1973.

Howard, George. *Paul: Crisis in Galatia: A Study in Early Christian Theology.* 2d ed. SNTSMS 35. Cambridge: Cambridge Univ. Press, 1990.

Hultgren, Arland J. *Christ and His Benefits: Christology and Redemption in the New Testament.* Philadelphia: Fortress Press, 1987.

————. *1 and 2 Timothy, Titus.* ACNT. Minneapolis: Augsburg, 1984.

————. "Jesus and Gnosis: The Saying on Hindering Others in Luke 11:52 and Its Parallels." *FFF* 7/3–4 (1991): 165–82.

————. *Paul's Gospel and Mission: The Outlook from His Letter to the Romans.* Philadelphia: Fortress Press, 1985.

————. "The Self-Definition of Paul and His Communities." *SEÅ* 56 (1991): 78–100.

Hultgren, Arland J., and Barbara Hall, eds. *Christ and His Communities: Essays in Honor of Reginald H. Fuller.* Cincinnati: Forward Movement Publications, 1990.

Hummel, Reinhart. *Die Auseinandersetzung zwischen Kirche und Judentum im Matthäusevangelium.* BEvT 33. Munich: Kaiser Verlag, 1963.

Hurd, John C., Jr. *The Origin of I Corinthians.* 2d ed. Macon, Ga.: Mercer Univ. Press, 1983.

Hurtado, Larry W. *One God, One Lord: Early Christian Devotion and Ancient Jewish Monotheism.* Philadelphia: Fortress Press, 1988.

Jacobson, Arland D. *The First Gospel: An Introduction to Q.* Sonoma, Calif.: Polebridge Press, 1992.

————. "The Literary Unity of Q." *JBL* 101 (1982): 365–89.

Jeremias, Joachim. *The Parables of Jesus.* Rev. ed. New York: Charles Scribner's Sons, 1961.

Jewett, Robert. "The Agitators and the Galatian Congregation." *NTS* 17 (1971): 198–212.

————. *A Chronology of Paul's Life.* Philadelphia: Fortress Press, 1979.

————. *The Thessalonian Correspondence: Pauline Rhetoric and Millenarian Piety.* Philadelphia: Fortress Press, 1986.

Jonas, Hans. *The Gnostic Religion: The Message of the Alien God and the Beginnings of Christianity.* 2d ed. Boston: Beacon Press, 1963.

Jonge, Marinus de. *Christology in Context: The Earliest Christian Response to Jesus.* Philadelphia: Westminster Press, 1988.

————, ed. *L'Évangile de Jean: Sources, rédaction, théologie.* BETL 44. Gembloux: Duculot, 1977.

————. *Jesus: Stranger from Heaven and Son of God: Jesus Christ and the Christians in Johannine Perspective.* SBLSBS 11. Missoula, Mont.: Scholars Press, 1977.

Judge, Edwin A. *Rank and Status in the World of the Caesars and St. Paul.* Univ. of Canterbury Publications 29. Christchurch, New Zealand: Univ. of Canterbury, 1982.

————. *The Social Pattern of Christian Groups in the First Century.* London: Tyndale Press, 1960.

Karris, Robert J. "The Background and Significance of the Polemic of the Pastoral Epistles." *JBL* 92 (1973): 549–64.

Käsemann, Ernst. *Esays on New Testament Themes.* SBT 41. Naperville: Alec. R. Allenson, 1964.

————. *New Testament Questions of Today.* Philadelphia: Fortress Press, 1969.

————. *Perspectives on Paul.* Philadelphia: Fortress Press, 1971.

————. *The Testament of Jesus: A Study of the Gospel of John in Light of Chapter 17.* Philadelphia: Fortress Press, 1968.

Keck, Leander E. "On the Ethos of Early Christians." *JAAR* 42 (1974): 435–52.

————, and J. Louis Martyn, eds. *Studies in Luke-Acts: Essays Presented in Honor of Paul Schubert.* Nashville: Abingdon Press, 1966.

Kee, Howard C. *Christian Origins in Sociological Perspective.* Philadelphia: Westminster Press, 1980.

————. *Jesus in History: An Approach to the Study of the Gospels.* 2d ed. New York: Harcourt Brace Jovanovich, 1977.

Kelly, J. N. D. *A Commentary on the Epistles of Peter and Jude.* HNTC. New York: Harper & Row, 1969.

Kilpatrick, G. D. *The Origins of the Gospel according to St. Matthew.* Oxford: Clarendon Press, 1946.

Kingsbury, Jack D. "The Figure of Peter in Matthew's Gospel as a Theological Problem." *JBL* 98 (1979): 67–87.

————. *Matthew.* 2d ed. PC. Philadelphia: Fortress Press, 1986.

————. *Matthew: Structure, Christology, Kingdom.* Philadelphia: Fortress Press, 1975.

Kittel, Gerhard, and Gerhard Friedrich, eds. *Theological Dictionary of the New Testament.* 10 vols. Grand Rapids: Wm. B. Eerdmans, 1964–76.

Klijn, A. F. J. *The Acts of Thomas: Introduction, Text, Commentary.* NovTSup 5. Leiden: E. J. Brill, 1962.

Kloppenborg, John S., and Leif E. Vaage, eds. *Early Christianity, Q and Jesus. Semeia 55.* Atlanta: Scholars Press, 1992.

———. *The Formation of Q: Trajectories in Ancient Wisdom Collections.* Philadelphia: Fortress Press, 1987.

———, ed. *The Shape of Q: Signal Essays on the Sayings Gospel.* Minneapolis: Fortress Press, 1994.

———, et al. *Q-Thomas Reader.* Sonoma, Calif.: Polebridge Press, 1990.

Knight, George W. *The Pastoral Epistles: A Commentary on the Greek Text.* NIGTC. Grand Rapids: Wm. B. Eerdmans, 1992.

Knox, John. *Chapters in a Life of Paul.* Rev. ed. Macon, Ga.: Mercer Univ. Press, 1987.

Knox, W. L. "Parallels to the N.T. Use of Sōma." *JTS* 39 (1938): 243–46.

Koenig, John. *New Testament Hospitality: Partnership with Strangers as Promise and Mission.* Philadelphia: Fortress Press, 1985.

Koester, Craig. "The Origin and the Significance of the Flight to Pella Tradition." *CBQ* 51 (1989): 90–106.

Koester, Helmut. *Ancient Christian Gospels: Their History and Development.* Philadelphia: Trinity Press International, 1990.

———. *Introduction to the New Testament.* 2 vols. Philadelphia: Fortress Press, 1982.

———. "Jesus the Victim." *JBL* 111 (1992): 3–15.

———. *Synoptische Überlieferung bei den apostolischen Vätern.* TU 65. Berlin: Akademie Verlag, 1957.

Kraabel, A. Thomas. "The Disappearance of the 'God-Fearers.'" *Numen* 28 (1981): 113–26.

Kraft, Robert A., ed. *The Apostolic Fathers: 3, Barnabas and the Didache.* New York: Thomas Nelson, 1965.

Krodel, Gerhard. *Acts.* ACNT. Minneapolis: Augsburg, 1986.

Kümmel, Werner G. *Introduction to the New Testament.* Rev. ed. Nashville: Abingdon Press, 1975.

———. *The New Testament: The History of the Investigation of Its Problems.* Nashville: Abingdon Press, 1972.

———. *The Theology of the New Testament: According to Its Main Witnesses, Jesus-Paul-John.* Nashville: Abingdon Press, 1973.

Kysar, Robert. *John.* ACNT. Minneapolis: Augsburg, 1986.

Lake, Kirsopp, trans. *The Apostolic Fathers.* 2 vols. LCL. New York: G. P. Putnam's Sons, 1912–13.

Lamouille, Arnaud. *L'Évangile de Jean.* Paris: Cerf, 1977.

Layton, Bentley, ed. *The Gnostic Scriptures*. Garden City, N.Y.: Doubleday, 1987.

———, ed. *The Rediscovery of Gnosticism*. 2 vols. SHR 41. Leiden: E. J. Brill, 1980–81.

Leeuw, Gerardus van der. *Religion in Essence and Manifestation*. New York: Harper & Row, 1963.

Lieu, Judith. *The Second and Third Epistles of John: History and Background*. Edinburgh: T. & T. Clark, 1986.

Lightfoot, J. B., and J. R. Harmer. *The Apostolic Fathers*. 2d ed. Ed. Michael W. Holmes. Grand Rapids: Baker Book House, 1989.

Lindars, Barnabas, and Stephen S. Smalley, eds. *Christ and Spirit in the New Testament: In Honour of Charles Francis Digby Moule*. Cambridge: Cambridge Univ. Press, 1973.

Lindars, Barnabas. *New Testament Apologetic: The Doctrinal Significance of the Old Testament Quotations*. Philadelphia: Westminster Press, 1961.

Livingstone, Elizabeth A., ed. *Studia Evangelica 7*. TU 126. Berlin: Akademie Verlag, 1982.

Loader, W. R. G. "The Central Structure of Johannine Christology." *NTS* 30 (1984): 188–216.

Logan, A. H. B., and A. J. M. Wedderburn, eds. *The New Testament and Gnosis: Essays in Honour of Robert McL. Wilson*. Edinburgh: T. & T. Clark, 1983.

Lohfink, Gerhard. *Jesus and Community: The Social Dimensions of the Christian Faith*. Philadelphia: Fortress Press, 1984.

Lohmeyer, Ernst. *Kyrios Jesus: Eine Untersuchung zu Phil. 2, 5-11*. 2d ed. Heidelberg: Carl Winter, Universitätsverlag, 1961.

Lohse, Eduard. *Colossians and Philemon*. Hermeneia. Philadelphia: Fortress Press, 1971.

———. *Theological Ethics of the New Testament*. Minneapolis: Fortress Press, 1991.

Luedemann, Gerd. "The Acts of the Apostles and the Beginnings of Simonian Gnosticism." *NTS* 33 (1987): 420–26.

———. *Opposition to Paul in Jewish Christianity*. Philadelphia: Fortress Press, 1989.

———. *Paul: Apostle to the Gentiles: Studies in Chronology*. Philadelphia: Fortress Press, 1984.

———. *Untersuchungen zur simonianischen Gnosis*. GTA 1. Göttingen: Vandenhoeck & Ruprecht, 1975.

Lührmann, Dieter. *Galatians: A Continental Commentary*. Minneapolis: Fortress Press, 1992.

———. "The Gospel of Mark and the Sayings Collection Q." *JBL* 108 (1989): 51–71.

————. *Die Redaktion der Logienquelle.* WMANT 33. Neukirchen-Vluyn: Neukirchener Verlag, 1969.

Luz, Ulrich. *Matthew 1–7: A Commentary.* Minneapolis: Fortress Press, 1991.

————. "The Primacy Text (Mt. 16:18)." *PSB* 12 (1991): 41–55.

Luz, Ulrich, and Hans Weder, eds. *Die Mitte des Neuen Testaments: Einheit und Vielfalt neutestamentlicher Theologie: Festschrift für Eduard Schweizer zum siebzigsten Geburtstag.* Göttingen: Vandenhoeck & Ruprecht, 1983.

MacDonald, Margaret Y. *The Pauline Churches: A Socio-Historical Study of Institutionalization in the Pauline and Deutero-Pauline Writings.* SNTSMS 60. Cambridge: Cambridge Univ. Press, 1988.

Mack, Burton. *The Lost Gospel: The Book of Q and Christian Origins.* San Francisco: HarperSanFrancisco, 1993.

Malherbe, Abraham. *Paul and the Thessalonians: The Philosophic Tradition of Pastoral Care.* Philadelphia: Fortress Press, 1987.

————. *Social Aspects of Early Christianity.* 2d ed. Philadelphia: Fortress Press, 1983.

Manson, T. W. "A Parallel to a N.T. Use of *Sōma.*" *JTS* 37 (1936): 385.

————. *The Sayings of Jesus.* London: SCM Press, 1949.

Marshall, I. Howard. "The Christology of the Pastoral Epistles." *SNTU* 13 (1988): 157–77.

————. *1 and 2 Thessalonians.* NCB. Grand Rapids: Wm. B. Eerdmans, 1983.

Martyn, J. Louis. "A Law-Observant Mission to Gentiles: The Background of Galatians." *SJT* 38 (1985): 307–24.

————. *The Gospel of John in Christian History: Essays for Interpreters.* New York: Paulist Press, 1979.

————. *History and Theology in the Fourth Gospel.* Rev. ed. Nashville: Abingdon Press, 1979.

Marxsen, Willi. *The Beginnings of Christology: A Study in Its Problems.* FBBS 22. Philadelphia: Fortress Press, 1969.

————. *Introduction to the New Testament.* Philadelphia: Fortress Press, 1968.

Massaux, Édouard. *The Influence of the Gospel of Saint Matthew on Christian Literature before Saint Irenaeus: The First Ecclesiastical Writers.* NGS 5/1. Macon, Ga.: Mercer Univ. Press, 1990.

Maurer, Christian. *Ignatius von Antioch und das Johannesevangelium.* Zurich: Zwingli Verlag, 1949.

Mauser, Ulrich. "Paul the Theologian." *HorBT* 11 (1989): 80–106.

McCue, James F. "Orthodoxy and Heresy: Walter Bauer and the Valentinians." *VC* 33 (1979): 118–30.

McInnes, Val A., ed. *Renewing the Judeo-Christian Wellsprings.* New York: Crossroad Publishing Company, 1987.

Meeks, Wayne A. *The First Urban Christians: The Social World of the Apostle Paul.* New Haven: Yale Univ. Press, 1983.

Meeks, Wayne, and Robert L. Wilken. *Jews and Christians in Antioch in the First Four Centuries of the Common Era*. SBLSBS 13. Missoula, Mont.: Scholars Press, 1978.

Mellink, M. J. "Archaeology in Asia Minor." *AJA* 81/3 (1977): 289–321.

Metz, Johann-Baptist, and Edward Schillebeeckx, eds. *Orthodoxy and Heterodoxy*. Edinburgh: T. & T. Clark, 1987.

Metzger, Bruce M. *The Canon of the New Testament: Its Origins, Development, and Significance*. Oxford: Clarendon Press, 1987.

———. *The Early Versions of the New Testament: Their Origin, Transmission, and Limitations*. Oxford: Clarendon Press, 1977.

Meyer, Paul D. "The Gentile Mission in Q." *JBL* 89 (1970): 405–17.

Michaels, J. Ramsey. *1 Peter*. WBC. Waco, Tex.: Word Books, 1988.

Miller, Donald G., and Dikran Y. Hadidian, eds. *Jesus and Man's Hope*. 2 vols. Pittsburgh: Pittsburgh Theological Seminary, 1970–71.

Moore, George Foot. *Judaism in the First Centuries of the Christian Era: The Age of the Tannaim*. 3 vols. Cambridge, Mass.: Harvard Univ. Press, 1927–30.

Moulton, James H., and George Milligan. *The Vocabulary of the Greek Testament Illustrated from the Papyri and Other Non-Literary Sources*. Grand Rapids: Wm. B. Eerdmans, 1949.

Munck, Johannes. *The Acts of the Apostles*. AB 31. Garden City, N.Y.: Doubleday, 1967.

Neill, Stephen, and Tom Wright, *The Interpretation of the New Testament 1861–1986*. 2d ed. New York: Oxford Univ. Press, 1988.

Neirynck, Frans. "Once More—The Symbol Q." *ETL* 55 (1979): 382–83.

Neufeld, Vernon H. *The Earliest Christian Confessions*. NTTS 5. Grand Rapids: Wm B. Eerdmans, 1963.

Neusner, Jacob, ed. *Christianity, Judaism and Other Greco-Roman Cults: Studies for Morton Smith at Sixty*. 4 vols. SJLA 12. Leiden: E. J. Brill, 1975.

———. *Jews and Christians: The Myth of a Common Tradition*. Philadelphia: Trinity Press International, 1991.

———, and Ernest S. Frerichs, eds. *To See Ourselves as Others See Us*. Chico, Calif.: Scholars Press, 1985.

———. *Understanding Seeking Faith: Essays on the Case of Judaism*. BJS 153. 3 vols. Atlanta: Scholars Press, 1986–88.

Nock, Arthur Darby. *Early Gentile Christianity and Its Hellenistic Background*. New York: Harper & Row, 1964.

———. "The Historical Importance of Cult Associations." *CR* 38 (1924): 105–09.

Ogden, Schubert, ed. *Existence and Faith: The Shorter Writings of Rudolf Bultmann*. New York: Meridian Books, 1960.

Orton, David E. *The Understanding Scribe: Matthew and the Apocalyptic Ideal*. JSNTSup 25. Sheffield: JSOT Press, 1989.

Overman, J. Andrew. "The God-Fearers: Some Neglected Features." *JSNT* 32 (1988): 17–26.

―――. *Matthew's Gospel and Formative Judaism: The Social World of the Matthean Community.* Minneapolis: Fortress Press, 1990.

Pagels, Elaine H. *The Gnostic Gospels.* New York: Random House, 1979.

―――. *The Gnostic Paul: Gnostic Exegesis of the Pauline Letters.* Philadelphia: Fortress Press, 1975.

―――. *The Johannine Gospel in Gnostic Exegesis: Heracleon's Commentary on John.* SBLMS 17. Nashville: Abingdon Press, 1973.

Painter, John. *The Quest for the Messiah: The History, Literature and Theology of the Johannine Community.* Edinburgh: T. & T. Clark, 1991.

Pannenberg, Wolfhart. *Jesus, God and Man.* 2d ed. Philadelphia: Westminster Press, 1977.

Patterson, Stephen J. *The Gospel of Thomas and Jesus.* Sonoma, Calif.: Polebridge Press, 1992.

Pearson, Birger A. "Early Christianity and Gnosticism: A Review Essay." *RSR* 13 (1987): 1–8.

―――. "1 Thessalonians 2:13-16: A Deutero-Pauline Interpolation." *HTR* 64 (1971): 79–94.

―――, ed. *The Future of Early Christianity: Essays in Honor of Helmut Koester.* Minneapolis: Fortress Press, 1991.

―――. *Gnosticism, Judaism, and Egyptian Christianity.* Minneapolis: Fortress Press, 1990.

―――, and James E. Goehring, eds. *The Roots of Egyptian Christianity.* Philadelphia: Fortress Press, 1986.

Perkins, Pheme. *The Gnostic Dialogue: The Early Church and the Crisis of Gnosticism.* New York: Paulist Press, 1980.

―――. *Gnosticism and the New Testament.* Minneapolis: Fortress Press, 1993.

Perrin, Norman. *The New Testament: An Introduction.* New York: Harcourt Brace Jovanovich, 1974.

Pesch, Rudolf. *Die Apostelgeschichte.* 2 vols. EKKNT 5. Neukirchen-Vluyn: Neukirchener Verlag, 1986.

Pétrement, Simone. *A Separate God: The Christian Origins of Gnosticism.* San Francisco: Harper & Row, 1990.

Piper, Ronald A. *Wisdom in the Q-Tradition: The Aphoristic Teaching of Jesus.* SNTSMS 61. Cambridge: Cambridge Univ. Press, 1989.

Plevnik, Joseph. "The Center of Pauline Theology." *CBQ* 51 (1989): 461–78.

Pokorný, Petr. *The Genesis of Christology: Foundations for a Theology of the New Testament.* Edinburgh: T. & T. Clark, 1987.

Polag, Athanasius. *Fragmenta Q: Textheft zur Logienquelle.* 2d ed. Neukirchen-Vluyn: Neukirchener Verlag, 1982.

Preisker, Herbert. *Das Ethos des Urchristentums*. 2d ed. Gütersloh: Verlagshaus Gerd Mohn, 1949.

Quasten, Johannes. *Patrology*. 4 vols. Westminster, Md.: Christian Classics, 1983–86.

Quinn, Jerome D. *The Letter to Titus*. AB 35. New York: Doubleday, 1990.

Quispel, Gilles. "The Gospel of Thomas and the New Testament." *VC* 11 (1957): 189–207.

Radcliff-Brown, A. R. *Structure and Function in Primitive Society: Essays and Addresses*. London: Cohen & West, 1952.

Rahner, Karl. *On Heresy*. QD 11. New York: Herder & Herder, 1964.

Reitzenstein, Richard. *Hellenistic Mystery-Religions: Their Basic Ideas and Significance*. PTMS 15. Pittsburgh: Pickwick Press, 1978.

Reumann, John. *Variety and Unity in New Testament Thought*. Oxford: Oxford Univ. Press, 1991.

Reynolds, Joyce M., and Robert Tannenbaum. *Jews and God-fearers at Aphrodisias: Greek Inscriptions with Commentary*. CPSSV 12. Cambridge: Cambridge Philological Society, 1987.

Richards, G. C. "Parallels to a N.T. Use of *Sōma*." *JTS* 38 (1937): 165.

Richards, Kent H., ed. *Society of Biblical Literature 1987 Seminar Papers*. SBLSPS 26. Atlanta: Scholars Press, 1987.

Riches, John. *Jesus and the Transformation of Judaism*. New York: Seabury Press, 1981.

Roberts, Alexander, and James Donaldson, eds. *The Ante-Nicene Fathers*. 10 vols. Buffalo: Christian Literature Company, 1885–96.

Roberts, Colin H. *Manuscript, Society and Belief in Early Christian Egypt*. London: Oxford Univ. Press, 1979.

Robinson, John A. T. *Redating the New Testament*. Philadelphia: Westminster Press, 1976.

Robinson, James M. "Jesus from Easter to Valentinus (or to the Apostles' Creed)." *JBL* 101 (1982): 5–37.

————, ed. *The Nag Hammadi Library in English*. 3d ed. San Francisco: Harper & Row, 1988.

————, and Helmut Koester. *Trajectories through Early Christianity*. Philadelphia: Fortress Press, 1971.

Robinson, Thomas A. *The Bauer Thesis Examined: The Geography of Heresy in the Early Christian Community*. SBEC 11. Lewiston, N.Y.: Edwin Mellen Press, 1988.

Roetzel, Calvin J. *The Letters of Paul: Conversations in Context*. 3d ed. Louisville: Westminster/John Knox Press, 1991.

Roloff, Jürgen. *Der erste Brief an Timotheus*. EKKNT 15. Zurich: Benziger Verlag, 1988.

————. "Der Kampf gegen die Irrlehrer: Wie geht man miteinander um?" *BK* 46 (1991): 114–20.

Rudolph, Kurt. *Gnosis: The Nature and History of Gnosticism.* San Francisco: Harper & Row, 1983.

Sanders, E. P. *Jesus and Judaism.* Philadelphia: Fortress Press, 1985.

————. *Paul and Palestinian Judaism: A Comparison of Patterns of Religion.* Philadelphia: Fortress Press, 1977.

————. *Paul, the Law, and the Jewish People.* Philadelphia: Fortress Press, 1983.

————, and Margaret Davies. *Studying the Synoptic Gospels.* Philadelphia: Trinity Press International, 1989.

————, et al., eds. *Jewish and Christian Self-Definition.* 3 vols. Philadelphia: Fortress Press, 1980–82.

Sanders, J. N. *The Fourth Gospel in the Early Church.* Cambridge: Cambridge Univ. Press, 1943.

Sanders, Jack T. *The New Testament Christological Hymns: Their Historical Religious Background.* SNTSMS 15. Cambridge: Cambridge Univ. Press, 1971.

Sato, Migaku. *Q und Prophetie: Studien zur Gattungs- und Traditionsgeschichte der Quelle Q.* WUNT 2/29. Tübingen: J. C. B. Mohr (Paul Siebeck), 1988.

Schillebeeckx, Edward. *Jesus: An Experiment in Christology.* New York: Crossroad, 1981.

Schleiermacher, Friedrich. *On Religion: Speeches to Its Cultured Despisers.* New York: Harper & Brothers, 1958.

Schmidt, Daryl. "1 Thess. 2:13-16: Linguistic Evidence for an Interpolation." *JBL* 102 (1983): 269–79.

Schmithals, Walter. *Gnosticism in Corinth: An Investigation of the Letters to the Corinthians.* Nashville: Abingdon Press, 1971.

————. *Jesus Christus in der Verkündigung der Kirche: Aktuelle Beiträge zum notwendigen Streit um Jesus.* Neukirchen-Vluyn: Neukirchener Verlag, 1972.

————. *Paul and the Gnostics.* Nashville: Abingdon Press, 1972.

Schnackenburg, Rudolf. "Ephesus: Entwicklung einer Gemeinde von Paulus zu Johannes." *BZ* 35 (1991): 41–64.

————. *The Gospel according to St. John.* 3 vols. New York: Herder & Herder, Seabury, Crossroad, 1968–82.

Schoedel, William R. *The Apostolic Fathers: 5, Polycarp, Martyrdom of Polycarp, Fragments of Papias.* New York: Thomas Nelson, 1967.

————. *Ignatius of Antioch.* Hermeneia. Philadelphia: Fortress Press, 1985.

Schoeps, Hans-Joachim. *Jewish Christianity: Factional Disputes in the Early Church.* Philadelphia: Fortress Press, 1969.

Schrage, Wolfgang. *The Ethics of the New Testament.* Philadelphia: Fortress Press, 1988.

————, ed. *Studien zum Text und zur Ethik des Neuen Testaments: Festschrift zum 80. Geburtstag von Heinrich Greeven.* Berlin: Walter de Gruyter, 1986.

Schulz, Siegfried. Q: Die Spruchquelle der Evangelisten. Zurich: Theologischer Verlag, 1972.

Schürer, Emil. The History of the Jewish People in the Age of Jesus Christ (175 B.C.–A.D. 135). Rev. Geza Vermes, Fergus Millar, and Martin Goodman. 3 vols. Edinburgh: T. & T. Clark, 1973–87.

Schweizer, Eduard. Church Order in the New Testament. SBT 32. Naperville, Ill.: Alec R. Allenson, 1961.

————. The Good News according to Matthew. Atlanta: John Knox Press, 1975.

————. The Letter to the Colossians. Minneapolis: Augsburg, 1982.

————. Lordship and Discipleship. SBT 28. Naperville, Ill.: Alec R. Allenson, 1960.

————. A Theological Introduction to the New Testament. Nashville: Abingdon Press, 1991.

Scott, Bernard B. Hear Then the Parable: A Commentary on the Parables of Jesus. Minneapolis: Fortress Press, 1989.

Seeley, David. "Jesus' Death in Q." NTS 38 (1992): 222–34.

Segal, Alan F. Paul the Convert: The Apostolate and Apostasy of Saul the Pharisee. New Haven: Yale Univ. Press, 1990.

————. Two Powers in Heaven: Early Rabbinic Reports about Christianity and Gnosticism. SJLA 25. Leiden: E. J. Brill, 1977.

Simpson, John W., Jr. "The Problems Posed by 1 Thessalonians 2:15-16 and a Solution." HorBT 12 (1990): 42–72.

Smalley, Stephen S. 1, 2, 3 John. WBC. Waco, Tex.: Word Books, 1984.

————. John: Evangelist and Interpreter. Exeter: Paternoster Press, 1978.

Smith, D. Moody. John. 2d ed. PC. Philadelphia: Fortress Press, 1986.

Snodgrass, Klyne R. "Matthew's Understanding of the Law." Int 46 (1992): 368–78.

Stambaugh, John E. The Ancient Roman City. Baltimore: John Hopkins Univ. Press, 1988.

Stambaugh, John E., and David L. Balch. The New Testament in Its Social Environment. Philadelphia: Westminster Press, 1986.

Stanton, Graham. "The Communities of Matthew." Int 46 (1992): 379–91.

————. A Gospel for a New People: Studies in Matthew. Edinburgh: T. & T. Clark, 1992.

————. "The Gospel of Matthew and Judaism." BJRL 66 (1984): 264–84.

————, ed. The Interpretation of Matthew. IRT 3. Philadelphia: Fortress Press, 1983.

Steck, Odil H. Israel und das gewaltsame Geschick der Propheten: Untersuchungen zur Überlieferung des deuteronomistischen Geschichtsbild im Alten Testament, Spätjudentum und Urchristentum. WMANT 23. Neukirchen-Vluyn: Neukirchener Verlag, 1967.

Stendahl, Krister. *The School of St. Matthew and Its Use of the Old Testament.* 2d ed. Philadelphia: Fortress Press, 1968.

Strack, Hermann, and Paul Billerbeck. *Kommentar zum Neuen Testament aus Talmud und Midrasch.* 6 vols. Munich: C. H. Beck'sche Verlag, 1922–61.

Stuhlmacher, Peter, ed. *The Gospel and the Gospels.* Grand Rapids: Wm. B. Eerdmans, 1991.

Suggs, M. Jack. *Wisdom, Christology, and Law in Matthew's Gospel.* Cambridge, Mass.: Harvard Univ. Press, 1970.

Sullivan, Thomas J., and Kendrick S. Thompson. *Sociology: Concepts, Issues, and Applications.* 2d ed. New York: Macmillan, 1990.

Sykes, Stephen. *The Identity of Christianity: Theologians and the Essence of Christianity from Schleiermacher to Barth.* Philadelphia: Fortress Press, 1984.

Tannehill, Robert C. "The Functions of Peter's Mission Speeches in the Narrative of Acts." *NTS* 37 (1991): 400–14.

Tannenbaum, Robert F. "Jews and God-Fearers in the Holy City of Aphrodite." *BAR* 12/5 (1986): 54–57.

Theissen, Gerd. *The Gospels in Context: Social and Political History in the Synoptic Tradition.* Minneapolis: Fortress Press, 1991.

———. "Itinerant Radicalism: The Tradition of Jesus Sayings from the Perspective of the Sociology of Literature." *RadRel* 2 (1975): 84–93.

———. "Jesusbewegung als charismatische Wertrevolution." *NTS* 35 (1989): 343–60.

———. *The Social Setting of Pauline Christianity: Essays on Corinth.* Philadelphia: Fortress Press, 1982.

———. *Sociology of Early Palestinian Christianity.* Philadelphia: Fortress Press, 1978.

Thompson, Marianne Meye. *The Humanity of Jesus in the Fourth Gospel.* Philadelphia: Fortress Press, 1988.

Thurston, Bonnie Bowman. *The Widows: A Woman's Ministry in the Early Church.* Philadelphia: Fortress Press, 1989.

Tödt, Heinz E. *The Son of Man in the Synoptic Tradition.* Philadelphia: Westminster Press, 1965.

Tönnies, Ferdinand. *Community and Society.* New York: Harper & Row, 1957.

Trebilco, Paul R. *Jewish Communities in Asia Minor.* SNTSMS 69. Cambridge: Cambridge Univ. Press, 1991.

Trilling, Wolfgang. *Das wahre Israel: Studien zur Theologie des Matthäusevangeliums.* SANT 10. 3d ed. Munich: Kösel Verlag, 1964.

Troeltsch, Ernst. *The Absoluteness of Christianity and the History of Religions.* Richmond: John Knox Press, 1971.

Tröger, Karl-Wolfgang, ed. *Gnosis und Neues Testament: Studien aus Religionswissenschaft und Theologie.* Gütersloh: Gerd Mohn, 1973.

Turner, H. E. W. *The Pattern of Christian Truth: A Study in Relations between Orthodoxy and Heresy in the Early Church.* Bampton Lectures 1954. London: A. R. Mowbray, 1954.

Tyson, Joseph B. *Luke-Acts and the Jewish People: Eight Critical Perspectives.* Minneapolis: Augsburg, 1988.

————. "Paul's Opponents in Galatia." *NovT* 10 (1968): 241–54.

Unnik, W. C. van. *Newly Discovered Gnostic Writings: A Preliminary Survey of the Nag Hammadi Find.* SBT 30. Naperville, Ill.: Alec R. Allenson, 1960.

Van Voorst, Robert E. *The Ascents of James: History and Theology of a Jewish-Christian Community.* SBLDS 112. Atlanta: Scholars Press, 1989.

Verseput, D. J. "Paul's Gentile Mission and the Jewish Christian Community: A Study of the Narrative in Galatians 1 and 2." *NTS* 39 (1993): 36–58.

Volf, Judith M. Gundry. *Paul and Perseverance: Staying In and Falling Away.* Louisville: Westminster/John Knox Press, 1991.

Wach, Joachim. *Sociology of Religion.* Chicago: Univ. of Chicago Press, 1944.

Wagner, Walter H. *After the Apostles: Christianity in the Second Century.* Minneapolis: Fortress Press, 1994.

Wanamaker, C. A. "Christ as Divine Agent in Paul." *SJT* 39 (1986): 517–28.

Washington, James M. *A Testament of Hope: The Essential Writings of Martin Luther King, Jr.* San Francisco: Harper & Row, 1986.

Watson, Francis. *Paul, Judaism and the Gentiles: A Sociological Approach.* SNTSMS 56. Cambridge: Cambridge Univ. Press, 1986.

Weber, Max. *Gesammelte Aufsätze zur Religionssoziologie.* 3 vols. Tübingen: J. C. B. Mohr (Paul Siebeck), 1920.

Weiss, Johannes. *Earliest Christianity: A History of the Period A.D. 30–150.* 2 vols. New York: Harper & Row, 1959.

————. "Die Verteidigung Jesu gegen den Vorwurf des Bündnisses mit Beelzebul." *TSK* 63 (1890): 555–69.

Whitacre, Rodney A. *Johannine Polemic: The Role of Tradition and Theology.* SBLDS 67. Chico, Calif.: Scholars Press, 1982.

Widengren, Geo. *The Gnostic Attitude.* Santa Barbara, Calif.: Institute of Religious Studies, Univ. of California, 1973.

Wilckens, Ulrich. *Die Missionsreden der Apostelgeschichte.* 2d ed. WMANT 5.2. Neukirchen-Vluyn: Neukirchener Verlag, 1963.

Wiles, Maurice F. *The Spiritual Gospel: The Interpretation of the Fourth Gospel in the Early Church.* Cambridge: Cambridge Univ. Press, 1960.

Wilken, Robert L., ed. *Aspects of Wisdom in Judaism and Early Christianity.* Notre Dame, Ind.: Univ. of Notre Dame Press, 1975.

————. "The Durability of Orthodoxy." *WW* 8 (1988): 124–32.

Williams, David S. "Reconsidering Marcion's Gospel." *JBL* 108 (1989): 477–96.

Williams, Frank, trans. *The Panarion of Epiphanius of Salamis*. NHS 35. Leiden: E. J. Brill, 1987.

Williams, Rowen, ed. *The Making of Orthodoxy: Essays in Honour of Henry Chadwick*. Cambridge: Cambridge Univ. Press, 1989.

Wilson, Bryan R. *Religion in a Sociological Perspective*. Oxford: Oxford Univ. Press, 1982.

――――. *Sects and Society*. Berkeley: Univ. of California Press, 1961.

Wilson, Robert McL. *Gnosis and the New Testament*. Philadelphia: Fortress Press, 1968.

――――. "How Gnostic Were the Corinthians?" *NTS* 19 (1972): 65–74.

――――. " 'Jewish Gnosis' and Gnostic Origins: A Survey." *HUCA* 45 (1974): 177–89.

――――. *Studies in the Gospel of Thomas*. London: A. R. Mowbray & Co., 1960.

Windisch, Hans. "Zur Christologie der Pastoralbriefe." *ZNW* 34 (1935): 213–21.

Witherington, Ben. *The Christology of Jesus*. Minneapolis: Fortress Press, 1990.

Yamauchi, Edwin M. *Pre-Christian Gnosticism: A Survey of the Proposed Evidences*. 2d ed. Grand Rapids: Baker Book House, 1983.

Yorke, Gosnell L. O. R. *The Church as the Body of Christ in the Pauline Corpus: A Re-examination*. Lanham, Md.: University Press of America, 1991.

Index of Ancient Sources

Old Testament

Old Testament Pseudepigrapha

New Testament

Other Early Christian Literature

Other Ancient Jewish Literature

Other Greco-Roman Literature

Index of Modern Authors